Health Policy Reform in America

Innovations from the States

Health Policy Reform in America
Innovations from the States

Howard M. Leichter

EDITOR

M.E. Sharpe Inc.

Armonk, New York · London, England

Library of Congress Cataloging-in-Publication Data

Health policy reform in America: innovations from the States /
Howard M. Leichter, editor.
p. cm.
Includes bibliographical references and index.
ISBN 1-56324-053-X.
ISBN 1-56324-054-8 (pbk.)
1. Medical policy—United States.
I. Leichter, Howard M.
RA395.A3H42564 1992
362.1′0973—dc20
92-22293
CIP

Printed in the United States of America

The paper used in this publication meets the minimum requirements of
American National Standard for Information Sciences—
Permanence of Paper for Printed Library Materials,
ANSI Z39.48–1984.

BB (c)   10   9   8   7   6   5   4   3   2   1
BB (p)   10   9   8   7   6   5   4   3   2

To Elisabeth

For everything forever

Contents

List of Figures and Tables

Figures

Tables

Preface

The 1990s may prove to be one of those rare decades in political astronomy in which the constellations of public and elite opinion will be in perfect alignment. According to an August 1991 Gallup Poll, 91 percent of the American people feel that the nation's health care system is in a state of crisis, an assessment, if the 1992 presidential campaign is any indication, uniformly shared by the nation's political leaders.[1] As Senator Paul Wellstone (D–MN) put it, health care reform "has become the functional equivalent of kissing babies."[2]

Reforming the nation's health care system has been catapulted to the top of state and national policy agendas by several factors. The first is the rapid increase in the number of Americans without health insurance: from 1989 to 1990 1.3 million people joined the ranks of the 35 to 38 million uninsured Americans. Significantly enough, three-quarters of the newly uninsured had annual family incomes of $25,000 or more. No longer is it simply the poor who must be concerned about access to health care. This factor alone changes the prospects and politics of health care reform.

Second, public opinion polls indicate that after years of being insulated from, and seemingly unconcerned about, rising health care costs because of third-party (e.g., private health insurance, Medicare, and Medicaid) reimbursement, even those with health care insurance now recognize the impact on their lives of skyrocketing costs. Gallup found that concern with the cost of health care and health insurance far outstripped all other health care–related problems: 42 percent of the respondents mentioned cost, while the next most frequently cited problem, the lack of coverage for the elderly, poor, or homeless, was mentioned by only 13 percent.[3]

Third, the 1991–92 recession demonstrated to millions of Americans just how tenuous an employment-based health insurance system can be. Over a two-year period, about 60 million people, including an increasing number of middle-income families, can expect to find themselves at least temporarily without health insurance.

If the country's political leadership needed to be educated about the need for health care reform—and its inability or unwillingness to address a problem that academics have been warning about for at least a decade suggests that it did—it received such instruction in November 1991. Harris Wofford, a Kennedy-era civil rights attorney and advocate, overcame a 44 point deficit to defeat George Bush's former attorney general, Richard Thornburgh, by 11 percentage points in a special United States Senate election in Pennsylvania. Wofford ran what amounted to a single-issue campaign that was encapsulated in a political advertisement announcing that "if criminals have a right to a lawyer, working Americans have a right to a doctor." Wofford's victory was a wakeup call to politicians of both political parties who would face an increasingly worried electorate in the 1992 election.

It is unclear, as of this writing, precisely what direction health care reform will take, how comprehensive it will be, or how quickly it will proceed. One thing is certain: the American health care system will experience its most significant transformation since the introduction of Medicaid and Medicare a quarter of a century ago. The purpose of this book is to contribute to this long overdue national debate. It is premised on the assumption that whatever happens, experiments that have been proposed by, or are already in place in, the states will, or at least should, provide lessons and context for that debate.

I would like to thank Michael Weber of M.E. Sharpe for recognizing, long before others, the need for a volume on health care reform. My own efforts have been made easier by the generous and highly professional assistance of Lynn Chmelir, Frances Rasmussen, Barbara Valentine, and Susan Whyte of Northrup Library, Linfield College. Vanessa Robin Weersing is one of the most extraordinarily talented research assistants I have ever known. Her help has been invaluable. Alexandra and Laurel have done what they do best, namely provide loving distractions. I dedicate this book to Elisabeth, a person of uncommon beauty and loving.

Howard M. Leichter
March 1992

Notes

1. Frank Newport and Jennifer Leonard, "The Crisis in National Health Care," *The Gallup Poll Monthly* 311 (August 1991): 4.
2. *Oregonian*, 23 January 1992.
3. Newport and Leonard, "The Crisis in National Health Care," p. 8.

Contributors

CAMILLE ASCUAGA works with the Neighborhood Health Plan in Dorchester, Massachusetts. From 1988 until 1990 she was the Small Business Liaison with the Massachusetts Department of Medical Security, the agency responsible for implementing that state's universal health care law. From 1982 to 1983 she was Assistant to the Regional Director, U.S. Department of Health and Human Services in San Francisco.

DELL ENSLEY is a Research Assistant in the Long Term Care Resources Program at Duke University.

DAVID J. FALCONE is Associate Professor of Health Administration and Associate Program Director, Long Term Care Resources Program Center for the Study of Aging and Human Development, Duke University Medical Center.

DANIEL M. FOX is the President of the Milbank Memorial Fund. Before coming to that position in January 1990, he was Professor of Social Sciences and Medicine, and Director of the Center for Assessing Health Services at the State University of New York, Stony Brook.

MALCOLM L. GOGGIN is a Professor of Political Science at the University of Houston. His publications include *Implementation Theory and Practice: Toward a Third Generation*, with Ann O'M. Bowman, James P. Lester, and Laurence J. O'Toole (1990), and *Policy Design and the Politics of Implementation: The Case of Child Health Care in the United States* (1987).

BRUCE JENNINGS is Executive Director of The Hastings Center in Briarcliff Manor, New York.

STEVEN LAUBACHER is currently on the faculty of Roosevelt University in Chicago. He formerly was Executive Director of the Association for Retarded Citizens of Illinois.

HOWARD M. LEICHTER is Professor of Political Science at Linfield College in McMinnville, Oregon, and Clinical Professor of Public Health and Preventive Medicine at the Oregon Health Sciences University.

CECILIA B. MOORE is a Research Assistant in the Long Term Care Resources Program at Duke University.

DEANE NEUBAUER is Professor of Political Science at the University of Hawaii. His work includes *Empirical Democratic Theory* (1969), and *Readings in Modern Political Analysis* (1968), as well as numerous articles in scholarly journals.

SAUNDRA K. SCHNEIDER is an Assistant Professor in the Department of Government and International Studies at the University of South Carolina. She previously served as the Health Planning Administrator and the Medicaid Program Administrator for the State of Ohio.

Health Policy Reform in America

Innovations from the States

1

The States and Health Care Policy: Taking the Lead

Howard M. Leichter

. . . the sorry fact is that most state and local governments—with some notable exceptions—are poorly structured and poorly staffed to carry out new and innovative tasks. They have a hard time even meeting their routine commitments.

—E. Ginsberg and R. Solow, "Some Lessons of the 1960s," *The Public Interest*, 1974.

But suddenly the states are where much of what is vital, new, interesting and important in American politics is going on.

—Morton Keller, *Governing*, 1988.

What a difference a decade makes! After years of being overshadowed by the federal government and "neglected," "maligned," and derided by many national interest groups and scholars, the states are reemerging, "reformed, reinvigorated, [and] resourceful."[1] Suddenly pundits, policymakers, and political scientists have found "a burst of innovation at the state level,"[2] and "a level of liberal and minority political activism heretofore unknown in state capitals."[3] The perception among political observers that domestic political power is gravitating toward, and policy creativity is emerging from, the states is accompanied by a favorable public attitude toward state governments. Opinion polls

3

show that Americans today have more faith in their state governments than in the federal government.[4]

Predictably the vitality of state governments has been most apparent in such traditional areas of state responsibility as education, criminal justice, and taxation. Increasingly, however, the states have entered new policy territories, including comparable worth, exploring new foreign markets for state products, regulating toxic waste and other environmental hazards, testing AIDS vaccines, and determining when life begins and when and under what circumstances it should end.[5]

Although it would be misleading to suggest that the states have shown greater inventiveness in one particular area of public concern than in others, few areas have stimulated as much creativity, activity, and interest as that of health policy. Faced with problems involving access, cost containment, the quality of health care, and the promotion of responsible life-styles, state governments have assumed new roles and obligations in the area of health policy. This book is about some of the recent state efforts to meet these challenges.

The purpose of this chapter is to examine both the conditions that have fostered increased state policy innovation and reform in general and those that relate specifically to the health field. The story that will unfold is one of federal retreat, unprecedented demands on the health care system, and a fundamental reorientation in the way both medical professionals and the general public have come to think about the problem of ill health. Political, philosophical, epidemiological, and life-style changes have conspired to relocate the locus of health policymaking in this country to the state capitals. All this is not to suggest that the federal government has meekly abandoned the field to the states. The chapters in this book tell a story of continued active federal involvement and rekindled interest in the health policy arena. Yet that involvement and interest is often in the form of piecemeal responses to chronic health policy problems rather than attempts at fundamental policy change. Nothing the federal government has done in the last decade in health policy has been as innovative or controversial, as, say, the Oregon experiment in health care rationing for Medicaid recipients. Nor has the national government been as attentive or responsive to the health care needs of the American people as many of the state governments described in the chapters in this volume.

The era of federal quiescence appears to be at an end. As I noted in the Preface, health care reform is now a national, not simply a state, problem, and federal officeholders of all political persuasions have announced their support for changing a system in which an estimated 35 to 38 million people, including 12 million children, are without health insurance, and one in which cost increases have been running at a rate twice that of overall inflation. Thus, for example, in January 1992 there were 30 health insurance bills before Congress, and George Bush, who has yet to claim the title of "health care president," unveiled a plan for a national health policy in his State of the Union Address. Clearly the federal government's role in the delivery of health care is about to change significantly.

Yet even in this environment of federal activism, I predict that national policymakers will look to state experiments and experiences when they grapple with health care policy reform. Indeed, several proposals offered by congressional Democrats, including an insurance pool for people who cannot purchase coverage because of preexisting conditions and requiring employers either to provide insurance for their employees or pay a tax, were first proposed in various state experiments. Either as models upon which federal policy is crafted, or as the innovative provider and regulator in the first instance, the states will play a major role in the shaping of health policy into the next century.

New Federalism and Its Aftermath

It was not that long ago, as the Ginsberg and Solow quotation at the head of this chapter suggests, that the states were routinely dismissed, by former state officials as well as academicians, as too administratively inept and politically corrupt to respond effectively to pressing public problems. This was an attitude taken especially by liberal policymakers and political observers. In the 1960s, for example, then-senator and former governor of Maine Edmund Muskie (D) complained that "because of antiquated, patronage oriented personnel systems which hinder the hiring and keeping of good people, state administration is often . . . lacking in quality and experience, is unimaginative, and too subject to negative political and bureaucratic pressures."[6]

The sixties in particular was a time when state governments suffered the reputation as obstructionist and recalcitrant troops in the war on the various social evils identified by liberals. James Sundquist dubbed this the "Alabama syndrome." He explains: "In the drafting of the Economic Opportunity Act, an 'Alabama syndrome' developed. Any suggestion within the poverty task force that the states be given a role in the administration of the act was met with the question, 'Do you want to give that kind of power to [Alabama Governor] George Wallace?' "[7] Liberals, then, viewed the states with suspicion, favoring social policy leadership from the national government. Gary Clarke summarizes the liberal indictment of the states in the following manner:

> Being smaller than the national government, they are more prone to special interest group favoritism; being less professional, they are less likely to be vigilant enforcers of the public interest; and having less money, they are less likely to devote sufficient resources to do a thorough job of regulation and enforcement.[8]

Conservatives, on the other hand, have long argued that state governments were politically and administratively better situated than the national government to gauge popular sentiment and to resist the temptations of prolific spending and social nannyism. This conservative affection for "leaving it up to the states" was reiterated by George Bush in his 1991 State of the Union Address when, explaining a proposal to turn over $20 billion in programs to the states, he said: "It moves power and decision-making closer to the people. And it reinforces a theme of this administration: appreciation and encouragement of the innovative power of 'states as laboratories.' "

Despite President Bush's endorsement of the "states as laboratories" thesis, his is one of a dwindling number of conservative voices praising state activities of late. Indeed, conventional ideological distinctions seem to have gone awry: liberals now view the states as progressive, while many conservatives bemoan their new activism. "Conservatives who gleefully assumed that shifting responsibility for social programs to the states would mean the end of the programs have discovered that state governments were not as conservative as they thought."[9] Richard Nathan believes that this reversal reflects historical cycles of federalism in this country. He makes the case that,

> Typically the national government has been the source of innovations and policy initiatives in liberal (prospending and expansive) periods of our history; the states (not all states, but many of them) have been the

centers of activism and innovation in conservative (retrenchment and contractive) periods.

Thus, as the "conservative" 1980s replaced the "liberal" 1960s and early 1970s, each ideological group has had to readjust its view of the national and state governments.[10] This explanation, convincing as it is, begs the question: How and why did this reversal occur? The answer lies in forces at work both within and outside of the states themselves.

A Federal Retreat

To begin, the states were able to emerge from the shadow of federal activism and dominance in part because that shadow has shrunk. The retreat from federal social policy hyperactivism began during the Nixon administration. Nixon was committed to what he called a "New Federalism" in which there would be a rearrangement or rationalization of national and state/local responsibilities with an aim toward "strengthen[ing] the capacity of States and localities to make decisions which reflect their own priorities and needs."[11] The main tools in accomplishing this rationalization were block grants and revenue sharing, both of which were intended to give subnational governments greater autonomy and flexibility.

Whatever Nixon's intentions, the immediate results were quite different. Federal aid to states and localities increased appreciably during the Nixon–Ford years, as did categorical grants. But perhaps most significantly, "The Nixon administration also presided over and contributed to the greatest expansion of federal regulation of state and local government in American history."[12] Yet a case can be made that Nixon (and later Ford) was responsible for beginning the shift in domestic political power from the national government to state governments. Ironically this occurred not by design but because of the virtual paralysis of the federal government in the wake of Watergate, the Arab oil embargo, and the fall, under Gerald Ford, of South Vietnam and the accompanying dramatic decline in citizen support for national institutions.[13] The national malaise and citizen disenchantment with the national government following the troubled Nixon–Ford administrations continued during the Carter years and was epitomized by the energy and the Iran hostage crisis. In the early 1980s public opinion polls were reporting rather significant disenchantment with the federal government and considerably more faith in state government. For example, Gallup found that in 1981 by a margin of 67 percent to 18 percent the American people believed that state governments were more likely to run social programs efficiently than the federal government, while by a margin of 67 percent to 15 percent they believed the states were more understanding of their needs than the federal government.[14]

It was against a backdrop, then, of both real and perceived impotence on the part of the national government that Ronald Reagan reached the White House, promising to restore America's greatness at home and abroad and to reduce the role of the national government in Americans' lives. Reagan adumbrated his view of the relative responsibilities of the federal and state governments by proclaiming in his first Inaugural Address a need "to curb the size and influence of the Federal establishment and to demand recognition of the distinction between the powers granted to the Federal Government and those reserved to the states or to the people."

Reagan officially launched his own version of a "New Federalism" in his 1982 State of the Union Address when he announced his intention "to make our system of federalism work again" and "to strengthen the discretion and flexibility of State and local governments." In practical terms this would be accomplished in three ways: reduce federal aid to the states and localities, consolidate remaining specific (i.e. categorical) programs into block grants, and permanently transfer various federal programs, worth $47 billion in 1982, to the state and local governments. In terms of the latter approach, the administration proposed a transitional period during which the federal government would help state and local governments pay for these programs through a trust fund financed by federal excise taxes that would be phased out in ten years. The centerpiece of the proposal was a so-called great swap: the federal government would assume full responsibility for Medicaid, while the states would take over the Aid to Families with Dependent Children and food stamp programs.

Although a definitive assessment of the New Federalism may be premature, it is clear that the results were at best mixed. First, the great swap never took place. State officials declined the offer because they claimed that the trust fund would not cover the costs of the programs for which the states would be responsible under Reagan's proposal. Second, the consolidation of scores of categorical grants into nine block grants actually involved only $7.5 billion of the total $88 billion of federal aid to states and localities.[15] Subsequent Reagan proposals for further consolidation and transfer of responsibility met with opposition and were ultimately rejected. Despite these setbacks, however, federal aid to the states and localities was reduced dramatically in the Reagan years: federal aid as a percentage of state and local outlays declined from a high in 1978 of over 26 percent to just under 17 percent in 1988.

In addition, along with the decline in the flow of money there was a reduction in the onerous regulations and administrative oversight imposed by the federal government on the states and localities. Reagan boasted in his 1982 State of the Union Address that there were 23,000 fewer pages in the *Federal Register* in 1981 than there had been in the previous year. Furthermore, John Kincaid has reported that "the Reagan administration also eliminated or modified 47 of 80 federal regulations identified by the National Governors' Association as being burdensome to states."[16] One unconventional measure of the success of the Reagan deregulation is that nearly 100 Washington law firms, specializing in regulatory law, closed their doors during the Reagan years.[17]

Finally the symbolic capstone to the Reagan deregulation effort came in the form of Executive Order 12612, issued in October 1987. The order was more a statement of philosophy than a plan of action but as such it wonderfully captures the *zeitgeist* of the Reagan administration. The purpose of the order was "to restore the division of governmental responsibilities between the national government and the States that was intended by the Framers of the Constitution and to ensure that the principles of federalism established by the Framers guide Executive departments and agencies in the formulation and implementation of policies." In effect, the order required executive departments and agencies routinely to consider the implications of federal action on the states in terms of limiting state power or impinging on state jurisdiction. Among the fundamental principles that should guide executive departments in this effort were two that go to the very heart of Ronald Reagan's philosophy of government:

1. "Federalism is rooted in the knowledge that our political liberties are best assured by limiting the size and scope of the national government";
2. "In most areas of governmental concern, the States uniquely pos-

sess the constitutional authority, the resources, and the competence to discern the sentiments of the people and to govern accordingly."[18]

The essence of the message was that whenever possible the national government should defer to the states in domestic policy, and in those areas where laws of national scope are necessary the states should be granted "the maximum administrative discretion possible." Kincaid thinks the order, which was intended to guide executive departments and agencies in policy planning, had as much educational as operational impact.

> The order was written in rather vague terms because it was deemed both impossible and unnecessary to stipulate detailed guidelines covering a diversity of agencies and policy issues. Instead, the order is intended to alert and sensitize executive officials to federalism principles and to require them to examine policies in the light of those principles.[19]

Other forces were at work reinforcing Ronald Reagan's commitment to redistributing domestic policy responsibility in the American system. Foremost among these were the mammoth budget deficits that emerged during the Reagan years and continue to influence policy in the Bush administration. In fact, one could argue that these deficits had more to do with propelling the New Federalism forward than an ideological concern, executive order, or legislative initiative.[20] When Ronald Reagan took office in 1981, the outstanding gross debt of the federal government was $914.3 billion, representing 34.2 percent of the Gross National Product (GNP); when he left office the outstanding debt was $2,581.6 billion or 54.9 percent of GNP.[21] Budget deficits, then, reinforced the message that was coming out of Washington: Do not expect any new programs or indeed continued levels of support for many existing programs from the federal government. The message, however, was as much symbolic as substantive. "Retrenchment involves more than money. *It sends a signal.* Reagan sent a signal to the domestic public sector . . . that the federal government should and would do less, and that states and localities, especially nonprofit institutions that provide social services and the private sector, should do more."[22]

The States Advance

In addition to those at work in Washington, there were forces in the states themselves that helped inspire and facilitate a rejuvenation of state policy activity.[23] In the last several years almost all the states have revised their constitutions to some degree. In some instances these changes were imposed by the national government, with U.S. Supreme Court reapportionment decisions and congressional civil rights legislation, while in others, such as education and tax reform, political change grew out of problems and pressures from within the states themselves.

These reforms have been facilitated, or prompted, by the modernization of state government. For example, state legislatures are now more likely to have annual sessions, streamlined committee systems, recorded roll-call votes, professional staffs, and access to computer-assisted data gathering capability than twenty or even ten years ago.[24] Similarly, the power of many chief executives has been strengthened through either constitutional revision or statute, so that governors today are more likely to be able to succeed themselves, serve four-year rather than two-year terms, and have larger professional staffs and broader appointive and budgetary power than their recent predecessors.

Finally, state courts have emerged in recent years as important actors in many critical policy areas, including minority and civil rights and environmental protection. Specifically with regard to the rights of individuals, Sol Wachtler, chief judge of the Court of Appeals of New York State says: "We are now experiencing a renaissance with respect to state constitutional rights. As the U.S. Supreme Court retreats from the field, or holds the line on individual rights, state courts and litigants seeking solutions to new problems are turning with greater frequency to the state constitutions, which for many years lay dormant in the shadow of the federal Bill of Rights."[25] Whatever the scope, focus, or impulse of these reforms, the results have been the same: "The cumulative effects of these independent reforms have been stronger, more capable governmental institutions and a desire on the part of state government officials to expand the scope of their responsibility even further."[26]

In addition to structural changes there have been a number of important behavioral changes in state government and politics. First, minority and female representation in elected and appointed state offices has increased substantially over the past few decades. For example, the percentage of female state legislators rose from 4 percent in 1969 to 18.1 percent in 1991. Similarly, the number of black elected state officials increased from 169 in 1970 to 417 in 1987.[27] This in turn almost certainly has enhanced the credibility, legitimacy, vitality, and responsiveness of state government. Second, state legislators, governors, judges, and a host of administrative officers now routinely share policy ideas, information, and experiences. This diffusion of information has enhanced the capacity of states to respond innovatively to public problems and demands. The ability to do so is particularly important in times of critical situations such as that posed by the AIDS epidemic. Particularly noteworthy in the area of interstate communications and cooperation have been the efforts of the National Governors' Association, which has been especially active in recent years in the areas of educational reform and environmental protection.

Third, one of the more interesting policy-related developments in recent years has been increased state-focused interest-group activity. Thus, as the federal deficit grew, aid to the states and localities declined, and federal regulations diminished, interest groups turned to state governments to fill the financial, regulatory, and programmatic void created by the federal retreat and retrenchment. Civil rights groups, advocates of the poor, environmentalists, educators, business groups, and others went to the state capitals seeking not only continued support for existing programs but also the initiation of new ones.

In sum, for reasons that were both internal and external to their own political environments, the structure and processes of state politics have changed significantly in the past two decades. The message from the Reagan and Bush administrations has been unambiguous: expect less from the federal government—less money, less regulation, less responsibility for domestic policy initiatives. As a result the states have become potentially far more formidable and effective policy actors in the American federal system. All this is not to suggest, however, that the states can or will fill the void left by the national government or fulfill the promise expected of them by interest groups. Foremost among the problems facing the states are the fiscal constraints that periodically and seemingly inevitably visit themselves on state governments. Much of the resistance among state governors to Reagan's new federalism proposals in the early 1980s was related to the severe budget problems faced by the states. And, as various authors in this volume demonstrate, the specter of recession and deficits has again come to dominate state budgets and other policy considerations. Nevertheless, the main point remains valid: The states have moved to a position of preeminence in domestic policy initiatives.

The Growing Health Policy Role of the States

The factors at work bringing about this transformation apply across virtually all areas of domestic policy. There are some, however, that have special relevance to the area of health policy. To begin, the states traditionally have maintained a high level of interest and activity in health policy. They are, after all, one of the largest purchasers and providers of health care services in the country. The astronomical increase in health care costs over the past decade—the $666 billion spent on health care in 1990 was twice the amount spent in 1982—alone would have warranted increased state concern and activity in this area. Beyond this, however, the states are the primary regulators of the health industry. States license physicians, nurses, pharmacists, and other health professionals; regulate the insurance, nursing home, and hospital industries; set rules governing workmen's compensation; and set standards for environmental pollution.

Finally, state and local governments have historically played the major role in public health. In this capacity they are responsible for laws and standards governing immunizations and inoculations, school health programs, public sanitation, waste disposal, and protection of food and water supplies. The regulatory, administrative, and provider roles of the states have all come at a high cost. "[W]hen the expense of *all* areas of state involvement in health care are considered, state governments now finance approximately one-third of all public health care services being provided to Americans."[28]

This investment would have warranted a high profile for state governments in health policy under "normal" circumstances. A number of unusual factors have conspired to increase that role greatly and turn the states into major health policy innovators. Two of these have already been mentioned. First, the federal government has cut, capped, or set limits to the growth of federal expenditures on social programs. One such program is Medicaid. Jointly financed by the federal and state governments, with the major portion coming from the federal government, Medicaid is administered by the states under federal guidelines. While Medicaid funding experienced a real growth of 33 percent during the Carter years, it increased just 2 percent under Reagan.[29] At the same time that real growth in spending on Medicaid came to a virtual halt, demand increased. This was the result of new people coming onto the Medicaid rolls because they lost their jobs during the recession in the early 1980s, and of new programs that were now funded under the program, including nursing home care and organ transplants. Although Medicaid cuts were never as draconian as those proposed by the Reagan administration, the constant specter of such cuts during those years spurred many states to find new ways to finance health care for those who might end up off the Medicaid rolls, and to expand coverage for the poor in general, while at the same time trying to contain costs.

Second, as part of the New Federalism's effort to reduce federal regulations and increase state discretion, changes were made in Medicaid rules that were intended to give the states increased leeway, although here too accomplishments fell short of expectations. In a review of the actual as opposed to hoped for changes in Medicaid, Frank Thompson has concluded that "viewing changes in the law with respect to health block grants and Medicaid, the president [i.e., Reagan] appears to have won a quarter of a loaf. While the modifications that occurred did not inevitably boost state discretion, the Reagan years provided states with new authority as implementing agents."[30]

Moreover, in many instances the federal government has actually increased the burden on the states by imposing mandates that require the states to provide expanded services or to expand the population served by the Medicaid program. Whether it is because of increased demand, overall medical cost inflation, or federal mandates, Medicaid has become, in the words of former Oregon Governor Neil Goldschmidt, "the monster that ate the states." Thus, while overall general fund expenditures increased 76 percent from 1980 to 1988, state Medicaid expenses rose on the average of 107 percent during this period, although in some states the increase was as much as 200 percent. Overall, Medicaid funding constituted about 9 percent of general fund spending in 1989, nearly twice what it had been in the mid 1960s. By some estimates, recent changes in Medicaid could cost the states an additional $3.2 billion by 1994 and increase the proportion of the general fund revenues allocated to Medicaid to 13 percent.[31] All this has placed an enormous burden on state policymakers, requiring of them, as this book demonstrates, considerable imagination and innovation as they try to balance budgets, provide nonhealth-related services, and satisfy the seemingly insatiable demand for more and better health care.

Yet another factor that explains the emerging dominance of the states in health policy can be traced to a fundamental shift in the field from an emphasis on access to one on prevention. This shift, which began in the early 1970s and continued through the 1980s, needs some elaboration.

For much of the last century or so, the prevailing wisdom has been that people can best maximize their prospects for good health through access to adequate health care. As a result, the emphasis in national debates on health policy has been on health care delivery. In this context, one major issue has been whether the government should help people secure access through a national health insurance system. Ultimately this nation decided that only certain vulnerable groups, like the needy and the aged, blind and disabled, or special groups, like veterans and members of Congress, should receive direct assistance from the government in getting health care. Many more, of course, receive indirect assistance through tax deductions on private health insurance.

In the past two decades there has been an important shift in the debate over how people can maximize their chances of staying healthy. Since the mid 1970s greater rhetorical and material emphasis has been placed on reducing environmental health hazards and encouraging more prudent life-styles. The "new perspective" on health, as it came to be known, heralded a new era in which health care professionals, public policymakers, academics, and the general public have come to believe that greater progress toward becoming a healthy people can be made through reducing both environmental hazards and self-indulgent, health-endangering personal behavior than by expanding access to health care. One crude measure of this shift was the virtual disappearance of the debate over national health insurance at the national level. In 1970 and 1971 the *Congressional Record* listed a total of 50 references to national health insurance; between 1981 and 1990 there were just three. The recent revival of interest at the state level in guaranteeing access to health care for those without insurance, noted in a number of selections in this book, has not replaced the important role of health promotion on state health policy agendas.

Because health promotion and disease prevention have traditionally been the primary responsibility of state and local governments, adoption of the "new perspective" on health has meant that the locus of health policy activity, and opportunities for innovative programs, have shifted to these arenas. The health policy agenda beginning in the late 1970s became crowded with such issues as mandatory seat belt and minimum drinking-age laws, restrictions on the sales pro-

motion and advertisement of tobacco and alcohol products, and distribution of free condoms and clean hypodermic needles, as well as various environmental health problems. Health politics became, to a
considerable extent, the politics of health promotion and disease prevention. And state governments have been at the very epicenter of the
action.

In the last decade the states have also been at the center of another
relatively recent health phenomenon, namely the battle against AIDS.
Rarely, if ever, in this century has any disease so captured popular fears,
frustrations, and prejudices as AIDS. Rarely, indeed, has any disease
emerged so rapidly and embedded itself so firmly in the health policy
landscape. While recent public health problems such as Legionnaires'
disease and Toxic Shock Syndrome enjoyed similarly rapid infamy,
their impact was much more circumscribed in terms of numbers affected and duration of the etiological mystery surrounding them. The
enormous burden AIDS has placed on the state and local governments
and the resulting "creative and compassionate" responses are discussed
by Daniel M. Fox in Chapter Two.

As Fox suggests, the cost of this disease will indeed be considerable: the bill for the 1990s may exceed $50 billion. In 1991, for
example, the estimated outlay was $5.8 billion and this is expected
to reach over $10 billion per year by 1994. AIDS will, of course,
further burden state Medicaid programs—estimates range from 20 to
60 percent of the cost absorbed by Medicaid—but the cost will also be
borne by public hospitals run by state and local governments. While
it is unclear exactly how the bill will be distributed, it is certain that
the states will continue to play a major role not only in the financing
of care for AIDS victims but in other AIDS-related policy efforts, including health education, protection of civil rights, and even research.

State policymakers will confront other major health problems that
will stretch both their resources and their ingenuity. These include the
care and treatment of the mentally ill, the aged, and people with chemical dependencies. Unlike many of the public health problems that
faced the states at the turn of the last century, such as tuberculosis,
influenza, measles, and other infectious or contagious diseases, these
problems will neither be episodic, as epidemics historically have been,
nor lend themselves to a "magic bullet" solution. Instead, state governments can expect to find pressing health issues high on the policy
agenda for decades to come, even if a cure for AIDS is found tomorrow.

Conclusion

Short of the adoption of a federally run national health insurance system, the states will play an increasingly prominent role in the provision, regulation, and financing of health care in this country. Beyond the important question of whether or not the states will have the financial ability to handle this challenge there lies a more fundamental, or at least interesting, one: What is the potential consequence or significance of this increased state responsibility in health care policymaking? Are the states likely to do a good job in guaranteeing the quality of care or the equitable distribution of resources? What about the commitment of state governments to insuring access to quality health care for all who need it? Proponents of state activism argue that the states will be more responsive to local needs and are in a better position to experiment and find innovative solutions to difficult health problems. The chapters in this book would lend credence to this perspective. In states as geographically, economically, and demographically diverse as Hawaii, Massachusetts, Oregon, and Texas, policymakers have shown extraordinary inventiveness and sensitivity in dealing with some of our most intractable health-related problems.

Yet not all observers are sanguine about the prospects of an increasing reliance on state governments as the main protectors of the public's health. Frank Thompson, for example, notes that there is considerable suspicion about the "commitment, capacity, and progressivity" of the states when it comes to social programs in general and health policy in particular. He suggests that some states have been reluctant to support redistributive social programs, including health care for the needy or publicly financed insurance systems. The explanation for this lack of commitment is often traced to a variety of economic pressures, including the power exercised by both industry and statewide medical providers. "Presumably, jurisdictions must above all be concerned with protecting their fiscal base and spurring economic growth. More generous health policies, especially redistributive ones, impede this development. Such generosity may drive up state taxes, thereby discouraging firms and affluent individuals from remaining in or moving to the state."[32]

Thompson also notes reservations about the fiscal and administrative capacity of the states to formulate and implement innovative health policies effectively and efficiently. Especially troubling to some critics is the lack of tax progressivity in the states caused by their heavy reliance on property and sales tax revenues. "Those less able to pay might, therefore, bear 'too much' of the costs of expanding health programs."[33]

The perennial concern, especially among liberals, over the commitment, capacity, and progressivity of the states is probably less valid today than in the past. Indeed, Thompson acknowledges that "while hard evidence remains elusive, a plausible case exists that any gap on these dimensions between state governments and Washington has declined. State capacity in particular has probably increased."[34] As I have noted above, this is certainly the case with regard to the administrative capacity of the states as their governments have become more professionalized. Yet the recession of the early 1990s was a reminder of how vulnerable the states are to economic cycles, regardless of structural political change. Innovative ideas and civic virtue often fall prey to budget shortfalls. This vulnerability has renewed the concerns of health care advocates that only a major federal presence and initiative can secure health care policy reform.

Whether or not these concerns are justified may be beside the point. "In spite of growing discontent about the system from providers and consumers, the federal government seems unable or unwilling to assume the leadership necessary for systemic change at the national level."[35] The inability and/or unwillingness of the federal government to address some of the more pressing health problems of our times will leave a policy void that the states will have to fill.

Plan of This Book

The contributors to this book focus on what are, in my judgment, some of the most critical and durable health care problems facing this nation. Daniel M. Fox opens with a discussion of how the states have responded to what might be called the defining disease of the last decade, namely AIDS. By early 1992 over one million Americans were thought to carry the virus, and nearly 135,000 had died from it. Fox describes the transformation in public perception, clinical treatment, and public financing of health care as HIV infection moved from being viewed as an episodic plague to a chronic illness. He shows how, during the period from 1986 to 1990, the states, largely in the absence of any national policy, responded to the AIDS crisis with creativity, compassion, and at considerable cost. His chapter, like others in this volume, reminds us how vulnerable the states are in trying to undertake and sustain innovative health care programs because of the fiscal and political uncertainties that are generic to a federal system.

In Chapter Three, Saundra Schneider shows how the states, working within the confines of the Medicaid program, have been the primary and creative forces in shaping maternal and child health care policy. She credits the Omnibus Budget and Reconciliation Act of 1981 with setting the stage for increased state autonomy, flexibility, and innovation in maternal and child care, but makes a convincing case that the states then seized the moment and gained effective control of this policy area. Schneider argues that in many instances federal changes in Medicaid were inspired by or merely endorsed existing state practices. She studies the experiences of four states—California, North Carolina, South Carolina, and Arkansas—to document her thesis.

As the country's population becomes older—the fastest growing segment of the American population for the next several decades will be those eighty-five years of age or older—long-term care for the elderly will become one of the most important, and potentially most costly, concerns of health care policy. David J. Falcone, Dell Ensley, and Cecilia B. Moore (Chapter Four) compare "aging policy" in Oregon and North Carolina. They conclude that Oregon's approach is superior in its ability to contain costs, assure access to those who need long-term care, and provide that care in an environment that best suits the needs and preferences of the elderly. The authors seek an explanation for Oregon's success and speculate on the exportability of the Oregon model. Their conclusion, that a variety of cultural and socioeconomic factors are involved but that the critical variable appears to be a "vigorous, sustained, informed, and effective advocacy" of the needs of the elderly, has important implications for the diffusion of innovation in this and other health policy areas as well.

In Chapter Five, Steven Laubacher and Malcolm Goggin describe Texas' success in dealing with one of the most troubling health care–related issues of the last decade, namely the deinstitutionalization of the mentally ill and retarded. Beginning in the 1970s, there was a national movement to relocate many of the mentally ill and retarded from mental institutions back into their communities. This seemingly enlightened effort had the unintended and unanticipated consequence of contributing to a new national problem; urban homelessness and the creation of a subclass of "street people." Laubacher and Goggin show how a policy of deinstitutionalization of the mentally retarded, if properly designed and administered, can apparently minimize the problem of creating homelessness and provide humane treatment of the mentally retarded.

Each of the next three chapters deals with state efforts to extend the protection of health insurance to all citizens. In Chapter Six, Oregon again comes under scrutiny when Leichter examines that state's "bold experiment" in health care rationing in its attempt to provide universal access to health care for all Oregonians. Few policy reforms have generated as much interest and controversy in recent years as the Oregon Basic Health Services Act. Oregon, under the talented leadership of its physician–Senate president, John Kitzhaber, and in the context of the moralistic political culture described by Falcone, Ensley, and Moore in Chapter Four, has proposed extending a basic or adequate level of health services to all people who fall below the federal poverty level and eventually to all Oregonians. The state has solicited citizen as well as expert opinion on what constitutes a "basic level of services" and will fund only those procedures and no more. This case illustrates, however, that innovation from below still often requires cooperation from above, that is, from the federal government. The final chapter on the Oregon story has not yet been written.

The state of Hawaii was one of the first in the nation to systematically address the problem of access to health care for the uninsured. In fact, Deane Neubauer (Chapter Seven) argues that Hawaii state officials see physical well-being as a critical ingredient in the economic vitality of their state. Hence, the promotion of Hawaii as a place of healthy living has become part of the state's tourism and economic development efforts. Indeed, so important is this goal, that state officials have taken to calling Hawaii "The Health State." Neubauer describes the series of policy steps Hawaii has taken to enhance its image as a place concerned with the good health of its population. It has done this by addressing such issues as expanding access to health care and promoting good health through environmental protection. Neubauer's account of the Hawaii "health culture" is a reminder of the central role that good health plays in the American value system and the potential political and economic advantages that go along with promoting this value.

"The story of universal health care in Massachusetts attests to the inherent vulnerability and fragility of state policy reforms." Thus begins Camille Ascuaga's account (Chapter Eight) of Massachusetts' much publicized experiment in guaranteeing universal access to health care. The Massachusetts law received national attention during the 1988 presidential campaign when the Democratic candidate, Massachusetts Governor Michael Dukakis, hailed it as a model for a nationwide effort at guaranteeing universal access. However, much like that state's "economic miracle," this Dukakis legacy has also fallen on hard times. Ascuaga's account is a sobering reminder of how quickly political and economic events can derail state policy reform. The Massachusetts experiment, whatever its fate—and it is still uncertain—provides important lessons for those interested in health care policy. Of particular significance was the effort to enlist the support of the small-business community in the policymaking and implementing process. Since small-business people are, for economic reasons, often opponents of expanding health care access to the working poor, the Massachusetts experiment remains important to students of health policy.

In the final chapter of the book, Bruce Jennings shifts the focus of the discussion from the substance of health policy innovation and reform to the moral and ethical nature of the process by which policy change takes place. In particular, he is concerned about the role of democratic values in helping reform the health policymaking process. He suggests that the innovative content of recent reform efforts has raised new ethical issues and generated innovative forms of policy discourse. Jennings argues that citizen involvement in health policy formation, illustrated most dramatically by the grass roots organization, Oregon Health Decisions, will be increasingly used to legitimize the allocation, prioritization, and, perhaps, rationing of health care resources in the future. In this sense, according to Jennings, democratic values will have an increasingly important role to play in the policymaking process. And, most importantly from the perspective of this book, this is most likely to occur at the subnational level.

Notes

1. Ira Sharkansky, *The Maligned States* (New York: McGraw-Hill, 1978); Malcolm E. Jewell, "The Neglected World of State Politics," *The Journal of Politics* 44 (August 1982): 638–657; Mavis Mann Reeves, "The States as Polities: Reformed, Reinvigorated, Resourceful," *The Annals of the American Academy of Political and Social Sciences* (hereafter *The Annals*) 509 (May 1990): 83–93.

2. David Osborne, *Laboratories of Democracy* (Boston: Harvard Business School Press, 1990), 1; Ann O'M. Bowman and Richard C. Kearney, *The Resurgence of the States* (Englewood Cliffs, NJ: Prentice Hall, 1986), 2.

3. Jerry Hagstrom, "Liberal and Minority Coalitions Pleading Their Cases in State Capitals," *National Journal* (23 February 1985): 426.

4. *The Economist,* 3 March 1990, 28.

5. For a review of some of these efforts see Robert Pear, "States Are Found More Responsive on Social Issues," *The New York Times,* 19 May 1985; Miles Benson, "States Take On Power as U.S. Government's Influence Ebbs," *Oregonian* (Portland), 22 April 1990; and John Herbers, "The New Federalism: Unplanned, Innovative and Here to Stay," *Governing* 1 (October 1987): 28–37.

6. Quoted in Gary J. Clarke, "The Role of the States in the Delivery of Health Services," *American Journal of Public Health* 71 (January 1981): 60.

7. James Sundquist, *Making Federalism Work* (Washington, DC: The Brookings Institution, 1969), 271.

8. Gary J. Clarke, "The Role of the States in the Delivery of Health Services," *American Journal of Public Health* 71 (January 1981): 60.

9. Jerry Hagstrom, "Liberal and Minority Coalitions Pleading Their Cases in State Capitals," *National Journal* 17 (25 February 1985): 426.

10. Richard P. Nathan, "Federalism—The Great 'Composition,' " in *The New American Political System,* 2d version, ed. Anthony King (Washington, DC: American Enterprise Institute, 1990), 241.

11. Richard M. Nixon, "White House Memorandum," June 1970, quoted in ibid., 251.

12. Timothy Conlan, *New Federalism: Intergovernmental Reform From Nixon to Reagan* (Washington, DC: The Brookings Institution, 1988), 84.

13. See Daniel Elazar, "Opening the Third Century of American Federalism: Issues and Prospects," *The Annals* 509 (May 1990): 14.

14. Dick Pawelek, "State vs. Federal Government: Which Is Most Trusted?" *Senior Scholastic,* 19 March 1982: 13.

15. Bowman and Kearney, *The Resurgence of the States,* 8.

16. John Kincaid, "The State of American Federalism—1987," Publius 18 (Summer 1988): 1.

17. Miles Benson, "States Take on Power as U.S. Government's Influence Ebbs."

18. *Public Papers of the Presidents of the United States: Ronald Reagan, 1987,* Book II (Washington, DC: Government Printing Office, 1989): 1235.

19. Kincaid, "The State of American Federalism," 8.

20. For such a view, see *The Economist,* 3 March 1990, 28.

21. U.S. Department of Commerce, *Statistical Abstract of the United States, 1989* (Washington, DC: Government Printing Office, 1989), 303.

22. Richard P. Nathan et al., *Reagan and the States* (Princeton: Princeton University Press, 1987), 14.

23. For the distinction between "external" (i.e., Washington) and "internal" (i.e., the states) factors stimulating state vitality, see Reeves, "The States as Polities," 86–93. This section draws heavily upon this work and Bowman and Kearney, *The Resurgence of the States,* 10–31.

24. Reeves, "The States as Polities," 88.

25. Sol Wachtler, "Constitutional Rights: Resuming the States' Role," *Intergovernmental Perspective* 15 (Summer 1989): 23.

26. Carl E. Van Horn, "The Quiet Revolution," in *The State of the States,* ed. Carl E. Van Horn (Washington, DC: CQ Press, 1989): 2.

27. Harold W. Stanley and Richard G. Niemi, *Vital Statistics on American Politics,* 2d edition (Washington, DC: CQ Press, 1990): 330; *Statistical Abstract of the United States, 1989,* 256.

28. Saundra K. Schneider, "Governors and Health Care Policy in the American States," *Policy Studies Journal* 17 (Summer 1989): 911. Emphasis supplied.

29. Frank J. Thompson, "New Federalism and Health Care Policy: States and the Old Questions," *Journal of Health Politics, Policy and Law* 11 (1986): 659.

30. Ibid., 654.

31. See Tony Hutchison, "The Medicaid Budget Tangle," *State Legislatures* 16 (March 1990): 15–19.

32. Frank J. Thompson, "New Federalism and Health Care Policy," 648.

33. Ibid., 649.

34. Ibid., 665.

35. Charles J. Dougherty, "Setting Health Care Priorities: Oregon's Next Steps," *Hastings Center Report* 21 (May–June 1991): 7.

2

The Once and Future Payers of Last Resort: The States and AIDS

Daniel M. Fox

Financing health care for persons with HIV infection and related diseases became a significant burden on the states and the taxpayers in the late 1980s. A number of states tried to meet this burden in ways that were innovative within the constraints imposed on state policymaking over many years by the United States Congress and regulators in the Health Care Financing Administration. By the end of 1990, this period of modest innovation was overtaken by events in the economy and in the public (and therefore the political) perception of AIDS. As one senior legislator put it, concern about AIDS in his state, even among liberals had been replaced by "massive apathy." A more scholarly assessment appeared in *The New England Journal of Medicine* in May 1991, where an article by Ronald Bayer, an expert on policy for AIDS, declared "An End to HIV Exceptionalism."

This chapter tells the story of that brief period of state innovation in financing for AIDS, the years between 1986 and 1990. In those years, the epidemic spread to every state and the federal government refused to make more than token gestures toward financing treatment. Estimates of the number of cases that would occur in the 1990s and of the cost per case caused great alarm in state capitols. The AIDS epidemic compounded the standard problems of financing health care for the poor and for everyone with chronic degenerative diseases.

This chapter, and the spirit of state innovativeness that it documents, was the fortunate product of a misjudgment in which I participated. The misjudgment was that AIDS would become increasingly important to the states in the 1990s. As a result of that misjudgment, Larry Gostin and William Curran of the Harvard University School of Public Health obtained a grant to commission papers on how the states could write better laws and regulations to cope with the epidemic. All of the commissions but mine went to academic lawyers. I was the odd person in the process because no academic lawyer shared my experience of helping out in policymaking in New York State in financing treatment for AIDS. Thinking, wrongly, that the state innovation would continue to be important in paying for AIDS treatment, I spent considerable time assembling documents from around the country and even more time conducting lengthy telephone interviews with key actors in a dozen states. The result was this chapter.

A knowledgeable political analyst writing about this subject in 1992 would not bother to catalogue state struggles to innovate within federally imposed constraints. Instead she or he would tell a story that had these elements: (1) the recession that began in 1990 (some would say earlier) made AIDS relatively much less important than it had been, even in the high-incidence states like New York, California, New Jersey, and Florida; (2) the failure of the epidemic to explode through heterosexual transmission made AIDS even more a disease of the black and Hispanic poor in the 1990s than in the 1980s, and thus relieved the states of pressures for action from white middle- and upper-class interest groups; (3) the tokenism of the appropriations transferred to local government in the federal Ryan White Act of 1990 made plain that it is now a national consensus that AIDS is a terrible problem, but not one that people who run for office have to be very concerned about.

What follows is a story of state innovation that turned out to be short-lived. It is, nonetheless, an important story because it reminds us that state officials often want to be innovators in policy and very often succeed, despite enormous obstacles put in their path by large constituencies of voters, economic interest groups, and the federal government. It is also a story that justifies political analysts tracking state policy with dedication and care. In retrospect, I am pleased about the misjudgment that led to the recording of this history and recognition of the people whose work I describe below.

By late 1989, 42 states had appropriated almost $100 million for patient care and support services in addition to their mandated contributions to Medicaid.[1] At least 12 states have used regulatory authority to organize treatment for persons with AIDS, 11 of these through their Medicaid programs.[2] Several states were purchasing private health insurance for persons with HIV infection.[3] Many states had established task forces on HIV and published plans for financing and organizing services during the epidemic.[4]

States regarded financing health care for persons with HIV-related disease as a growing problem for four reasons:

1. the increasing number and widespread geographic distribution of persons with HIV infection;
2. the increasing incidence of HIV among people who do not have or who lose private health insurance coverage;
3. the encouraging findings that expensive drugs can delay the onset and slow the progress of HIV-related diseases;
4. the unlikely prospect of a national solution to the growing burden on the states of the cost of health care for the poor, the uninsured, and the underinsured.

By mid 1989 state and local governments had paid a substantial proportion of the cost of caring for about 60 percent of the first 100,000 reported cases of AIDS through the state share of Medicaid and subsidies to finance the care of the uninsured and underinsured.[5] The state contribution to the cost of treating HIV-related disease is, moreover, likely to remain the same, especially because the politics of the federal budget deficit make major new redistributive national programs to finance care for any group of Americans unlikely. Many states have responded creatively and compassionately—and at considerable cost—to the challenge of the epidemic. This chapter describes the responses and the limited knowledge that has been acquired to date about their effectiveness.[6]

HIV infection was, for the first seven years of the epidemic in the United States, generally considered to be a plague called AIDS, a shocking affliction that rapidly destroyed its victims. By 1989, AIDS had been reconceived as HIV infection, a chronic illness of uncertain duration. As in other chronic illnesses, treatment of HIV infection and its consequences delayed the onset of symptoms or ameliorated them, but treatment did not cure the underlying disease. Therefore, the cost of care outside hospitals—of drugs, clinics, nursing homes, and home care—increased as a result of early detection and advances in therapeutics. The total cost of care for persons with HIV infection will increase by several billion dollars a year beyond existing estimates as a result of advances in drug therapy announced in the spring and summer of 1989.

The pressing problems raised by HIV infection for state policymakers in the 1990s will, therefore, be different from those of the 1980s. The dominant problems of the 1980s were how to organize and pay for hospital and physician services for people with AIDS who had lost or never had private health insurance, and how to provide nursing home and home health care during the few months, generally less than 18, between diagnosis of AIDS and death. The major problems for policymakers have changed. The new problems facing state policymakers in the 1990s are how to organize and finance early detection of infection and preventive drug treatment for persons without symptoms, and how to provide a full range of health and social services for infected persons whose life expectancy is unknown.

Uncertainty about how many people are infected and about how and to whom HIV will spread, complicates state efforts to design policies to finance care. In 1989 most federal and state officials assumed that one to one-and-one-half million people were infected and that the disease was spreading most rapidly among intravenous drug users. But there were still significant uncertainties regarding the rate of infection due to questions about the sexual practices and drug habits of Caucasians who live in suburban and rural areas, about the links between venereal disease, crack, and HIV in inner cities, and about the effectiveness of various educational strategies to prevent infection.

In June 1989, the General Accounting Office of the United States Congress estimated that current federal surveillance excluded one-third of present cases of AIDS and underestimated forecasts for the future.[7] An article in *Science* similarly suggested that Centers for Disease Control (CDC) data may underestimate "by a substantial margin the prevalence of AIDS in the white population of higher socioeconomic status."[8] What no one disputed, however, was that the number of cases of HIV-related disease would increase in each state and that the cost of care would increase for each case.

HIV Infection and the States: The Context

As a result of health policy in the United States during the past half century, the states have, largely by default, acquired an enormous residual responsibility. The states bear the burden of health care for people who lack or lose social or private insurance. These include people with disabilities who are ineligible for Medicare, those whose insurance benefits are exhausted or who have no insurance at all, and a majority of the people, of all ages, who need extensive long-term care.

HIV infection has rapidly become analogous to the major diseases of the 20th century: heart disease, cancer, stroke, diabetes, and arthritis.[9] Like these other chronic conditions, HIV-related disease is expensive to treat and to manage. Like them, HIV requires substantial expenditures for acute care in the closing months of life and demands considerable expenditures for drugs, physicians' services, and long-term care in institutions or other residential settings.

At the beginning of the epidemic, in the early 1980s, most of the people who provide and pay for health care assumed that AIDS would be a classic plague, rather than another problem of chronic illness. Plagues have historically risen quickly and unexpectedly, run rapidly through populations, and then have subsided forever or temporarily. Modern plagues of infectious disease, most people believed, yielded rather quickly to methods of science. These methods could isolate a microbial cause of disease and create vaccines and drugs to eliminate it. Most people sought analogies to AIDS in epidemics of influenza, polio, or cholera. Few believed, until very recently, that the more accurate analogue was tuberculosis, once called the "white plague," a chronic infection that was the most significant cause of death in the 19th century.[10]

As recently as 1985 and 1986, many people, using the classic plague model, expected that the cost of treating persons with AIDS would peak and then decline over a period of years. Thus, what many considered noteworthy about the early studies of the cost of treating persons with AIDS was the apparent sharp decline in the average number of days of hospital care used by patients in just a few years. This decline also caused a reduction in the aggregate cost per case. These data—

from studies in San Francisco, Boston, and New York City[11]—were often interpreted to suggest that within the foreseeable future the burden of paying for AIDS could be brought under control. Better management of patients was reducing costs, even in the absence of effective therapy. Moreover, under the plague model, AIDS was considered a distraction from the central problems of health policy for the nation and the states: how to contain costs while at the same time paying for care for people who were inadequately served by our payment systems—the poor and their children, low-paid workers, working people with disabilities, and the chronically ill elderly.[12]

AIDS is not a distraction from these problems but rather exacerbates them, particularly on the state level. The epidemic strikes hardest at those without insurance to underwrite the cost of an expensive chronic disease. Most premiums for private insurance are based on the illness experience of employees in particular firms or workplaces. As a result of both epidemiology and exclusions from coverage designed to contain the costs that insurers pass on to their customers, most employment-based health insurance does not pay for long-term care for chronic illness.[13] In addition, an increasing proportion of people with HIV infection lack private health insurance: intravenous drug users outside the labor market, their sexual partners, and their children. Medicare, our only social insurance program for health services, spreads the cost of care for chronic illness and disability over the entire working population. But most persons with HIV infection are ineligible for Medicare, by reason of age and previous employment history or inability to survive the 24-month waiting period after they meet the criteria for Social Security Disability Insurance.[14]

Pressure on the states to take action to finance health care for persons with HIV-related disease is strongly influenced by what the federal government does and does not do. Actions by the federal government have both relieved and added to state burdens. The requirement in the Consolidated Budget Reconciliation Act of 1986 that employers permit former employees to continue their health insurance payments at a capped premium has provided additional coverage for many persons with AIDS who were in the work force.[15] Similarly, the federal administrative ruling that a diagnosis of AIDS creates eligibility for disability benefits under the Supplemental Security Income entitlement has made it easier for many persons with the condition to qualify for Medicaid.[16] The availability of waivers of Medicaid regulations under authority in the Omnibus Budget Reconciliation Act of 1981 has enabled at least 11 states to propose targeting a particular range of services to persons with AIDS.[17] The federal program to subsidize purchases of AZT has also been helpful to the states, but its future is in doubt notwithstanding the 1989 finding that AZT delays the onset of HIV-related disease.[18]

Federal decisions have also added to state burdens. Most important has been the refusal of the Health Care Financing Administration (HCFA) to recommend that Congress eliminate the two-year waiting period before persons who qualify for Social Security Disability Insurance are eligible for Medicare. Such a change would cover most of the costs of care for many persons with HIV-related disease at a projected cost of less than $200 per year for each working person in the country.[19] This cost would be split evenly between employers and the employees. HCFA argues that eliminating the waiting period, for HIV or any other disabling condition, would be prohibitively expensive.[20] Similarly, HCFA has, in the view of some state officials, been slow to approve applications from states for waivers to permit more persons with AIDS to receive care in "home and community based" settings.[21]

Federal policy for paying hospitals under Medicare has increased the responsibilities of state governments as residual payers. In the early 1980s, the federal government changed the methodology of Medicare payments from a cost- to a price-based system called Diagnosis Related Groups (DRGs) in order to reduce, gradually, the rate of increase in hospital costs. For the first few years of the DRG system, however, Medicare remained the most generous and prompt institutional payer to hospitals. Many institutions continued to subsidize some of the costs of indigent care and graduate medical education from what, under a different accounting system, would have been called a surplus or a profit as a result of generous federal reimbursement. Then, as planned and announced, HCFA began to tighten its new system. Moreover, states began to adopt modified DRG systems for Medicaid and, in some instances, private and nonprofit insurers. Because DRGs seemed to permit no cross-subsidy for indigent care, shrewd hospital leaders had an opportunity to put additional pressure for funds on state government. At the same time, employers and insurers became more effective than ever before in forcing hospitals to restrain prices or offer discounts, thus further restricting cross-subsidies and adding to pressure on the states.

AIDS was an additional problem for hospitals: a syndrome that was apparently very expensive to treat at a time when third-party payments were less generous than in the past and state officials were becoming increasingly concerned about the costs of medical indigence. Many hospital leaders regarded AIDS as an opportunity to call attention to federal and state policies that, they insisted, underfunded their institutions.[22] They described AIDS, at public hearings and to the media, as a disease that required extraordinary expenditures for staff and supplies.[23] AIDS was a further drain on already limited resources.[24] Their campaign was successful: journalists and many state officials continued to accept the claim that AIDS was an unusually expensive affliction for hospitals to treat. However, as early as 1987, studies began to show that persons with AIDS did not use very many more resources during their hospital stays than other medical-surgical patients did and certainly no more than people dying of other diseases.[25]

In sum, HIV-related disease has been a growing problem for the states who have become the payers of last resort for health care in the United States. These patients have added to the burden carried by state taxpayers for Medicaid and indigent-care financing programs.

The cost of care for HIV-related disease is a burden for the states in other ways. For example, states have disincentives to require Blue Cross and other insurance companies to cover particular conditions or services. Under federal law since 1974, the states can regulate the business of insurance but not the provision of benefits to employees.[26] State-mandated health insurance benefits create pressure on employers to self-insure—that is, to escape state mandates by avoiding the "business" of insurance.[27] As a result, states are inhibited from requiring employers and fellow-employees to share the cost of treating persons with AIDS. They cannot, that is, regulate private insurance so that it serves more of the purposes that social insurance does in other countries.

The cost of AIDS is also a burden because of the states' responsibility for regulating and managing facilities. Every state has the opportunity to influence whether and how hospitals and nursing homes care for patients. States may regulate admission criteria, the number of beds available and whether patients with particular conditions are grouped or scattered. Furthermore, every state owns health facilities: mental hospitals, institutions for the mentally disabled, and nursing homes are the most common. Forty-six of the almost seventy university-owned teaching hospitals are owned or dominated by state government.[28] The others are chartered and regulated by the states.[29] Most of these state-owned or state-controlled facilities provide subsidized care to the uninsured and the under-insured. Because of this traditional state responsibility, any increase in expensive illness is translated into new public costs.

The cost of treating persons with HIV-related disease is a problem for all states but particularly for those with a high and growing number of cases. Startling increases in the rate of AIDS cases per 100,000 population have occurred in the past year in jurisdictions that have high proportions of intravenous drug users who are black or Hispanic. For example, in 1988 and 1989, striking increases in incidence occurred in Puerto Rico (from 8.0 to 43.4), Florida (13.6 to 23.8), New Jersey (22.7 to 32), Texas (9.5 to 13.8), and New York (23.4 to 39).[30] The growth in incidence has been less in some states, California (18.7 to 20.8) and Illinois (6.2 to 8.9), for example, where the total number of cases remains high in comparison to other jurisdictions.[31] Changes in both the rate of incidence and the total number of cases are important to state governments because these numbers drive both the size of the annual increment and the total amount of state expenditures.

Incidence is, however, only one of the uncertainties confronting state governments as they address the burden of financing the epidemic. Another factor is the difficulty of predicting what federal actions will demand state responses. Potential actions by Congress, the executive branch, and the courts include changes in Medicaid financing, mandated services or waiver policies, extension or curtailment of the AZT subsidy program, the availability of new drugs as a result of federally sponsored clinical trials and decisions by the Food and Drug Administration, and decisions by the federal courts on the constitutionality of state schemes to require employers to pay for health coverage for employees.

Another uncertainty is the effectiveness of state policies described in the next sections of this chapter. Despite what appears to be considerable research activity, too little is known about the cost-effectiveness of the various policies instituted in this decade to address the problems of managing care for the chronically ill, especially the elderly. (An exception to this is the work of Falcone and his colleagues in this volume. See Chapter Four.) The basis for applying these policies to persons with HIV-related disease is mainly conjecture and ideology.[32] Definitive research findings lag well behind the demand on state government to pay for care.

A Brief History of State Action to Finance AIDS Care

State governments have had a broad range of responses to the problems of financing care for persons with HIV-related disease. Several states have enacted legislation on the assumption that everyone with HIV infection should have access to state-financed care. At the other extreme are a few states that have adopted no legislation or regulations directed specifically at financing the cost of HIV infection and related disease. In between are the majority of states, which have adopted policies that address financing of care for all persons with a diagnosis of AIDS, though not HIV infection, or all persons with a diagnosis who are eligible for Medicaid.

Another way of examining how state governments have addressed problems of financing and organizing care is to divide the brief history of the epidemic into stages. These stages occur at different times in different states, depending in part on the number of cases of infection and disease but also on the traditional stance of state officials toward policy to finance health care. Three stages can be discerned.

In the first stage, a state relies on its existing policies for financing health care and regulating the institutions that provide it. These policies include those that regulate companies offering health insurance. The states with the highest number of cases, New York and California, attempted to prevent health insurance companies from testing applicants for antibodies to HIV. Most states have adopted regulations prohibiting discriminatory practices and protecting confidentiality in testing by insurance companies.[33] Toward the end of the first stage, states earmark appropriations to pay for care of persons with AIDS. New York was the first to earmark funds[34], but by 1986 the list included, among others, California, New Jersey, New Mexico, and Ohio.

In the second stage, states make a deliberate decision about how to adapt their Medicaid policies and regulations and often initiate state-only programs to address the problems of financing and organizing care for persons with HIV-related disease. By the spring of 1989, a variety of explicit Medicaid policies were in place. The most common policies concerned "waivers," essentially agreement by HCFA that a state may make a particular mix of Medicaid services available to some people, but not to all beneficiaries, on the condition that the proposed services will not add to federal costs. By the end of 1988, six states had received "home and community-based care waivers" to substitute for acute hospital care for persons with AIDS reimbursed care in homes or community facilities or nursing homes (skilled or intermediate) that could or would not provide such care. These states are California, Hawaii, New Jersey, New Mexico, Ohio, and South Carolina.[35] The states of Florida, Pennsylvania, and Texas had waivers pending.[36] Other states, Illinois and North Carolina for instance, were treating persons with AIDS as part of a broader grant of waiver authority (for the aged and disabled) from HCFA. According to HCFA staff, it is difficult to know precisely how many states are using broad waiver authority to treat persons with HIV-related disease.

Other states decided not to seek a waiver. Some have failed to do so in order to avoid potential costs to the state as a result of additional services or because they believe that the problem of financing care for HIV-related disease is not yet pressing. A few state legislatures have not granted or have not been asked to grant the executive branch the authority to seek waivers from HCFA.[37] In other instances the decision not to seek a waiver has different sources. In New York, for example, officials decided that Medicaid was already covering "almost everything that was waiverable [sic] except perhaps in-home pastoral counseling."[38] In Michigan, the decision not to seek a waiver was based on officials' belief that in addition to a "rich service package," waivers are difficult to administer and "hard to renew."[39]

In 1989, 27 states appropriated funds for patient care for persons with HIV-related diseases in addition to their Medicaid programs. Eighteen of these states also made appropriations for support services. Most of these funds subsidized inpatient care, but they were also used for hospices, outpatient clinics, case management, and, in ten states, to purchase and administer AZT.[40]

The third stage has been reached only in California, New York, and, to a lesser extent, Michigan and New Jersey. In this stage, states collaborate with other payers and institutions to adopt policies for organizing and financing care that go beyond the population eligible for Medicaid services. In New York, for example, the AIDS Treatment Center program, begun in 1986, provides enhanced reimbursement to hospitals for both inpatient care and case management of ambulatory and long-term care. New York also provides enhanced reimbursement rates in long-term care facilities, one of which has begun to accept persons with AIDS.[41] The California Department of Health Services (CDHS) has used authority provided in an amendment to the Health and Safety Code to fund 26 pilot projects to provide home health and attendant care.[42] CDHS has also devised regulations for providing hospice services to persons with AIDS and other terminal diseases and is sponsoring legislation to establish a new category of "licensed health care facility for persons with AIDS."[43] In the Newark–Jersey City region of New Jersey, the state is participating in a comprehensive case management program using funds from the Medicaid waiver, federal drug abuse treatment grants, a grant from the Robert Wood Johnson Foundation, and state appropriations.[44] In the summer and fall of 1989, New Jersey established a new program of "assessment centers" to encourage early detection, regular testing for the level of T-4 cells and the use of AZT to retard the onset of symptoms. The state provided the start-up costs for this program; Medicaid and private insurers will cover most of the ongoing costs.

A 1989 law in Michigan attempts to reduce the financial consequences of HIV infection for the state by continuing coverage by private insurance. This legislation requires the Department of Social Services to "identify potential Medicaid recipients who test HIV positive and pay their insurance premiums so that they can maintain their health insurance policies."[45] The project will be implemented initially as a pilot in three counties and limited to participants whose income is likely to fall below 200 percent of the poverty level within three months as a result of HIV-related disease. The sponsors of the program predict significant savings to the state when it is implemented: the difference between a premium of approximately $135 per month and an average monthly cost to Medicaid of $1,600 for each person with AIDS.[46]

The Michigan program is one of several whose sponsors explicitly engage the issue of financing health care for all citizens with chronic illnesses, not just those with AIDS. The state of Washington is implementing a similar HIV/AIDS insurance continuation program.[47] As one Michigan official said, "[w]hat is occurring with AIDS is true of other chronic illnesses which cause people to leave employment."[48] He could have added that these are illnesses for which the insurance industry would have been pleased to have the states as payers of last resort.

State Initiatives

Medicaid Waivers

Medicaid waivers and state-only insurance programs are probably the most interesting current options for the states that do not have them. Insurance "buy-in" legislation, of the kind passed in Michigan and Washington, is too new and too closely related to general strategies for providing health insurance for the uninsured and the underinsured to be the subject of further analysis in this chapter.

There is considerable state interest in waiver programs. While six states had approved waiver programs for persons with HIV infection by late 1989, others were awaiting approval by HCFA. Nine states were considering applying for waivers for persons with HIV; 13 others were considering applications under other waiver authorities, most of them for chemically dependent and HIV-positive children.[49]

The administrators of the waiver programs in both the federal government and states have similar views of progress to date. Both HCFA staff and respondents in each of the six states with active waivers for persons with AIDS in the spring of 1989 said, in interviews conducted for this chapter, that the programs had increased the availability of out-of-hospital services. Both federal and state officials cautioned that the AIDS waivers were too new to be properly evaluated. Both identified problems with HCFA polices for eligibility, paperwork, and reimbursement with state reimbursement levels and with the unwillingness of particular providers in the states to provide long-term care services to persons with AIDS. The analysis that follows focuses on problems of broad health policies raised by the programs. It ignores the intricate problems of managing waivers, which deserves a separate study.

The fundamental question raised by the waiver programs, and by many of the state-only programs of financing support services, is the value of case management as a fundamental strategy for providing equitable and effective health care. Case management has become a panacea of our time, one whose definition and substance vary enormously among programs.[50] It has been the conventional wisdom of the Medicaid waiver program since its inception in 1981. The authors of an early study of applications for waivers for mentally retarded and aged and disabled populations reported that "case management is the service most often requested in a state's waiver request."[51]

Case management strategies interpose a new professional role, typically performed by nurses or social workers, between patients and the institutions that provide and pay for services. Beginning in the late 1970s, a number of demonstration projects financed by the federal government and foundations tested the assumption that case management would improve the quality of care and perhaps even health status, especially for elderly people requiring long-term care. Most of the demonstrations also tested the hypothesis that case management would reduce or contain costs by eliminating expensive hospital stays.[52]

Some case managers simply brought expertise and compassion to their clients. Others had some control over reimbursement for the bills their clients incurred. Most of the managers were nurses and social workers, though some projects used other professionals, including physicians. Some managers worked for provider organizations—home health care agencies or hospitals or aftercare programs—others were employed by public agencies, insurance companies or other private payers. Some proponents of case management hoped that coordination and even advocacy could substitute for cash; they often described it as a strategy for cost containment.[53]

Research on the impact of case management programs has not sustained the high hopes of their proponents. A recent survey of this research concluded that "generally, provision of case management services increased the cost of care provision without producing commensurate reductions in the utilization of what are considered inappropriate services, specifically hospital and nursing home care."[54] Nevertheless, case management generally seems to produce "some positive outcomes for patients" but without considerable impact on clients' health and functioning.[55] Within the Medicaid program "case management continues to attract enthusiastic attention" amid confusion and disagreement about its definition and goals.[56] Moreover, case management continues to be associated with "cost-containment goals despite mounting evidence that case management increases the cost of service provision. . . ."[57]

An evaluation sponsored by HCFA reached similar conclusions. It confirmed that home and community-based care programs, almost all of which used case management, "supplement rather than replace expenditures for institutional care," although they appear to cut annual Medicaid expenditures "per waivered applicant *at least* in half."[58] The unanswered question is whether the expenditures would have been a charge on public budgets at all in the absence of a waiver.[59]

Despite these generally negative research findings, proper policy for case management has been the most controversial issue in the AIDS waiver program. The opposite extremes of the debate are represented by South Carolina and California. A senior official in South Carolina insisted that "case management is better when it is not done by the vendor, when there are checks and balances."[60] A leading proponent of the California plan, in contrast, insists that it is better to "put the responsibility on agencies coming in under the waiver to do case management and maintain the [clients'] budgets."[61]

The dispute about who should be case managers is subordinate to the problems of who should employ them and whether their employers should have a stake in reimbursement. Almost everyone agrees that nurses should be case managers, and that social workers can, in many situations, adequately perform the role. But there is disagreement about including other professions and about what level of training beyond the professional credential should be required.

Waiver programs and case management strategies were devised to meet the needs of the chronically ill and the disabled. State officials initially viewed these programs as an expedient way to treat persons with AIDS. Now that HIV infection is perceived as a chronic disease, these programs are likely to be expanded in scope and therefore in cost.

Other Medicaid Issues

Although waiver programs are the most important state initiatives, others are significant. By late 1989, 9 states covered hospice services for persons with AIDS; another 12 were considering coverage. Six states provided enhanced reimbursement to nursing homes, 2 for home health aides; 6 others are considering such programs. Four states in addition to those with waivers offered targeted case management, with 17 others considering it. In sum, all 50 states had either modified or were considering changes in their Medicaid programs to take account of the epidemic of HIV infection and the concomitant rise in demands upon states' health care resources.[62]

The most important state decisions with regard to Medicaid coverage in the near future will most likely be about prescription drugs. In the spring of 1989, 45 states included in their Medicaid formularies the two most effective drugs approved by the FDA for treating persons with HIV-related disease: AZT and aerosolized pentamidine. Most states covered other drugs used to treat diseases secondary to HIV infection. Most states did not, however, routinely cover investigational new drugs.[63]

Just covering the purchase costs of newly approved drugs would not be sufficient. Administration of both AZT and aerosolized pentamidine requires establishment of a network of services for assessing and testing patients and for administering the drugs. A survey of 11 states, 6 counties, and 13 cities by the Intergovernmental Health Policy Project in the summer of 1989 revealed that most of them anticipated that their costs would increase by millions of dollars as a result of these innovations in treatment.[64]

The uses for which drugs were covered varied widely among states and began to change radically as a result of clinical trials concluded in the spring and summer of 1989. Prior to the announcement of the prophylactic benefits of AZT in certain circumstances in August 1989, 36 states covered it for seropositive persons,[65] while 45 covered it for persons with AIDS as defined by the CDC. A similar situation existed for aerosolized pentamidine. Both the extent of coverage and the cost of these drugs were uncertain when this article was written. Similarly, whether the federal government would continue to subsidize states to purchase AZT was unknown: in 1989 states spent $20 million for AZT purchases. Not in dispute, however, was the assumption that prophylactic treatment of people with HIV infection but without symptoms could cost several billion dollars over the next few years.[66]

The amount of Medicaid expenditures in each state for persons with HIV infection and its adequacy for the covered populations has not been calculated. Because Medicaid is a federal–state matching program that is driven by eligibility policies that vary among states, comparisons have usually involved policies rather than expenditures. Because, until recent court decisions, Medicaid operated as a vendor program, requiring providers to accept its reimbursement levels as payment in full, physicians and hospital leaders frequently criticized its inadequacy. From the perspective of recipients, however, Medicaid is more generous than most private insurance in payments for pharmaceuticals, ambulatory care, long-term care and support services. The problem is the wide variety in covered benefits among the states. Medicaid remains, however, the most generous program for the increasing number of persons with HIV infection who are poor. Moreover, because of the federal matching funds, Medicaid reduces the burden that patient care for the poor places on state and local funds.

State-Only Programs

New York and California have instituted the most extensive state-only programs for financing and organizing services for persons with AIDS. Neither state has completed even a preliminary evaluation of the effectiveness of their programs. Officials in both states claim that it is too soon to make effective judgements about programs that are still being established.

The New York program is more comprehensive than the one in California, which consists of pilot grants for home health and attendant care. Beginning in 1987, the New York State Health Department (NYSHD) designated as AIDS Treatment Centers hospitals that agreed to meet particular standards such as clustering beds for the care of persons with AIDS and proposing a case management system. By mid 1989, 15 hospitals had been accepted into the program and were receiving enhanced reimbursement (the precise amount determined by negotiation), from federal, state and private payers, of what one official estimated to be approximately $200 per day above the Medicaid rate, or an average $800 to $1000 for each patient day. This enhanced reimbursement ranged from 39 to 54 percent, depending on the provider. The regulations creating the designated center hospitals were the first of a series issued by the NYSHD; subsequent regulations addressed residential health care facilities and home care services for persons with AIDS. Proposed or draft regulations describe the conditions for state approval of AIDS Home Care Programs, pediatric, and maternal services, and case management. The legislature amended the ten-year-old Nursing Home Without Walls program to authorize the provision of special home care services to persons with AIDS.

Anecdotal evidence suggests that there are conflicting judgements among providers about the effectiveness of the New York State program. The regulatory arm of the NYSHD, the Office of Health Systems Management (OHSM), is frequently criticized in the industry for heavy-handedness and capriciousness. These criticisms have influenced the attitude of physicians and hospital staff toward the way the

AIDS treatment programs are monitored. Despite these criticisms, staff of several centers report high morale and a feeling of accomplishment. In 1989, the treatment center hospitals accounted for 34 percent of the hospital discharges of persons with AIDS in the state, and applicants for the program accounted for another 30 percent.[67]

Some of the satisfaction with the treatment center program may be a result of deliberate overpayment by Medicaid and private insurers due to a state policy to encourage hospitals to provide enhanced services for persons with AIDS. In an off-the-record discussion in 1989, a senior official at OHSM acknowledged that current reimbursement was excessive. The medical director of a major treatment center in New York City said in public that he worked out both "profit and loss statements." [68] Notwithstanding these comments, the first study to compare utilization and charges for patients with AIDS in a treatment center with those in scattered beds in the same hospital concluded, tentatively, that the patients in the AIDS unit were more expensive because they were sicker.[69]

Despite the strong regulatory strategy of the NYSHD, however, staff of the treatment centers still find it difficult to discharge their patients to appropriate long-term care facilities. A recent study found that 53 percent of patients with AIDS were discharged only to return home, many because there was no alternative. An unreleased needs assessment conducted by the NYSHD in Manhattan revealed that a substantial number of hospital patients were eligible for placement in a skilled nursing or health-related facility, but that few places were available. At the time of the study, only one skilled nursing facility in the city accepted persons with HIV-related disease. A systematic study of a stratified sample of 30 patients from three state-designated treatment centers on Long Island revealed that the costs of treating patients from diagnosis to death would have been reduced by 12 percent, on average, if skilled nursing care outside hospitals had been available. At the time the study was conducted, however, no AIDS patients had been accepted by a nursing home in this region of 2.6 million people.[70]

Alternatives

Financing the epidemic of HIV infection and related disease will cause increasing problems for the states. The states will continue to bear much of the burden of financing care and managing services, particularly long-term care services, for HIV-related disease. In the immediate future, the greatest additional burden on the states will be to pay the cost of prophylactic treatment with AZT for patients without symptoms of the disease.

The easiest conclusion from the analysis in this chapter would be that, because the epidemic of HIV infection has overwhelming costs, the best policy for states is to mobilize support for more extensive federal subsidy. The states with the most cases would have the strongest interest in federal action. The arguments for such a strategy are obvious as are the fiscal and political impediments to its success in the immediate future. This is an unlikely time for generous federal social programs.

The most compelling argument against HIV-specific advocacy in Washington is that, although the diseases that follow infection with the virus are terrible and expensive, HIV is one among many areas of inadequacy in health care financing and organization. Advocacy for more federal participation in HIV financing would make political sense to most state officials only if it were part of a larger national campaign to solve problems of access to health care for the uninsured, the underinsured, and the poor. Assessing the prospects and, more importantly, the participants in such a campaign is beyond the scope of this chapter.

Another conclusion, much more modest, from the analysis here, would be that as the recession recedes, states should address the problems of financing care for persons with HIV infection as part of their strategy for addressing the needs of the uninsured and underinsured among their citizens. A comprehensive state solution would be next best to an elusive federal remedy. Such a policy would be attractive to many constituencies: to health providers, especially hospitals, to large employers, many labor unions, and advocates for the poor and for persons with HIV infection. A comprehensive state solution would, in current politics, be opposed by employers whose costs would increase, by many taxpayers, and by fiscal conservatives. In sum, there is no compelling political incentive to advocate comprehensive state solutions to any problems of health care financing any more than there is for a national health policy.

Comprehensive state solutions to the general problems of health care finance are unlikely, except in a few states. The past and present health care politics of each state, including its long-term relationship with the Medicaid program, is likely to be the most important predictor of how that state addresses the HIV epidemic. States with a dominant university-owned hospital serving a general population and a relatively generous Medicaid program are going to finance and organize health care for persons with AIDS differently from states where the university hospital has traditionally served the indigent and Medicaid has been relatively ungenerous. In the HIV epidemic, as with most other serious illnesses, equality of access to health care is not yet an attainable entitlement for Americans.[71] For Americans of working age and their children, where one lives and for whom one works continue to be the major determinants of what care one can have and how it will be financed.

In this context, what matters is not what model legislation intellectuals suggest but rather the cogency of the analysis by which officials and people in the health industry in each state address the questions raised in the preceding sections of this chapter. There is no prescription; there is only the experience of people in other states with different resources and political environments. All that outsiders can bring to such reasoning is information, some analytical skill, and the conviction that, if research is good enough and timely, some issues can, at least temporarily, be transferred from politics to expertise.

State policy for financing and organizing services for persons with HIV infection must now start with the assumption that it is a chronic illness. Moreover, it is one of many chronic illnesses that have become the central problems of health policy at the end of the 20th century. The problems of financing and organizing care for AIDS, at whatever level of government or the private sector they are addressed, should be conceived as part of this larger issue. There are many expensive chronic diseases, some infectious, all degenerative; there will be more. AIDS is not a plague, a passing affliction: it is part of our society for some indefinite time to come. We cannot avoid the costs of chronic illnesses but we can influence their rate of incidence and how equitably the burden of payment is spread among employers, employees, and taxpayers.

To make policy for HIV infection as a chronic illness is hardly to trivialize it, as some AIDS advocates have claimed. Making policy for HIV infection as a chronic illness puts the epidemic in its proper context. HIV infection is a terrible affliction. But state officials must address a great many terrible afflictions, for many of which there is considerable and often justifiable special pleading.

Because HIV infection is new, spreads so rapidly, and is expensive to treat, it reveals more clearly than most illnesses the flaws in the collection of laws and customs we call our health policy. Recognizing flaws, as everyone in public life knows, creates both problems and opportunities. There is no lack of solutions to the problems of health policy. There is, however, no politically effective coalition at present willing to pay the price of legislating any of the more fundamental solutions.

Acknowledgments

A number of people provided data and informed opinions that have been essential to preparing this article. Their names follow in alphabetical order. It is important to emphasize that none of them is responsible for the author's opinions, including his conclusions about the organization or the jurisdiction for which they work.

The author is indebted to: Lawrence Bartlett, A.E. Benjamin, Stephen Boese, Charles Bruner, Richard Chambers, Benny Clark, Georgia Cleverly, Marianne C. Fahs, Ira Feldman, Rashi Fein, Larry Gostin, Katie Hammer, David C. Hollister, Robert Hummel, Kenneth W. Kizer, Carol Levine, Richard Merritt, Frank Pistella, Lori Preschuk, Stephen Rose, Kevin Seitz, Elmer Smith, Sandra Tannenbaum, Emily H. Thomas, and Robert Wardwell. An earlier version of this chapter appeared as "Financing Health Care for Persons With HIV Infection: Guidelines for State Action," *American Journal of Law & Medicine* 16 (1990): 223–247. The author would like to thank the journal for permission to reproduce that material here.

Notes

1. At least thirteen cases of AIDS have been reported in each of the states. *Centers for Disease Control, HIV/AIDS Surveillance Report* 5 (July 1989) [hereinafter *HIV/AIDS Surveillance*]. At least 60 percent of these patients were financed under either Medicaid or state-only programs of indigent care. See note 5 below and accompanying text. For a discussion of non-Medicaid spending for AIDS in 42 states, see Monica Rowe and Stephanie Keintz, "National Survey of State Spending for AIDS," *Intergovernmental State Reports* (September–October, 1989): 1–10.

2. These figures were provided to the author by staff of the Health Care Financing Administration [hereinafter HCFA Staff Information]. For a different number, see *Intergovernmental Health Policy Project, State AIDS Reports* (February–March, 1989): 8.

3. Social Security Appropriations Act of 1988/89, 1989 Michigan Legislative Service 322, §1626 (West). The author is grateful to the Hon. David C. Hollister of the Michigan legislature for calling his attention to this initiative and providing him with a history of it. See also Department of Social and Health Services, State of Washington, "New HIV/AIDS Insurance Continuation Program" (Memorandum June 26, 1989); Department of Health Services, State of California, Medi-Cal's

Health Insurance Premium Payment Program (undated memorandum). Lawrence Bartlett provided references for Washington and California.

4. Daniel M. Fox and Emily H. Thomas, "Methods of Projecting AIDS Services Utilization," slides presented at the Annual Meeting of the American Public Health Association (Boston, November 1989) (unpublished).

5. Daniel M. Fox and Emily H. Thomas, "AIDS Cost Analysis and Social Policy," *Law, Medicine & Health Care* 15 no. 186 (1987): 203 (synthesized data from nine studies in Table 4). For a recent summary of data on the burden of costs on public hospitals, see Dennis P. Andrulis, Virginia B. Weslowski, and Larry Gage, "The 1987 U.S. Hospital AIDS Survey," *JAMA* 262 (1989): 784–794. For calculation of federal expenditures, see William Winkenwerder, Austin R. Kessler, and Rhonda M. Stolec, "Federal Spending for Illness Caused by Human Immunodeficiency Virus," *New England Journal of Medicine* 320 (1989): 1598–1603.

6. However, much of our current knowledge about the effects of state policies may be obsolete.

7. "CDC AIDS Surveillance Data Omits One-Third of Current Cases; Total for 1991 May be Underestimated—GAO," *The Blue Sheet* 32 no. 26 (F-D-C Reports, Inc., June 28, 1989): 3 [hereinafter "CDC AIDS Surveillance"]; Edward O. Laumann, J.H. Gagnon, S. Michaels, R.T. Michael, and J.S. Coleman, "Monitoring the AIDS Epidemic in the United States: A Network Approach," *Science* (9 June 1989): 1186–1189.

8. "CDC AIDS Surveillance."

9. For further exploration of this argument in an international context, see Daniel M. Fox, Patricia Day, and Rudolf Klein, "The Power of Professionalism: Policies for AIDS in Britain, Sweden and the United States," *Daedalus* 118 (1989): 93–112.

10. Elizabeth Fee and Daniel M. Fox, "Contemporary Historiography and AIDS" in Elizabeth Fee and Daniel M. Fox, eds., *AIDS: The Making of a Chronic Disease* (Berkeley, CA: University of California Press, 1992).

11. Daniel M. Fox and Emily H. Thomas, "AIDS Cost Analysis and Social Policy," 189–190; Anne A. Scitovsky, Mary Cline, and Philip R. Lee, "Medical Care Costs of Patients with AIDS in San Francisco," *JAMA* 256 (1986): 3103–3106; Jerome R. Seage, Stewart Landers, M. Anita Barry, Jerome Groopman, George A. Lamb, and Arnold M. Epstein, "Medical Care Costs of AIDS in Massachusetts," *JAMA* 256 (1986): 3107–3109; Peat, Marwick, and Mitchell (Inc.), *Study of Routine Costs of Treating Hospitalized AIDS Patients* (New York: Greater New York Hospital Association, 1986).

12. Fox and Thomas, "AIDS Cost Analysis and Social Policy,": 189–191.

13. Office of Technology Assessment, U.S. Congress, *AIDS and Health Insurance: An OTA Survey* (1988); Daniel M. Fox, "Policy and Epidemiology: Financing Health Services for the Chronically Ill and Disabled, 1930–1990," *Milbank Quarterly* 67 (August 1989): 257–287.

14. Requirements for Supplemental Medical Insurance Enrollment and Entitlement, 42 C.F.R. §§405, 1988: 205–226.

15. Consolidated Omnibus Budget Reconciliation Act (COBRA) of 1985, Pub. L. No. 99–272, §10001, 100 Stat. 222, 1986: 223–224.

16. 50 *Federal Register*, 5,573 (1985) (interim regulations taking effect February 11, 1985).

17. Omnibus Budget Reconciliation Act of 1981, Pub. L. No. 97–135, 95 Stat. 357, in ibid.

18. Every state, the District of Columbia, and most U.S. territories had received federal funds to purchase AZT by mid 1989.

19. For documentation of HCFA policy and a description of these calculations, see Fox and Thomas, "AIDS Cost Analysis and Social Policy," 192.

20. Ibid.

21. Conversation with South Carolina Department of Social Services (source elected to remain anonymous); Conversations with Michigan Department of Social Services (source elected to remain anonymous).

22. Fox and Thomas, "AIDS Cost Analysis and Social Policy," 187, 189, 190, 205.

23. Ibid.

24. Ibid.

25. For a list of sources, see ibid., 186, 189; Daniel M. Fox and Emily H. Thomas, eds., *Financing Care for Persons with AIDS: The First Studies,* (Frederick, MD: University Publishing Group, 1989), 1985–1988.

26. Employment Retirement Income Act of 1974, Pub. L. No. 93–406, 88 Stat. 829 (codified as amended in 29 U.S.C. §§1001–1461 (1982)).

27. Daniel M. Fox and Daniel C. Schaffer, "Interest Groups and ERISA: The Politics of Semi-Preemption," *Journal of Health Politics, Policy, and Law* 14 (1989): 239, 251.

28. See Rowe and Keintz, "National Survey of State Spending for Aids," 1–10.

29. Ibid.

30. *HIV/AIDS Surveillance,* 5.

31. Ibid.

32. A.E. Benjamin, "Long Term Care and AIDS: Perspectives from Experience with the Elderly," *Milbank Quarterly* 66 (1988): 415, 434.

33. National Association of Insurance Commissioners, Model Regulation, "Medical/Lifestyle Questions and Underwriting Guidelines," (July, 1989): 3–8.

34. Department of Health State of New York, *AIDS, New York's Response: A 5-Year Inter-Agency Plan* (Jan. 1989) [hereinafter *AIDS, New York's Response*]. Much of the data from other states are in lengthy documents submitted by the states in order to apply for Medicaid waivers. When these applications are approved, the language in them is translated into regulations governing state Medicaid programs. These regulations are then transmitted to providers. See Rowe and Keintz, "National Survey of State Spending for AIDS," which arrays some of the same data but without any hypotheses about stages of state response.

35. HCFA Staff Information.

36. Ibid.

37. HCFA staff do not have a list of these states. Its compilation awaits further research.

38. Conversation with New York State Health Department (source elected to remain anonymous).

39. Personal interview with Kevin Seitz, Director, Michigan Medicaid Program (March 1989) [hereinafter Seitz Interview].

40. Rowe and Keintz, "National Survey of State Spending for Aids," 7.

41. *AIDS, New York's Response,* 61–67; Department of Health, State of New York, *Memoranda, Health Facilities* Series H–38, NH–32, HRF–32 (n.d.).

42. For a description of programs and citations to pertinent laws and regulations, see Kenneth Kizer, "California's Approach to AIDS," *AIDS and Public Policy Journal* 3 (1988): 1–10. The author is grateful to Dr. Kizer for additional information provided in conversation and documents.

43. Ibid.

44. Molly J. Coye et al. "Funding AIDS Services and Prevention from Public and Private Sources, New Jersey's Experience," *AIDS and Public Policy Journal* 20 (1988): 20–28. Robert Hummel, Assistant Commissioner for AIDS Services, provided information about more recent initiatives in New Jersey.

45. Social Securities Appropriations Act of 1988/1989, 1989 Michigan Legislative Service 322, §1626 (West); Seitz interview.

46. Seitz interview.

47. California and New York City have continuation programs but only for persons who already qualify for Medicaid.

48. Seitz interview.

49. "AIDS and Medicaid," National Governors' Association (March 1989).

50. The author is grateful to Dr. A.E. Benjamin and Dr. Stephen Rose for useful conversations on this subject.

51. K.C. Lakin, J.N. Greenburg, M.P. Schmitz and B.K. Hill, "A Comparison of Medicaid Waiver Applications for Populations That Are Mentally Retarded and Elderly/Disabled," *Mental Retardation* (22 August 1984): 187.

52. Benjamin, "Long Term Care and AIDS," 415–434.

53. Ibid.

54. For a more optimistic view of case management for AIDS services in San Francisco, see A.E. Benjamin, Philip R. Lee, and Leslie Solkowitz, "Case Management of Persons with Acquired Immunodeficiency Syndrome in San Francisco," *Health Care Finance Review* 1988 (Annual Supplement 1988): 69–73.

55. Benjamin, "Long Term Care and AIDS," 415–434.

56. Ibid.

57. Ibid.

58. Lucy Johns and Gerald Adler, "Evaluation of Recent Changes in Medicaid," *Health Affairs* 8 (Spring 1989): 171–181 (emphasis added).

59. Ibid.

60. Conversation with California Department of Health Services (source elected to remain anonymous).

61. Ibid. He was convinced, not without reason according to sources in the federal government, that HCFA approval of the California waiver was held up for almost a year over this issue.

62. For a summary of these data, see Rowe and Keintz, "National Survey of State Spending for AIDS." Other state initiatives include: 1987 Connecticut Acts 553 (Spec. Sess.) (creating a pilot program to assist homeless persons with AIDS); 1987 Connecticut Acts 789 (Special Session) (providing grants to agencies for "services including but not limited to education, counseling and prevention"); Act approved July 6, 1988, ch. 88, 1988 Fla. Sess. Law Serv. 380 (West) (mandating education and planning activities).

63. National Gay Rights Advocates, *Access to AIDS-Related Drugs under*

Medicaid: A Fifty State Analysis (May 1989); "State Medicaid Does Not Routinely Cover Treatment IND AIDS Drugs: Private Insurers Often Reimburse," *The Blue Sheet* 32 no. 27 (F-D-C Reports, Inc., 5 July 1989): 3.

64. *Intergovernment Health Policy Project, T-Cell Testing Recommendations Affect Planning Activities* 1–3, 10–11 (July–August 1989).

65. Five other states covered the cost of drugs for seropositive persons in a limited number of cases.

66. National Gay Rights Advocates, *Access to AIDS-Related Drugs under Medicaid.*

67. The first publicly available evaluation data about the New York AIDS Treatment Center program were described at a conference on May 2, 1989 sponsored by the United Hospital Fund. No publications from that conference are available.

68. Conversation with Dr. Michael Grieco, Director of St. Luke's/Roosevelt Hospital Center, in New York City (May 1989).

69. Marianne Fahs, Research Presented at the 5th International Conference on AIDS, Montreal, Canada (June 1989).

70. *AIDS, New York's Response,* Conversation with New York State Health Department (source elected to remain anonymous); Roy Steigbigel and Emily H. Thomas, "Report of the Medical Panel for the Nassau–Suffolk Regional AIDS Planning Study," (September 1988).

71. For a recent analysis of geographic inequities in entitlement, see Dennis P. Andrulis, Virginia B. Weslowski, and Larry S. Gage, "The 1987 U.S. Hospital AIDS Report," *Journal of Medicine* 262 (1989): 1598–1603.

3

Improving the Quality of Maternal and Child Health Care in the United States: State-Level Initiatives and Leadership

Saundra K. Schneider

Maternal and child health care is an important public policy issue in the United States. First, and foremost, it is a barometer of the overall well-being and conscience of the nation.[1] Women and children are two of the most vulnerable groups in American society. Consequently, they should receive appropriate and effective medical treatment. The extent to which women and children are actually shielded from preventable and unnecessary medical problems tells us a great deal about the value priorities and moral commitment of the country.

Second, the issue is important for pragmatic reasons. Stated simply, maternal and child health care is cost-effective. It has an immediate impact on the health care status of pregnant women and infants. It also has long-range societal consequences. Healthy mothers are more likely to deliver healthy babies. Healthy babies have a better chance of becoming healthy children. And healthy children do better in school and are more apt to grow up to become productive citizens. By improving the health care status of mothers and children, we are able to deal with a host of important social issues.

Maternal and child health care is also a very symbolic and politically expedient issue. Most Americans believe that "mothers," "babies," and "children" deserve *special* care and treatment. So, it is relatively easy to focus public attention on this problem area. It is also much easier for public officials to push for government-sponsored maternal and child health care programs. No one wants to be *against* providing services to pregnant women and infants. This, in turn, helps to legitimize and stimulate governmental activity.

In order to understand governmental involvement in this area, we must focus on the role of the states. State governments have always played a role in America's maternal and child health care system. During the 1980s, however, they became more actively involved in this policy area. The states helped focus national attention on the problems faced by poor women and children. And they served as the testing grounds for major policy initiatives aimed at alleviating these problems. In essence, the states became key actors in the development of maternal and child health care programs across the United States.

This chapter examines the role of the American states in contemporary maternal and child health care policymaking. The analysis focuses specifically on how the states have shaped recent changes in Medicaid—the nation's largest and most influential medical assistance program for low-income women and children. The chapter is divided into four sections. The first briefly discusses the causes and consequences of the nation's maternal and child problems. The next examines how the states use Medicaid to address these issues. The third section describes why the states became more involved in this process, and it presents several examples of state-level activity. The final section assesses the accomplishments of these governmental efforts and identifies remaining problems and challenges in this area.

Maternal and Child Health Care Issues in the United States

The issues surrounding maternal and child health care illustrate many of the strengths and weaknesses of the entire American health care system. On the positive side, there is a relatively clear understanding of the factors that contribute to poor health outcomes. Specifically, there is a strong, positive relationship between the medical care women and children receive and their subsequent health care status. Young children who see a doctor on a regular basis are less likely to develop serious medical conditions and more likely to recover from the illnesses they do experience.[2] Similarly, women who obtain early, continuous, and appropriate treatment during pregnancy are less likely to experience serious maternity problems and less likely to give birth to premature, underweight infants.[3] The birth weight of an infant is the major determinant of infant disability and death.[4]

There have also been significant improvements in the treatment of many critical health care problems. Medical advances in the diagnosis and care of high-risk pregnancies have allowed many more women to deliver full-term, healthy babies. Technological developments in neonatal intensive care have prevented millions of infants from dying prematurely.[5] Breakthroughs in the treatment of children's diseases and illnesses have prolonged the lives of thousands of young Americans.[6]

Despite the advances mentioned above, the United States continues to have serious maternal and child health problems. The infant mortality rate—the percentage of all infants who die before the first year of life—is often used as the primary indicator of a nation's health. The United States has the dubious distinction of having a higher infant mortality rate than any other advanced, industrialized nation, and its rate is more than twice as high as those in Japan, Sweden, and Finland.[7] Moreover, for certain subgroups of the American population, infant mortality is significantly more severe. Infants born to mothers who are poor, young, unmarried, and nonwhite are twice as likely as other American infants to die before their first birthday.[8]

The cost of obtaining adequate medical care is both a cause and a consequence of this situation. Clearly health care is expensive, especially if it involves a serious or complicated condition. In order to pay for needed medical care, most Americans rely on private health insurance, public health care programs, and/or their own personal funds. However, between 32 and 37 million Americans have no medical insurance of any kind.[9] Low-income women and children comprise two of the largest and most recognizable elements within the country's uninsured/underinsured population.[10] It is estimated that 17 million American women and children—about one-half of the country's total uninsured/underinsured population—have no public or private health insurance coverage.[11] These women and children are simply unable to pay for timely, appropriate, and continuous care. This, in turn, leads to more serious health care problems that are also more difficult and expensive to treat. As an example, consider the financial cost of caring for one underweight infant. The average hospital bill for a low birth weight infant is 22 times the amount of a normal, healthy newborn. If the infant is extremely premature and underweight (under 750 grams), the costs are astronomical, ranging from $31,000 to $150,000.[12] Thus, the costs of health care prevent many women from seeking and obtaining appropriate care; and inadequate medical treatment ends up contributing to even higher health care expenses.

As the magnitude of the maternal and child health problem has increased, so too has governmental involvement in this policy area. There now exists a myriad of public programs designed to address certain aspects of the problem—the Title V Maternal and Child Health Block Grant Program, the Special Supplemental Food Program for Women, Infants, and Children (WIC), the Community Health Centers Program, and so on. Many of these measures are federal programs. The federal government establishes general program parameters, and it provides technical and financial assistance to facilitate the implementation of services. However, it is the *states,* not the federal government, that shape the actual structure and impact of these programs. The Medicaid program provides an excellent example of this system.

The Basic Structure of Medicaid:
State and Federal Responsibilities

Medicaid is the primary mechanism for financing maternal and child health care services in the United States.[13] It is used to address many of the causes and symptoms of the nation's problems in this area. It is used to help reduce the incidence of teen pregnancy, out-of-wedlock births, maternal deaths, infant mortality, and a variety of children's diseases. The federal government has allowed the Medicaid program to expand in this area. But it is the states, not the federal government, that have pushed for and shaped developments within the program. Let us briefly examine the basic structure of the Medicaid program and the evolution of federal versus state responsibilities in Medicaid policymaking.

Medicaid was created in 1965 as a joint federal–state initiative. The basic idea was that both the federal and state governments were to work together to provide medical assistance to the poor.[14] The federal government was to encourage each state to set up a unified system of health care for low-income individuals. It was to establish the general parameters for program eligibility and service provision, and it was to provide federal matching funds to states that agreed to participate in Medicaid. Essentially, the federal government's primary responsibility was to stimulate, not control, state action.

The states were placed in charge of implementing their own Medicaid programs.[15] They were given three important responsibilities, all of which they still retain. First, they determine who actually qualifies for program benefits. Although the federal government specifies the groups to be covered, each state sets the income, asset, and family-status criteria for program eligibility. They also have the discretion to extend Medicaid coverage to other groups of needy citizens.

Second, the states determine the scope of health care coverage. Again, states have to provide a basic set of services to their Medicaid populations, but beyond this minimum benefit package they have the option of adding other types of services. They also have the authority to establish their own Medicaid reimbursement and service delivery mechanisms. This means that they determine how much money health care professionals receive for providing services to program recipients.

Finally, states develop their own administrative system for the program. They determine the organizational location of the Medicaid program within each state—that is, whether Medicaid is placed under the jurisdiction of the state health department, social services agency, or public welfare office. Moreover, they also have the option of centralizing administrative functions at the state level as opposed to delegating responsibilities to local governmental jurisdictions.[16] As long as it abides by several general federal guidelines, such as comparability of services and "statewideness," a state can design its own unique administrative structure.

State Influence as a Result of Federal Action

As we have just seen, the states have always exerted an important impact on the Medicaid program. However, in the early 1980s, they were given more flexibility and control over program components. In response to the Reagan administration's "New Federalism" plan, the U.S. Congress passed the Omnibus Budget Reconciliation Act of 1981 (OBRA–81). This act decreased federal controls and increased state discretion in Medicaid policymaking. Although OBRA–81 maintained the basic structure and entitlement nature of the program, it increased the range and type of policy choices available to the states.[17] More specifically, OBRA–81 totally eliminated many federal restrictions and established other procedures that would allow the states to experiment with new reimbursement methodologies and service delivery systems (see Table 3.1). In terms of maternal and child health care, the OBRA–81 provisions gave the states greater leeway to pursue more cost-effective payment policies for hospital-related maternity and infant care. For example, it allowed states to experiment with all-payer, multiple-rate, and diagnostic-related-group prospective payment systems. It encouraged the development of "alternative delivery systems," such as health maintenance organizations and case management systems, for the provision of both primary and institutional prenatal care. OBRA–81 also gave the states more freedom to target subgroups of the population, such as women and infants, with special health care needs for Medicaid coverage. This provision is referred to as a "targeted" medically needy option. States choosing this option have to cover all pregnant women and all children (up to the age of eighteen) who meet the state's categorical Medicaid guidelines. OBRA–81 required that the states selecting this option provide ambulatory services to the children and prenatal and delivery care to the pregnant women in this newly eligible population. Beyond this, however, states were given the responsibility of defining the full range of medical benefits that would be available to this new "medically needy" group of recipients.[18] Overall, the OBRA–81 changes were designed to give the states more control over the management and implementation of Medicaid.

OBRA–81 did have a noticeable impact on state-level activity. Following the passage of this legislation, a number of states took advantage of the targeted medically needy option. They extended Medicaid coverage to low-income women and their children who met the categorical but not the financial criteria for regular Medicaid eligibility.[19]

States also relaxed the categorical restrictions for Medicaid eligibility. For example, "first-time" pregnant women who met the program's income criteria began receiving Medicaid as soon as their pregnancy was verified. States also extended coverage, for the first time, to "children" between the ages of eighteen and twenty-one who remained in school.[20] A year after the passage of OBRA–81, 18 states revised their eligibility requirements to cover this group of individuals.

The states also made changes in the type and scope of services

Table 3.1
Summary of Major Legislative Changes Affecting Medicaid's Coverage of Maternal and Child Health Care

Legislation	Changes	Implications
Omnibus Budget Reconciliation Act of 1981	Relaxed federal controls over the administration, financing, and operation of Medicaid.	Allowed states to experiment with alternative payment, reimbursement, delivery, and eligibility systems in Medicaid.
Consolidated Omnibus Budget Reconciliation Act	Waived federal requirements specifying that states provide "comparable" medical coverage to all Medicaid recipients.	Allowed states to target "at risk" or "high risk" women/infants for more intensive, managed health care services in their Medicaid programs.
Omnibus Budget Reconciliation Act of 1986	Relaxed federal Medicaid eligibility standards. Created several entirely new optional groups of Medicaid recipients.	Severed the traditional link between Medicaid and AFDC eligibility. Allowed states to expand Medicaid, without extended cash assistance, to low-income pregnant women and children in families up to 100% of poverty.
Omnibus Budget Reconciliation Act of 1987	Made further changes in federal Medicaid eligibility standards.	Allowed states to expand Medicaid to low-income women and children (up to age 8) in families up to 185% of poverty.
Family Assistance Act (Welfare Reform Act) of 1988	Extended medical care coverage to former welfare recipients.	Allowed states to continue providing Medicaid coverage to former AFDC recipients for up to twelve months.
Medicare Catastrophic Care Amendments of 1988	Set specific guidelines for the states implementation of Medicaid eligibility changes for pregnant women and children.	Mandated the states to expand Medicaid eligibility to cover pregnant women and children in families up to 100% of poverty by July 1990.
Omnibus Budget Reconciliation Act of 1989	Revised the Medicare Catastrophic Care eligibility thresholds and timetables.	Mandated the states to expand Medicaid eligibility for pregnant women and children (up to age 6) in families at 133% of poverty by April 1990.

available to their Medicaid populations. Under OBRA–81, they were allowed to experiment with "alternative" health care delivery systems. As a result, many states encouraged Medicaid recipients, especially women and children, to use primary care case management systems.

The basic idea behind this approach was to provide more timely and continuous care, thereby improving the health care status of recipients and reducing the overall costs of providing medical care.

State-Initiated Changes in Medicaid

OBRA–81 represented a major change in Medicaid policymaking. It shifted the locus of decisionmaking from the federal government to the states. Although OBRA–81 initiated this intergovernmental transfer of power,[21] it did not give the states enough freedom to take the lead in program developments. As we shall see, it was the states themselves that pushed for additional Medicaid changes. These changes allowed the states to take control of the program's maternal and child health care policies.

In 1984, a coalition of 19 southern governors established the Southern Regional Task Force on Infant Mortality. The Task Force was created "to draw attention to the critical problem of infant mortality in the South" and to promote preventive measures to reduce its incidence.[22] First, the Task Force collected relevant information to document the severity of the problem. It found that 10 of the 12 states with the highest rates of infant mortality were in the South. Then, the Task Force issued a series of policy recommendations. It identified a number of specific strategies and programs that the states could pursue to improve the health care status of poor women and children, such as establishing special adolescent health care clinics, mobile units for rural areas, and family planning services for young, child-bearing women. The Task Force also recommended that further changes and revisions be made in the Medicaid program so that the states could focus more specifically on maternal and child health care issues.

Although their immediate goal was to focus the direct attention of the southern states on the problem of infant mortality, the Southern Regional Task Force had a much broader impact. It raised the awareness of public officials across the country of the extent and severity of America's infant mortality problems.[23] Indeed, many of the ideas from the Task Force Report were later advocated by the National Governors' Association,[24] the National Conference of State Legislators, and the National Association of State Budget Officers.[25] Its recommendations were also echoed in reports issued by the Institute of Medicine, the Children's Defense Fund,[26] the Guttmacher Institute,[27] and the National Commission to Reduce Infant Mortality.[28]

The Federal Government Responds to the States

In response to the initiatives taken by state governments, the federal government made further changes in Medicaid's coverage of maternal and child health care. These changes further enhanced state powers. For example, in 1986 Congress passed the Consolidated Omnibus Reconciliation Act (COBRA) of 1985 (see Table 3.1). COBRA created another new opportunity for the states. It "waived" the federal comparability rule requiring states to finance the same services for *all* Medicaid recipients. Under COBRA, states could now add *extra* benefits and/or finance *greater* amounts of care for pregnant women and their infants. A number of options were possible. States could expand the traditional types of benefits, such as physician services, home health care, and the like. Or, they could develop new ways of delivering services. For example, they could identify pregnant women "at risk" and then channel them into more "managed,"[29] and intensive forms of care.[30] Prior to COBRA, only one state (South Carolina) had been allowed to pursue these options. After COBRA's passage, Massachusetts, Minnesota, and Ohio immediately adopted this provision. By 1990, a total of 33 states had implemented this option.[31]

Several months after the enactment of COBRA, Congress made yet another major change in Medicaid. The Omnibus Budget Reconciliation Act of 1986 (OBRA–86) created several entirely new categories of Medicaid recipients. One of these was an optional coverage group of poor pregnant women and children. Beginning on April 1, 1987, states could provide Medicaid services to pregnant women and infants in families with incomes between the state Aid to Families with Dependent Children program (AFDC) threshold and the federal poverty rate. The following year (1988), states could expand eligibility even further, and continue providing Medicaid to eligible children up to the age of five. OBRA–86 also allowed the states to decide whether they would impose "resource" standards for these newly eligible groups. This meant that the states, not the federal government, were to determine how assets, such as automobiles, would be considered in making eligibility decisions. Finally, OBRA–86 made it possible for the states to bring pregnant women onto Medicaid more quickly. States could give qualified medical providers the ability to make immediate "presumptive eligibility" determinations, thereby enabling them to deliver early and more effective prenatal care services before a woman's Medicaid application had even been processed (see Table 3.1).

OBRA–86 reinforced and expanded upon the earlier Medicaid changes. It also made an important distinction between Medicaid and the AFDC program. Traditionally, Medicaid had been viewed simply as the health care counterpart of AFDC. In order to receive medical assistance, low-income women and children first had to qualify for AFDC. OBRA–86 made it possible for states to expand their Medicaid populations without enlarging their AFDC programs. Thus, the linkage between AFDC eligibility and Medicaid eligibility was officially severed.[32] It was clear that pregnant women and children were now perceived as a group with special needs; hence, they did not have to meet the traditional welfare criteria. However, it was left up to the states to determine if and how they would provide this group with medical care. OBRA–86 is considered to be the "single most important piece of legislation affecting pregnant women and children" passed during the 1980s.[33] It opened the door for the states to expand Medicaid coverage to thousands of low-income women and children across the country.

The states responded quickly to the OBRA–86 changes. By 1988, one year after the legislation's implementation, over one-half of the states had expanded Medicaid coverage to pregnant women with incomes up to 100 percent of the poverty rate. By the end of 1989, all but six states had adopted this option.[34] A number of states had even established eligibility standards that were more generous than the OBRA–86 guidelines.[35]

Federal Actions Legitimize State Initiatives

Medicaid was revised several more times during the late 1980s. But, in each case the federal government's actions merely legitimized efforts that the states were already undertaking. The first of these was part of the Omnibus Budget Reconciliation Act of 1987. This legislation gave states the authority to expand Medicaid eligibility to pregnant women and infants up to 185 percent of the federal poverty rate, and it also permitted states to continue Medicaid coverage for children (admitted through the OBRA–86 revisions) beyond the age of five, up to eight years of age. However, a number of states had already established eligibility standards that were as generous as these provisions.

The following year, the Welfare Reform Act of 1988 was enacted (see Table 3.1). Although this legislation focused primarily on AFDC, it also made some significant revisions in Medicaid. For example, welfare recipients who lose their AFDC benefits because they are working can still receive Medicaid coverage for 12 months. This enables low-income mothers trying to move off of welfare to retain medical assistance for themselves and their children during this difficult transitional period. Once again, several states, including New Jersey, Wisconsin, Washington, and Ohio had already enacted this type of program.

Later in 1988, Congress passed the Medicare Catastrophic Care Amendments. Like the Welfare Reform Act, this legislation was not aimed directly at the Medicaid program. It did, however, contain an important Medicaid policy extension. The Catastrophic Act mandated that all states expand Medicaid coverage for pregnant women and infants with incomes at or below 75 percent of poverty by July 1, 1989, and then up to 100 percent of poverty by July 1, 1990. Then, the following year, Congress passed the Omnibus Budget Reconciliation Act of 1989. Essentially, OBRA–89 altered the scope and timing of the earlier Medicaid changes. States were to extend program coverage to pregnant women and infants at 133 percent of the poverty rate; children were to be covered until the age of six; and the deadline for implementing these changes was moved up to April 1990. Here too, state actions preceded federal changes. Most states had already revised their eligibility standards, allowing more low-income pregnant women and children into the Medicaid program.[36]

The Impact of Recent Changes in Medicaid

Overall, the changes made in Medicaid during the 1980s illustrate two important points. First, the federal government made it increasingly easier for the *states* to expand their coverage of maternal and child health care. It is important to note that the federal government did not impose a uniform set of national standards or regulations on the states. Instead, the federal government *relaxed* its controls and influence, thereby allowing the states to assume more responsibilities in this area. The states, not the federal government, were given the lead to develop more comprehensive and extensive maternal and child health services.

Second, the states were active participants in this process. They played a key role in the initiation, as well as the implementation, of maternal and child health care policy changes. The states pushed the issues onto the federal government's agenda, and they served as the testing grounds for major policy efforts. In addition, they have continued to stimulate interest and action in the health care problems of poor women and children. In the next section of this chapter, I will describe four examples of state-level activity in this area. Each represents a different type of initiative or response. Taken together, they demonstrate the influence of the states on maternal and child health care policymaking.

State Initiatives and Experiments in Maternal and Child Health Care

The states have been actively involved in reshaping governmental assistance for low-income women and children. It would be impossible to describe all the state-level efforts in this area. However, we can use the experiences of four states to illustrate the range and depth of this activity. The first two examples, California and South Carolina, show how state precedents guided subsequent federal actions. The next two examples, Arkansas and North Carolina, demonstrate how state interpretations of federal guidelines can actually determine the very nature of the policy itself.

California's Obstetrical -Access Projects

California was one of the first states to experiment with Medicaid as a way of dealing more directly with the health care needs of women and children. In 1979, California implemented an "Obstetrical-Access Project" (OB-Access) on a demonstration basis in 13 counties. The overall goal of the project was to reduce the incidence of infant mortality in the state.[37] In order to accomplish this goal, pilot projects were set up in the poorest, most underserved areas of the state. Although each project operated somewhat differently, all of them concentrated on improving the accessibility and usage of Medicaid services for pregnant women and children. Some of the projects experimented with outreach programs, such as using public service announcements on local television channels, to publicize their efforts. Others worked closely with local health care providers to develop more appropriate reimbursement systems and more comprehensive packages of maternal and child health care. Overall, the OB-Access Project tested the feasibility and viability of alternative Medicaid service provision and reimbursement mechanisms.[38]

The OB-Access project operated from 1979 to 1982, during which time it provided care to over 7,000 women and infants. At the end of this period, a full-scale comprehensive evaluation of all of the individual projects was conducted. The evaluation indicated that the projects had achieved two extremely important objectives: (1) They improved the accessibility of Medicaid benefits for pregnant women and children; and (2) The projects had a positive impact on maternal and child health care by enhancing the program's accessibility. In addition, the evaluations demonstrated the overall cost-effectiveness of such efforts. Every dollar spent on the OB-Access project led to a $1.70 to $2.20 savings in total health care expenses.[39]

The successes of the OB-Access projects led to further action. In 1989, the California legislature extended the program to all pregnant women enrolled in Medi-Cal (California's Medicaid program). In a related measure, the Community-Based Perinatal Services Program was later introduced in California to provide similar services to low-income women who did not qualify for Medi-Cal.

The OB-Access Program also had an impact on policymaking across the country. Other states, including Massachusetts and New York, experimented with similar types of projects. All of these efforts demonstrated that the states could design more effective and cost-efficient maternal and child health care provisions. This information was then used to stimulate and justify federal changes in Medicaid policy. These revisions, initiated by the federal government in the mid 1980s, effectively gave the states authority and incentives to conduct more comprehensive experiments in this area. Thus, California's efforts have had a truly national impact on the Medicaid program.

South Carolina's High Risk Perinatal Channeling Program

In 1986, South Carolina implemented a statewide High Risk Perinatal Channeling Program. The program created a standardized assessment system to identify all high-risk pregnancies.[40] Essentially, the program operates like this: As soon as a woman's pregnancy is established, she is screened and evaluated by a qualified professional to determine if she is likely to experience a poor birth outcome. If she is found to be "at risk," the woman is then channeled to a network of providers and given more specialized and enriched medical care.

This program embodies a number of innovative ideas. First, it stresses the early identification of maternal health care problems. Second, it emphasizes the provision of a highly enriched set of prenatal care services, including physician services, nutritional assessments, case management, home visiting benefits, and specialized hospital care. Third, it demonstrates the need to tailor Medicaid services to the specific needs of the women and children it serves: "High-risk" women should receive more intensive and more comprehensive care than healthy ones who are not likely to experience serious complications or problems. Finally, the project promotes collaboration between Medicaid and other participants in the system. In order to channel high-risk patients to appropriate services, the Medicaid agency works closely with state and local health care providers.

It is important to point out that South Carolina undertook these initiatives on an experimental, self-directed basis. The federal government did not mandate this effort. Indeed, these steps conflicted with federal provisions contained in Medicaid legislation. Therefore, South Carolina had to obtain waivers from the federal government in order to conduct its experimental program.[41]

Like California's OB-Access Program, South Carolina's initiative was used as a model for later Medicaid changes. In particular, two of the most important Medicaid provisions contained in COBRA–85[42] were based on South Carolina's maternal and child health care experiment: (1) the provision to offer specialized services for pregnant women without requiring that these services be extended to the entire Medicaid population; and (2) the provision to develop targeted case management programs so that "at risk" pregnant women could receive additional help in obtaining medical, social, clinical, and educational services.

The South Carolina and California experiences demonstrate the impact that state-level initiatives can and have had on policymaking across the country. In each case, it was the states that pursued and experimented with new systems of care. The federal government embraced these initiatives and passed legislation to encourage further state experimentation and activity. The states quickly and eagerly responded to this situation. The next two examples, Arkansas and North Carolina, clearly demonstrate how the states continue to influence Medicaid policymaking.

Arkansas' Presumptive Eligibility System

Arkansas was one of the first states to take *full* advantage of the Medicaid provisions contained in OBRA–86 by quickly expanding program coverage to pregnant women and infants with incomes up to 75 percent of the poverty line. The state also authorized a major change in its eligibility determination process. Arkansas was the first state to implement a presumptive eligibility system in its state Medicaid program.

The basic idea of "presumptive eligibility" is quite simple. It allows a state to provide Medicaid coverage to poor women at the "earliest point of contact between the patient and the provider."[43] Health care providers document the woman's pregnancy, assess her financial status, and make the initial determination of Medicaid eligibility. A low-income pregnant woman does not have to go to the local welfare office or wait months for her application to be processed before she can qualify for Medicaid coverage. Instead, she can receive essential medical care, paid for by Medicaid, in the early, critical days of her pregnancy. In theory, presumptive eligibility is an easy way of bypassing the normal, but cumbersome and stigmatizing, process of establishing Medicaid eligibility. In practice, however, it is an extremely difficult initiative to adopt and implement. Arkansas' efforts in this regard illustrate two important points. First, the states are often ready and willing to undertake extremely complicated, difficult program changes. Second, state efforts constitute the actual responses to maternal and child health problems. Therefore, it is the states that effectively make public policy in this area.

When Arkansas decided to implement a presumptive eligibility system, it had to determine how this system would operate.[44] The federal government delineated only the basic parameters and then left it up to the states to design workable procedures. This meant that Arkansas had to determine which health care professionals would actually have the ability to grant "presumptive eligibility" status to pregnant woman. It had to develop mechanisms whereby these qualified providers could notify the state Medicaid agency of their determinations. Arkansas also had to devise other procedures so that the applications of the "presumptively eligible" women could be reviewed and processed.[45] In essence, Arkansas was faced with the difficult task of designing another eligibility determination system that would operate alongside its "normal" administrative apparatus.

Arkansas' "presumptive eligibility" program was enacted completely within previously existing guidelines. Arkansas demonstrated that the states could overcome the administrative difficulties and complexities of implementing a workable presumptive eligibility system. Thus, it illustrates how the states can interpret the Medicaid program in ways that enhance their own powers and responsibilities. As the first state to pursue this option, Arkansas played an influential role in defining critical aspects of the program. The lessons learned in Arkansas were used to help other states design their own eligibility reform initiatives.[46] By July 1990, 28 states had implemented presumptive eligibility systems.[47]

North Carolina's First Step and Baby Love Programs

Several years ago North Carolina's Medicaid program was ranked among the "worst" in the country. The Public Citizen Health Research Group described North Carolina's program as "wholly inadequate across the board."[48] The only area in which North Carolina's Medicaid program scored well was in its coverage of services for pregnant women and infants.

Over the last several years, North Carolina has taken steps to strengthen and build upon its maternal and child health care benefits. In 1988, it introduced a set of comprehensive initiatives to reduce infant mortality across the state.[49] Major changes were made in the state's Medicaid program. Eligibility criteria were liberalized so that more pregnant women could qualify for program coverage, and eligibility procedures were streamlined to expedite the receipt of needed medical care. In addition, physician fees for maternity care were increased in order to encourage more doctors to participate in Medicaid and to give them the financial incentive to continue providing care throughout a woman's pregnancy. It was hoped that these efforts would have a positive impact on the health care status of low-income and pregnant women in the state.

Unfortunately, the initial results of these efforts were not encouraging. The year after the changes were implemented, North Carolina had the highest infant mortality rate of any state in the nation. Consequently, the state took another look at its maternal and child health care system.[50] One basic problem stood out. There was no way of reaching those who were in the greatest need of care and no way of linking them to appropriate medical services. Consequently, North Carolina launched a statewide outreach campaign called "First Step." The campaign is designed to spread the message that early and continuous prenatal care is vitally important and to inform women about the availability of such treatment. In addition, it educates potentially eligible women about the possibilities of coverage under the new Medicaid provisions. First Step broadcasts public service announcements over television and radio channels urging pregnant women to obtain adequate prenatal care. It also uses a toll-free hotline to tell women where they can receive medical and social care during their pregnancies.

In concert with this outreach campaign, North Carolina also established a preventive care initiative called "Baby Love" in its Medicaid program. Baby Love picks up where First Step leaves off. It allows eligible women to move quickly and relatively smoothly into the Medicaid program, and it provides them with "managed," case-specific systems of medical and social care.

North Carolina's First Step and Baby Love programs illustrate the type of activities that states have been pursuing the past two-to-three years. Once again, the programs are established within existing Medicaid guidelines with an emphasis on finding ways to draw women and children into better systems of health care. The Medicaid program now covers many more pregnant women and children, and it finances fairly comprehensive packages of care. The problem is the link between the women and the program. North Carolina's First Step and Baby Love initiatives are attempting to alter the public's perception of Medicaid and to attract more women to the program.

Summary and Conclusions

In summary, the states are powerful actors in the nation's maternal and child health care system. As we have seen, they have experimented with and pushed for major changes in Medicaid's coverage of pregnant women and children. They have capitalized on the flexibility and influence now available to them, and they are continuing to develop new initiatives and strategies.

The role of the states in maternal and child health care policymaking is indicative of a general trend. The states are assuming more control and more leadership over important health care issues in the United States. The federal government encouraged this development in the early 1980s when it relaxed federal regulations over programs like Medicaid. The states, however, have taken the initiative and addressed many health care concerns. As a result, it is accurate to say that the states are now the leaders in this policy area. They are not merely reacting to federal initiatives.

At the same time, however, there is one aspect of maternal and child health care that makes it unique compared to other, related concerns. The states have been much more willing, and in some cases even eager, to take an active role in this area. This is because of the type of issue involved. There are compelling practical and political reasons for the states to address the health care needs of women and children. In South Carolina, North Carolina, and Arkansas, for example, the problems are so severe that they are difficult to ignore. Therefore, it is very reasonable that these states have targeted maternal and child health care as an important public policy concern. It is also the case, however, that the states now recognize the practical implications of improving medical services for pregnant women and infants. It is clearly a cost-effective way of dealing directly with some of our most serious and expensive health care problems (for example, low birth weight infants), and it also has an indirect impact on many other social problems (such as teenage pregnancy and out-of-wedlock births).

Maternal and child health care is also a politically expedient issue for states to pursue. There are no powerful interest groups trying to prevent or shape government activity in this area, as there are in many other health issues (witness the role of the nursing home industry in aging policy). As a result, state governments have much more leeway to develop their own response to maternal and child health care problems. Because of the symbolic importance of "womanhood" and "childhood" in American society, state officials also have much less difficulty getting the public to accept their proposals. Consequently, although there are important similarities to other health care policy developments, the states' activity in this area has been somewhat different.

There are several specific consequences of the states' efforts in this field. First, they have succeeded in making maternal and child health care problems major policy issues.[51] Although the states have not been the only ones to draw attention to these problems, they have certainly played a critical role in the agenda-setting process. They helped to make the general public and the national government more aware of the extent and severity of the country's maternal and child health problems. The changes that have occurred within the Medicaid program over the last decade are clear indications of this increased attention.

Second, the states are now viewed as the major testing grounds for governmental activity in this policy area. As discussed earlier, California's OB-Access Project and South Carolina's High Risk Channeling Program are two examples of models that guided federal Medicaid changes in the mid 1980s. Similarly, Arkansas' and North Carolina's efforts to develop new eligibility and outreach programs illustrate that the states continue to be the main innovators in this area. Overall, these state-level initiatives and experiments have had a dramatic impact on the Medicaid program's coverage of maternal and child health care.[52] Although it is too early to determine the precise consequences of these changes, it is clear that the Medicaid program is now in a much better position to provide more and better care to low-income pregnant women and children. Third, there is good news to report about the health care status of pregnant women and children in the United States. The national infant mortality rate is now the lowest in history: 9.8 deaths per 1,000 live births. In some states, there have been more dramatic improvements. Over the last three years, the infant mortality rates in Oregon, Washington, Maryland, and Maine have been steadily dropping.[53] The states' efforts to address health care problems in this area are not the sole determinants of these developments. But, it is certainly reasonable to conclude that they have been at least partially responsible for these trends.

Despite these achievements, America's maternal and child health care problems have not been eradicated. Indeed, there are still some alarming statistics. Although the national infant mortality rate has been declining, the downward trend has slowed for all segments of the population.[54] It is quite possible that we have reached the limits of our technological and medical ability to save sick and premature babies. Now, we are faced with the more difficult task of preventing these conditions from occurring in the first place. The data pertaining to the availability of preventative medical services is not very positive. Over one-half of all children in the United States have some trouble obtaining regular and continuous health care services,[55] and the percentage of all American women who have access to prenatal care actually declined in the 1980s.[56]

There is also concern about whether government can continue to direct resources toward this problem. The Medicaid program itself provides benefits to a diverse population with quite varied health care needs.[57] It is used to finance the treatment of AIDS patients, nursing home care for the elderly, and institutionalized services for disabled adults. Although women and children comprise the largest segment of the Medicaid recipient population, they are neither the fastest *growing* nor the most *expensive* coverage group. The aged, blind, and disabled population is growing at a faster rate, and it already consumes the largest percentage of all program expenditures.[58] Obviously this means that fewer and fewer resources can be devoted to maternal and child health care.

The preceding problem is so serious that states are questioning their ability to provide health care for all those in need. Medicaid is already the largest single item in most state budgets. Faced with budget deficits and revenue crises, states are taking a closer look at the scope and coverage of their Medicaid programs.[59] A few, such as Oregon, whose story Howard Leichter chronicles in Chapter Six, are experimenting with ways of "rationing" Medicaid services or targeting only those who are truly in need. Other states are considering cutting back the eligibility and service expansions they pursued in the 1980s in order to avoid shortfalls in Medicaid spending.[60]

It is unlikely that the states will abandon their commitment to low-income families, pregnant women, and children. They are, however, being forced to make difficult policy choices concerning whom they will cover and how they will administer program services. The policy choices that the states are now making, particularly concerning the size, scope, and focus of their Medicaid programs, will have a profound effect on the future well-being of America's women and children.

Notes

1. Dana Hughes, Kay Johnson, Sara Rosenbaum, Janet Simons, and Elizabeth Butler, *The Health of America's Children: Maternal and Child Health Data Book* (Washington, DC: Children's Defense Fund, 1988).

2. J.L. Wagner, R.C. Herdman, and D.W. Alberts, "Well-Child Care: How

Much is Enough?" *Health Affairs* 8 no. 3 (1989): 147–157; Gretchen V. Fleming and Beth K. Yudkowsky, *Preventive Health Care for Medicaid Children: Related Factors and Costs* (Baltimore: Health Care Financing Administration, 1990); Beth K. Yudkowsky and Gretchen V. Fleming, "Preventive Health Care for Medicaid Children," *Health Care Financing Review* (Annual Supplement, 1990): 89–96.

3. United States General Accounting Office, *Prenatal Care: Medicaid Recipients and Uninsured Women Obtain Insufficient Care* (Washington, DC: Government Printing Office, 1987); Hughes, Johnson, Rosenbaum, Simons, and Butler, *The Health of America's Children.*

4. Institute of Medicine, *Preventing Low Birthweight* (Washington, DC: National Academy Press, 1985); Institute of Medicine, *Prenatal Care: Reaching Mothers, Reaching Infants* (Washington, DC: National Academy Press, 1988).

5. Margaret McManus, "Medicaid Services and Delivery Settings for Maternal and Child Health," in *Affording Access to Quality Care: Strategies for Medicaid Cost Management* (Washington, DC: Health Policy Studies, Center for Policy Research, National Governors' Association, 1986).

6. C.C. White, J.P. Koplan, and W.A. Orenstein, "Benefits, Risks and Costs of Immunization for Measles, Mumps and Rubella," *American Journal of Public Health* 75 no. 7 (1985): 739–744.

7. Hughes et al., *The Health of America's Children.*

8. National Center for Health Statistics, "Births, Marriages, Divorces, and Deaths for August 1990," *Monthly Vital Statistics Report* 39 no. 8 (1990): 1–5; National Center for Health Statistics, "Advance Report of Final Mortality Statistics, 1988," *Monthly Vital Statistics Report* 39 no. 7 (1988): 1–47.

9. Louis P. Garrison, "Medicaid, The Uninsured, and National Health Spending: Federal Policy Implications," *Health Care Financing Review* (Annual Supplement, 1990): 167–170; National Center for Health Statistics 1990.

10. Jeffery C. Merrill, "State Initiatives for the Medically Uninsured," *Health Care Financing Review* (Annual Supplement, 1990): 161–166.

11. R.B. Gold, A.M. Kenney, and S. Singh, *Blessed Events and the Bottom Line: Financing Maternity Care in the United States* (New York: Alan Guttmacher Institute, 1987); McManus 1986.

12. Office of Technology Assessment, *Neonatal Intensive Care for Low Birthweight Infants: Costs and Effectiveness* (Washington, DC: Government Printing Office, 1987).

13. McManus, "Medicaid Services and Delivery Settings for Maternal and Child Health"; Ian T. Hill, "Improving State Medicaid Programs for Pregnant Women and Children," *Health Care Financing Review* (Annual Supplement, 1990): 75–87.

14. Robert B. Stevens and Rosemary Stevens, *Welfare Medicine in America: A Case Study of Medicaid* (New York: Free Press, 1974).

15. Randall R. Bovbjerg and John Holahan, *Medicaid In the Reagan Era: Federal Policy and State Choices* (Washington, DC: The Urban Institute Press, 1982).

16. Saundra K. Schneider, "Intergovernmental Influences on Medicaid Program Expenditures," *Public Administration Review* 47 no. 6 (1988): 479–484.

17. Bovbjerg and Holahan, *Medicaid In the Reagan Era.*

18. Ian T. Hill, *Medicaid Eligibility: A Descriptive Report of OBRA, TEFRA,*

and DEFRA Provisions and State Responses (Baltimore: Office of Research and Demonstration, Health Care Financing Administration, U.S. Department of Health and Human Services, Medicaid Program Evaluation Working Paper 5.2, 1984).

19. Hill, 1986.

20. These are sometimes referred to as "Ribicoff children" because former Senator Abraham Ribicoff (D–CT) played an instrumental role in establishing their eligibility for Medicaid.

21. After the passage of OBRA–81, the federal government enacted two other pieces of legislation that affected the Medicaid program: the Tax Equity and Fiscal Responsibility Act of 1982 (TEFRA) and the Deficit Reduction Act (DEFRA) of 1984. Although both of these acts contained provisions affecting the states' coverage of low-income women and children, they did not alter the basic transformations that were occurring in Medicaid policymaking. TEFRA gave the states another option. It allowed them to provide Medicaid coverage to disabled children who were not in institutionalized settings. DEFRA did require all states to cover "childless" pregnant women who would be eligible if the child were already born. But all but seven states already covered this group *prior* to the enactment of DEFRA.

22. Southern Regional Task Force on Infant Mortality, *Final Report: For the Children of Tomorrow* (Washington, DC: Southern Governors' Association and the Southern Legislative Conference, 1985).

23. Saundra K. Schneider, "Governors and Health Care Policy in the American States," *Policy Studies Journal* 17 no. 4 (1989): 909–926.

24. Ian T. Hill, *Broadening Medicaid Coverage of Pregnant Women and Children: State Policy Responses* (Washington, DC: Health Policy Studies, Center for Policy Research, National Governors' Association, 1987); *Implementing a Workable Presumptive Eligibility Program: The Experience in Arkansas* (Washington, DC: Health Policy Studies, Center for Policy Research, National Governors' Association, 1987); "Medicaid Eligibility Thresholds for Families and Pregnant Women Information Update" (Washington, DC: National Governors' Association, September 8, 1987); "Improving State Medicaid Programs for Pregnant Women and Children," *Health Care Financing Review* (Annual Supplement, 1990): 75–87; and J. Breyel, *Coordinating Prenatal Care: Strategies for Improving State Perinatal Programs* (Washington, DC: National Governors' Association, 1989).

25. Heather Fairburn Haggard, "Medicaid Eligibility: New State Options" (Washington, DC: National Conference of State Legislatures, 1987).

26. Hughes, Johnson, Rosenbaum, Simons, and Butler, *The Health of America's Children* (1988); *The Health of America's Children* (1989).

27. Gold, Kenney, and Singh, *Blessed Events and the Bottom Line*.

28. Many of the recommendations from the Southern Regional Task Force were incorporated into state and federal policy. Although the Task Force certainly influenced this activity, it was not the only stimulant for change. As mentioned in the body of this chapter, a number of state and national organizations pushed for new strategies and programs to deal with the nation's maternal and child health care problems. But the Southern Regional Task Force was one of the first and certainly one of the most influential advocates for change.

29. For a good description of "managed" systems of health care, see Bruce Spitz, "Medicaid Case Management Programs: A National Survey," *Focus On* 19 (Washington, DC: Office of Intergovernmental Affairs, Health Care Financing Administration, U.S. Department of Health and Human Services, November 1987): 1–10.

30. Sara Rosenbaum, "Financing Maternity Care for Low-Income Women: Results of a Nationwide Medicaid Survey" (Washington, DC: Children's Defense Fund, 1985).

31. Ian T. Hill, "Improving State Medicaid Programs for Pregnant Women and Children," *Health Care Financing Review* (Annual Supplement, 1990): 75–87; and T. Bennet, *Enhancing the Scope of Prenatal Services: Strategies for Improving State Perinatal Programs* (Washington, DC: National Governors' Association, 1990).

32. Ibid.

33. Ibid.

34. Ibid.

35. It is impossible to identify the precise impact of the OBRA–86 changes. Unfortunately, there are no reliable estimates of the total number of women and children affected or of the costs of the eligibility expansions. For example, the cost estimates in one state, Ohio, have varied from $5 million to over $52 million. This is due to different assumptions about the size of the affected populations, their utilization of health care services, and the cost-savings involved.

36. Hill, "Improving State Medicaid Programs for Pregnant Women and Children," 75–87; and Bennet, *Enhancing the Scope of Prenatal Services.*

37. Gregory Maridee, "Final Evaluation of the Obstetrical Access Pilot Project, July 1979–June 1982" (Sacramento: Department of Health Services, 1984).

38. Institute of Medicine, *Prenatal Care: Reaching Mothers, Reaching Infants* (Washington, DC: National Academy Press, 1988).

39. Maridee, "Final Evaluation of the Obstetrical Access Pilot Project."

40. "Request for Federal Waiver to Establish a High Risk Channeling Project Within the South Carolina Medicaid Program" (Columbia, SC: South Carolina Department of Health and Environmental Control, 1984); "Response to Federal Request for Additional Information Concerning the Establishment of a High Risk Channeling Project Within the South Carolina Medicaid Program" (Columbia, SC: South Carolina Department of Health and Environmental Control, 1985); "Medicaid High Risk Channeling Project Procedures Manual" (Columbia, SC: South Carolina Department of Health and Environmental Control, 1986).

41 Ibid.

42. COBRA–85 was enacted on April 7, 1986. This was several months before South Carolina actually implemented its High Risk Channeling Project. South Carolina first requested Medicaid waivers for the project in 1984, and it spent the next year and one-half submitting additional information and materials to obtain approval for its initiative. The federal government did not officially approve South Carolina's request until October 18, 1985; however, this was still six months before the passage of COBRA–85.

43. Ian T. Hill, *Broadening Medicaid Coverage of Pregnant Women and Children: State Policy Responses* (Washington, DC: Health Policy Studies, Center for Policy Research, National Governors' Association, 1987); Ian T. Hill, *Implement-*

ing A Workable Presumptive Eligibility Program: The Experience in Arkansas (Washington, DC: Health Policy Studies, Center for Policy Research, National Governors' Association, 1987); Ian T. Hill, "Medicaid Eligibility Thresholds for Families and Pregnant Women Information Update" (Washington, DC: National Governors' Association, September 8, 1987).

44. "Expanded Services for Pregnant Women and Infants," (Little Rock: Arkansas Department of Human Services, 1987).

45. Hill, *Broadening Medicaid Coverage of Pregnant Women and Children*; Hill, *Implementing A Workable Presumptive Eligibility Program*; Hill, "Medicaid Eligibility Thresholds for Families and Pregnant Women Information Update."

46. Ibid.

47. Hill, 1990.

48. Hill, 1987: 172.

49. "North Carolina Initiative to Reduce Infant Mortality" (Raleigh: North Carolina Medicaid Program, 1987).

50. "Hot Line Part of N.C.'s First Step to Reduce Infant Mortality," *The State*, 25 August 1990. sec. B.

51. Hill, 1990.

52. Ibid.

53. National Center for Health Statistics, *Births, Marriages, Divorces, and Deaths for August 1990* (Hyattsville, MD: Public Health Service, 1990); National Center for Health Statistics, "Advance Report of Final Mortality Statistics, 1988," *Monthly Vital Statistics Report* 39 no. 7 (1990): 1–47.

54. "Infant Mortality Rates Continue to Be Almost Stagnant," *The Nation's Health* (July 1989): 1, 9.

55. B. Bloom, "Health Insurance and Medical Care: Health of Our Nation's Children, United States, 1988," *Advance Data From Vital and Health Statistics* 188 (October 1): 1–8; Merit C. Kimball, "Children's Health: A System Full of Woe," *Health Week* 4 no. 17 (1990): 1, 38–40.

56. Karen Southwick, "Women Confront Second-Class Care," *Health Week* 4 no. 16 (1990): 1, 40–42.

57. Reilly, Clauser, and Baugh, 1990.

58. Marian Gornick, Jay N. Greenberg, Paul W. Eggers, and Allen Dobson, "Twenty Years of Medicare and Medicaid: Covered Populations, Use of Benefits, and Program Expenditures," *Health Care Financing Review* (Annual Supplement, 1985): 13–59.

59. David Sussman and Marilyn Wann, "Controlling Medicaid Costs a Lingering Concern in States," *Health Week* 4 no. 9 (1990): 1, 41.

60. David Profitt, "To Avoid Shortfall, Medicaid Cuts Likely," *The State*, 6 December 1990, sec. B.

4

Political Culture, Political Leadership, Sustained Advocacy, and Aging Policy Reform: The Oregon and North Carolina Experiences

David J. Falcone, with Dell Ensley and Cecilia B. Moore

This chapter compares health and social services policy targeted at the elderly in Oregon and North Carolina. (Hereinafter, such policy will be referred to as "aging policy.")[1] These states were chosen largely on the basis of the authors' intuitive insights rather than adherence to the canons of methodology. Still, the sites could be viewed as well-chosen from a policy analysis perspective. Oregon has a mature system of public and private provision of aging services that has been heralded as a national model and has been identified in a National Governor's Association study as one of six exemplars of community long-term care system reform.[2] North Carolina's aging policy is at a crossroads, where the Oregon approach is one path that might be taken.

In keeping with the theme of this volume, there is no doubt that effective aging policy reform, like reforms in other domestic policy areas, will be largely a subnational endeavor.[3] There is little doubt that the states now have the burden[4] or opportunity[5] to help meet the needs of the nation's aged population.

It would be difficult to overstate the magnitude of these needs. The demographic trends propelling increased need and demand for health and social services for the elderly are well-known. Life expectancy has been steadily increasing, as has the period of extended life that the elderly will likely spend in a morbid or disabled condition.[6] There is room for some optimism about the "compression of morbidity and disability" (that is, the reduction of extended lifetime spent function-ally impaired) based on evidence that improved life-styles and the increased socioeconomic status of the "new" older generation may eventually produce beneficial effects on functional independence.[7] However, it is highly improbable that such effects will occur in the near future. Nor will they offset increases in health care costs and the growth in utilization that will result from the fact that the fastest grow-ing segment of the population over the next 40 or so years will be made up of those eighty-five years of age or older, a group with a disproportionate need for health and social services.

One conservative estimate of the impending effects of these demo-graphic trends is that there will be 1.9 million nursing home residents in the year 2000, an increase of 800,000 since 1979; 111.3 million home care visits, or 65.4 million more than were made in 1979; and 12.9 million long-term care days in hospitals, versus 7.6 million in 1979. The financial impact of this increased utilization will be long-term care expenditures of $30.3 million, a $12.5 million or 70 percent growth since 1979 (in constant dollars).[8]

There is evidence that Americans sense what is coming and are appropriately concerned. Survey research conducted for the American Association of Retired Persons and the Villers Foundation documented the intensity of that concern and a willingness to support government sponsored long-term care insurance for everyone (61 percent); a mi-nority of 27 percent favored care for only the poor.[9] Of more import-ance, a solid majority of respondents in all income classes (68 percent) were willing to pay realistic taxes for such a program. (The lowest percentage of those willing to pay was 65 percent of the $20,000 to $30,000 income group.) More respondents (47 percent) preferred gov-ernment administration of a long-term care insurance program than administration by a private company. Of particular relevance to the concerns of this volume, when asked to state a preference for federal or state administration, 51 percent of the respondents favored state government versus 32 percent in favor of the federal government.

Neither Oregon nor North Carolina now has the long-term care program supported by the respondents to the AARP-Villers interview. But as mentioned, they have approached the exploitation of existing programs in quite different ways. In comparing these differences, we have not decomposed the Oregon and North Carolina contexts into clusters of variables, and, in violation of the Przeworski and Teune prescription for comparative analysis, we have explicitly examined only two cases.[10] But we have assembled enough socioeconomic data on the two cases/states to be able to suggest that the policy differences between them cannot be attributed to the environmental factors usually employed in "policy determinants" analyses. Rather, we will suggest that the differences in aging policy in Oregon and North Carolina result from political differences: Oregon's relatively more activist "moralistic," community-oriented political culture; its more effective sustained interest-group advocacy; a consolidated budget for aging services; and, perhaps most important, its exercise of public leadership. Of course, as always, idiosyncratic conditioning factors, such as the more profound impact of the last recession on the Oregon economy, also have to be taken into account in explaining the development of the Oregon model.

The ensuing discussion starts with a comparison of outputs and outcomes of aging policy in Oregon and North Carolina: quality of care, access improvement, and cost containment. We then review the political structures and processes that might plausibly be regarded as causes of the aging policy outcome/output variation, the political cultural variables that influenced the structures and processes, and, finally, the socioeconomic or "environmental" variables that might explain differences in both political structures and processes and policy outputs.

Aging Policies and Their Effects on
Quality, Cost, Access

Oregon

Quality

Oregon's aging services fulfill the state's mission to serve its elderly clients of all income classes in the least restrictive environment possible. A recent independent evaluation by two of the most respected researchers on aging programs has concluded that "judging from the absolute decline in nursing home beds over an eight-year period, Oregon's alternative programs have actually replaced nursing home care."[11] Robert Kane et al. report that an econometric analysis of Medicaid clients in foster care (the primary institutional alternative to nursing home care in place at the time of the analysis) showed that substitutability had occurred, as opposed to the complementarity that normally has been observed when encouragements to use options to nursing home care have been attempted.[12] And declines and improvements in residents' functional status were not significantly different in the two settings.

There is no significant hospital discharge delay problem in Oregon.[13] Elderly hospital patients in this state tend to be discharged when they are "medically ready." Partly as a result, the mean length of stay (LOS) in hospitals for the elderly in Oregon is 6.2 days compared to the national average of 8.9 days.[14] In this regard, Oregon has averted a national quality-of-care problem. Most hospitals are not set up to deliver "definitive" long-term care and reliance on hospitals for inappropriate, subacute care leads to increased system costs.[15] Although no general financial model is available, whatever payment hospitals are able to garner for inappropriate stays (principally Medicaid reimbursement at nursing home rates) are clearly insufficient to cover variable costs associated with those stays.[16] Quality and appropriateness of care in all settings in Oregon are continuously monitored through vigorous case management.

Costs

Oregon has thus far avoided the so-called "woodwork effect" that occurs when latent demand for long-term care services is activated by increases in supply. The increases in supply of lower unit-cost services (such as home care) for higher unit-cost services (nursing home care) result in increases in aggregate demand that wipe out the intended substitution effects. In other words, people needing low-cost services come out of the woodwork when such services become available and affordable. They consume so many of these services that the total cost of providing all types of services, low and high cost, then goes up.

The Federal Health Care Financing Administration (HCFA) and

Office of Management and Budget became preoccupied with the woodwork effect when the results of the extremely expensive "channeling" project, which used case management models at ten sites, were reported.[17] That project demonstrated that attempts to avert institutionalization of the elderly by providing affordable case-managed alternatives had only marginal effects on quality of care and that they substantially increased aggregate costs.[18]

A major flaw of the evaluation of the project, however, may be that it was done too early. The Kanes suggest in their study of long-term care in four Canadian provinces that once latent demand has been activated, an initial upsurge in costs may be followed by a plateauing of expenditure increases.[19] Thus, the Kanes imply that cost-effective reform requires commitment from officials: the title of their book, *A Will and a Way,* underscores that implication. Oregon has fulfilled that commitment and has reaped the rewards.

Oregon's health and social services fall under two Medicaid waivers, 1915 (c) and (d), which impose federal limits on cost increases and allow the state almost unlimited discretion as to how funds are spent. For example, the state can pay for services traditionally not covered, such as assisted living arrangements. In effect, this is a near-Canadian type of prospective block-budgeting. Partly as a result, the state's Medicaid expenditures for long-term care per person sixty-five years old or older are low by national standards, despite the fact that Oregon "has developed a wider range of long-term care programs funded under Medicaid and Medicaid waivers than has any other state."[20]

Access

Publicly funded health and social services for the elderly in Oregon are reimbursed on a sliding-scale basis. Two-thirds of foster care is consumed by private-paying clients: "Unlike other states where adult foster care tends to be a small program concentrating on poor, mentally ill people, in Oregon it has become a mainstream long-term care option."[21] "Assisted living" arrangements—such as apartments with supportive services available, a relatively new approach to demedicalization[22]—range from relatively modest but attractive Medicaid-reimbursed quarters to what one usually sees in an upscale continuing care retirement (CCRC) or life-style community.[23] Since no equity is required in assisted living quarters, residents do not incur the risk associated with CCRCs.

Assisted living, thus, is an affordable option for the middle-income elderly. These alternatives to nursing home services in large part account for the remarkably low average nursing home LOS in Oregon: 234 days compared to a national figure in excess of 600 days.[24]

In all three output/outcome domains, cost, access and quality, Oregon's success is atypical. North Carolina's is not.

North Carolina

Quality

No systematic study has focused on the overall quality of health and social services for the elderly in North Carolina. However, the consensus among analysts, activists, and officials is that, with few exceptions, the statewide delivery of services is uncoordinated.[25] Further, North Carolina has a distinctive supply characteristic that is suggestive of compromised quality of care: beds in homes for the aged (also known as old folks homes, rest homes, or domiciliary care homes) number almost three quarters of nursing home beds. That makes North Carolina uniquely reliant on this form of care,[26] which has been insufficiently evaluated in the state; when it has been examined on a national level, the results have been disturbing.[27]

It is important to distinguish rest home services in North Carolina from foster home services in Oregon. The latter are self-consciously viewed by the state as nursing home alternatives, and Medicaid clients in these settings are "case-managed"; that is, patients are regularly screened and, if required, assessed regarding functional status. Determinations, then, are made concerning the continued appropriateness of the setting for the patients' care needs.

Another warning sign of a breakdown in quality in the North Carolina aging services delivery network is the severity of the delayed hospital discharge syndrome in the state. One study of more than 3,100 hospital patients who were medically ready for discharge and awaiting placement in settings outside the hospital found an average of more than 16.5 days' delay.[28] The weight of opinion seems to be that hospitals are not a suitable environment for the frail elderly who are no longer in need of acute care, and most hospitals' services operations are not now geared toward the provision of high quality short-term–long-term care (that is, care that is not acute in the usual sense but is more intensive than traditional long-term care).[29] Delayed discharges do not seem to have a place in an efficient (cost-minimizing), effective (appropriateness-oriented), or efficacious (outcome-enhancing) system of care. "They, perhaps more than any other phenomenon, reflect a lack of coordination of service."[30]

The 16.5 day average delay in North Carolina compares to an average of 6.5 in Michigan, the only other state in which a similar study has been conducted.[31] As pointed out previously, Oregon does not experience the delayed discharge problem, despite its absolute reduction in the number of nursing home beds over the past decade. And nursing homes typically have been regarded as the most likely recipients of hospital patients whose discharges have been delayed, primarily because the delayed patients require "heavy care" (like ventilation and intubation). The delayed discharge problem is reflected in the high mean hospital LOS, 9.7 days, for elderly North Carolinians.[32] Recall that the national average is 8.9 days, and Oregon's is 6.2 days.

Cost

The possible deficiencies in the quality of services for the elderly in North Carolina are not inexpensive; the costs of long-term care rendered in hospitals that are staffed and equipped for acute care almost certainly far exceed the costs of care in more appropriate settings.[33]

Access

North Carolina's Medicaid program is one of the most income exclusive in the country, and the proportion of elderly persons "in poverty" relative to other age groups in this state is exceptionally high.[34] There are waiting lists for nursing home placements in all areas of the state as well as for home and community-based services. The CCRC industry is expanding but access to this option is limited, in general, to couples with approximately $100,000 in assets and a $25,000 to $30,000 annual income. The average nursing home LOS in North Carolina of 378 days is well below the national figure but higher than Oregon's. The average length of stay in rest homes, a mode of care upon which North Carolina is unusually reliant, is 426 days.

North Carolina's and Oregon's aging services policies, reflected in program performance regarding quality, cost-control and access, cannot be clearly assigned positions on a scale. However, there are enough indications of differential success to suggest that Oregon's status as a "model" is warranted. But is it exportable? To answer this question, we have to examine briefly the policy process that has produced the model results and the contextual underpinnings of that process.

Process and Structure

North Carolina: A Typical State

Figure 4.1 depicts the aging policy "network" found in North Carolina and most other states. Public financing comes to this state via a number of streams, but the ones listed in the exhibit cover almost all expenditures: federal funds from the Older American's Act (OAA), a social services block grant (SSBG), Medicaid (medical assistance), state and local matching funds, and state and local–only funds. The size of the Medicaid budget dwarfs all others. Medicaid is the chief source of public funding for long-term care, amounting to only slightly less than the main source, out-of-pocket payments by service recipients.

Some non-Medicaid funds flow through a designated state agency putatively responsible for planning and coordinating aging services, the Division of Aging (DoA), which, in turn, authorizes Area Agencies on Aging (AAAs, "triple As") to contract with providers for services at substate levels. There are 18 AAAs in North Carolina covering 100 counties.

The other major non-Medicaid actor in the aging policy arena is the Division of Social Services, which encompasses county social services departments with variable eligibility requirements for receipt of variable types and levels of service. This division, DoA, and Medicaid are housed in an umbrella agency, the Department of Human Resources (DHR).

In addition to the DHR divisions, there are state activities that Figure 4.1 puts in the elegant "others" category. One example of an "other" program is the Senior Volunteers Assistance Program in the Insurance Commission's Office, which mobilizes retirees to help educate the elderly about long-term care insurance options.

An "agency theory" is schematized in Figure 4.2. In this conceptualization, major state actors can be viewed as "contractors" for the "agents," the legislature and executive/administration, of the "princi-

Figure 4.1. **North Carolina State Aging Policy Network**

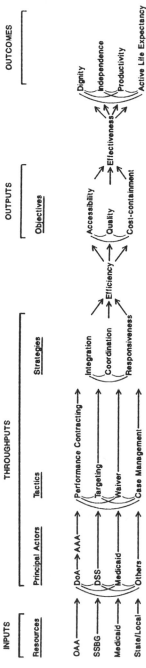

Figure 4.2. Principals, Agents, Contractors, and Subcontractors in the Aging Policy Network

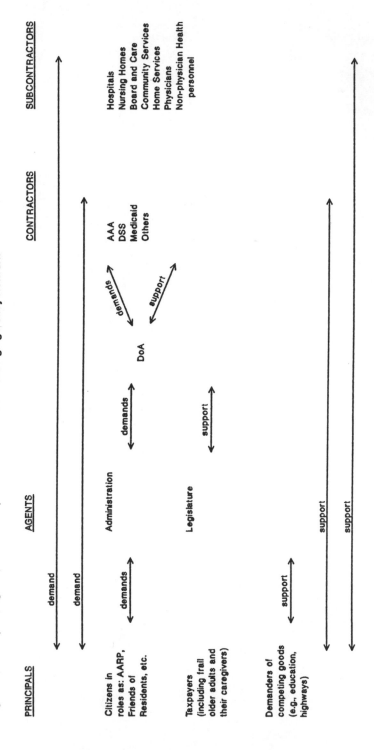

pals," who are the citizenry, organized to varying degrees. The contractors enter into subcontracts with providers. We will refer to this conceptualization in contrasting the way political advocacy has differed in Oregon and North Carolina.

The DoA is responsible for planning and coordinating aging policy, but it is independent of Medicaid. The DoA's budget is under $30 million; Medicaid's budget exceeds $1.6 billion. What Medicaid does not fund, such as case management or adult day care, is underfunded, or at least it is not funded statewide, regardless of what the alternative program's cost-effectiveness is likely to be. There are more than 40 Medicaid-waivered Community Alternatives Programs (CAPs) in the state in which home and community-based service (HCBS) can be funded for persons eligible for nursing home placement as long as the cost of providing that care is below the supposedly avoided nursing home costs that would have been incurred in treating such persons. The overall performance of the CAPs has not been evaluated and, in any event, their spread has been retarded by a HCFA "cold beds" rule, which ties the number of elderly persons who can be served under waivered programs to the number of nursing home beds in the state. The HCFA reasoning behind this rule is that waivered programs are meant to serve persons who otherwise would have been institutionalized. If a state does not have the nursing home beds to accommodate this population, that is virtually prima facie evidence that the demand was not there. Oregon, for reasons discussed below, has been exempted from this rule.

In sum, the responsibility for the allocation of public resources to the elderly in North Carolina is so complicated as to cause misunderstanding among legislators, activists, and those whom the system is intended to serve: the frail elderly and their care givers. There is no scarcity of public programs aimed at the needs of the frail elderly—one publication counted 24[35]—but there is little assurance that they will be on target.

Oregon: The Model

Figures 4.3 and 4.4 depict two variants of the Oregon "Senior Services System" or network. Figure 4.3 features "Type A" AAAs, which are vestiges of the prewaiver (1981) period. As can be seen, Title XIX and SSBG remain state functions in Type A agencies, which serve approximately ten percent of the elderly. Type B AAAs are shown in Figure 4.4 (page 85).

Figure 4.3. Oregon's Senior Services System: Type A Area

Seven Type A Area Agencies on Aging have been designated by the State Senior Services Division, representing nearly 10% of Oregon's elderly population.

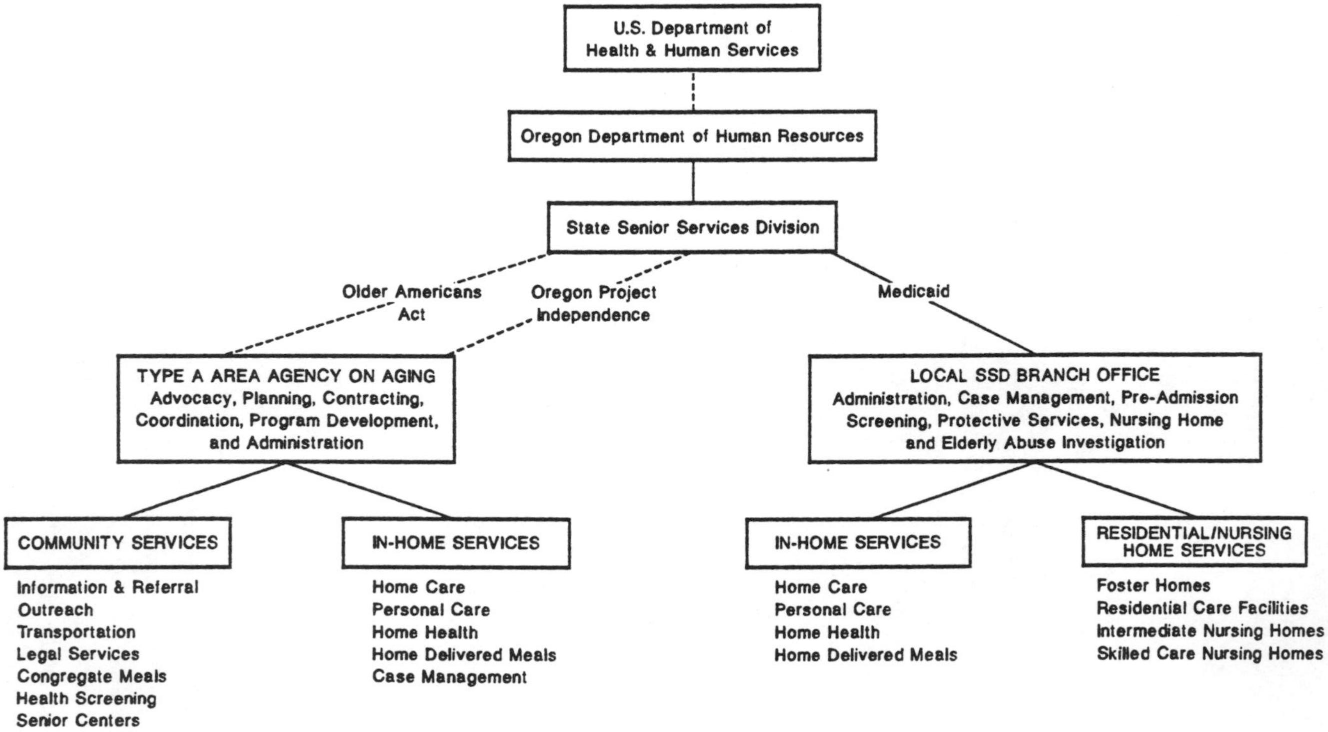

U.S. Department of Health & Human Services

Oregon Department of Human Resources

State Senior Services Division

Medicaid

LOCAL SSD BRANCH OFFICE
Administration, Case Management, Pre-Admission Screening, Protective Services, Nursing Home and Elderly Abuse Investigation

RESIDENTIAL/NURSING HOME SERVICES

Foster Homes
Residential Care Facilities
Intermediate Nursing Homes
Skilled Care Nursing Homes

IN-HOME SERVICES

Home Care
Personal Care
Home Health
Home Delivered Meals

Oregon Project
Independence

Older Americans Act

TYPE A AREA AGENCY ON AGING
Advocacy, Planning, Contracting, Coordination, Program Development, and Administration

IN-HOME SERVICES

Home Care
Personal Care
Home Health
Home Delivered Meals
Case Management

COMMUNITY SERVICES

Information & Referral
Outreach
Transportation
Legal Services
Congregate Meals
Health Screening
Senior Centers

Source: Oregon Association of Area Agencies on Aging, 1990.

Figure 4.4. **Oregon's Senior Service: Type B Area**

Eleven Type B Area Agencies on Aging have been designated by the State Senior Services Division, representing nearly 90% of Oregon's elderly population.

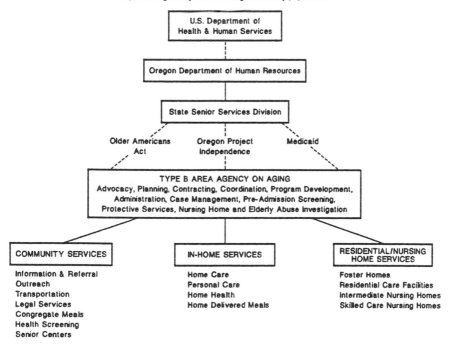

Source: Oregon Association of Area Agencies on Aging, 1990.

These agencies have responsibility for the allocation of all state funds for programs for the elderly and cover 90 percent of the state's elderly population. Type B agency responsibilities include planning, advocacy, service determination, coordination, and management and administration of all state programs. Technicalities aside, the most important feature of the Oregon agencies is that they ladle benefits from a "single pot" of money. In effect, then, the Oregon public services system is a monopsony, not unlike the systems in most Canadian provinces. The results are predictably the same: effective cost-containment and services coordination.[36] Benefits can follow the client, not the program. Turf battles are defined out of existence, although skirmishes regularly occur. A variety of services remain available, and these services are combined to maximize clearly stated goals:

- local advocacy, planning, program development, and service coordination;
- promote and provide for elderly participation in identifying and prioritizing needs, program planning and development, and service evaluation and monitoring;
- promote independent living, individual choice, and a range of options for elderly persons;
- provide for quality services in most appropriate, least restrictive settings;
- manage available private and public resources to the best interests of the older person;
- provide elder care management in the best possible interests of the older person.[37]

The Oregon model did not take shape without concerted effort. It was the result of interacting factors: dynamic official leadership (as opposed to management or administration), sustained informed advocacy, congressional support, a particular sensitivity to the economic recession of the past decade, and a distinctive moralistic political culture with a collective, community orientation. These factors will be discussed generally and contrasted with North Carolina's aging policy following a brief history of the Oregon and North Carolina experiences during the time just before the Oregon "system" gelled, while the North Carolina collage of services remained a "network."

Shared Problems: Different Policy Approaches to Solving Them

From the passage of Medicaid in 1965 through the 1970s, Oregon and North Carolina conformed to a well-documented national pattern in their approaches to aging policy. They expanded services that attracted a federal "match." Actually, the match in these two states amounted to an almost irresistibly seductive two federal (Medicaid) dollars collected for every state dollar spent. Skilled nursing facility care was covered by Medicaid from the outset; and, beginning in 1967, intermediate care facility services were covered as well.

Not surprisingly, the nursing home industry in each state grew, some would say hypertrophically, as did real relative price inflation in this sector of the health care industry.[38] People previously cared for in other settings were now being located in nursing homes. This may have been a well-intentioned incentive to lower hospital costs by allowing for more timely discharge, but, if such was the case, there is no evidence that the coverage had the intended effect.

The nursing home has never had a favorable public image. Most books about nursing homes have provocative titles such as *Tender Loving Greed*,[39] *Unloving Care: The Nursing Home Tragedy*,[40] and *Warehouses for Death*.[41] The homes are not generally thought to emphasize restoration of functional capability or even abatement of decline. However many grains of truth there are in the sensationalistic lambasting of the industry and the anecdotal accounts of abuse and neglect, the nursing home's ability to attract public funding clearly outstripped its ability to gain public respect.

Partly as a result of the perceived overreliance on nursing home services for care of the aged, Oregon, North Carolina, and most other states, largely on their own initiative but assisted by small OAA funding, took measures to avert institutionalization. Oregon funded, with state-only money, "Project Independence," but that project was more an expression of the commitment its name signifies than an effective force: its initial funding was $500,000. North Carolina also rode the waves of the HCBS movement with a similar paucity of state and OAA funding and with pockets of local innovation and project funding.

Expectedly, these counterinstitutionalization movements were largely unsuccessful. Services continued to follow funding. In the 1980s, however, the movements gained momentum and launched a battle against the concept of the nursing home as the care setting of "first resort" for persons needing long-term care services. The gain in momentum was occasioned by a change in federal Medicaid regulations under the Omnibus Budget Reconciliation Act (OBRA) of 1981 that allowed for coverage of nonmedical services outside of nursing homes. But the manifestation of the surge in momentum differed sharply in North Carolina, the typical state, and Oregon, the model state. North Carolina's major counterinstitutionalization measures were draconian in their negative aspect and piecemeal in their positive aspect. Oregon, on the other hand, developed a coherent policy, an implementation strategy, and a means for keeping the strategy in line with policy objectives.

The North Carolina Approach

The negative thrust of North Carolina's counterinstitutionalizational approach was a moratorium on new nursing home bed construction, in force from 1981 until 1984, followed by a restrictive Certificate-of-Need program designed to keep constant, until recently, the ratio of nursing home beds to the number of persons sixty-five years old or older. Some observers have held these restrictions on nursing home bed supply responsible for the aforementioned delayed hospital discharge problem in North Carolina. However, a review of the Oregon experience demonstrates that this causal relationship is questionable: in that state, the number of nursing home beds has declined, but the state has not experienced a significant delayed hospital discharge problem. What the North Carolina moratorium and subsequent more lenient supply constriction practices did accomplish was to produce waiting lists for nursing home placements. This result may be largely due, as the review of the Oregon experience will illustrate, to the failure of the positive thrust of the counterinstitutionalization effort.

At the statewide level, the positive thrust of the North Carolina approach took the form of HCBS expansion and encouragement of participation in the Community Alternatives Program. Of course, extensive participation in the CAP was limited by the already-cited "cold beds" rule; HCBS expansion, therefore, had to come from quite limited non-Medicaid funds or from funding secured through grants to localities for demonstration projects. Money incentives won out over idea incentives, but there were really no winners. Hospitals, particularly after the imposition of the Prospective Budgeting System, found themselves housing patients without reimbursement sufficient to cover hospitals' variable costs. Nursing homes ceased to be competitive, as virtually all had waiting lists. And HCBS did not have enough public funding to make them a realistic alternative to institutionalization for those with average incomes. The Oregon picture is about as stark a contrast to the North Carolina one as can be found in the United States.

The Oregon Approach

As the decade of the 1980s began, Oregon's system of services for the aged was beset by the same problems as that of North Carolina and other states: perceived inappropriate institutionalization and over-medicalization of care. Institutionalization and overmedicalization were perceived as inappropriate, not because Oregon's nursing home residents did not meet stipulated criteria of need for care, but because elder Oregonians did not want that type of care. Elderly advocates successfully mobilized opinion on the basis of that conviction. They then translated that conviction into a policy agenda, thus giving their agents, legislators, and bureaucrats a clear and irresistible mandate, and they maintained the agency relationship through sustained advocacy.

Catalysts in this solution were effective leadership on the part of Richard Ladd, Administrator of the Senior and Disabled Services Division (SDSD), and the 1915(c) and 1915(d) waiver options that Congress made available under Medicaid in 1981, which allowed the state to consolidate funding for nursing home services and HCBS in one administrative unit. Another catalyst may have been the relative severity of the recession which, as Kane et al. point out, made people more willing to care for the elderly in their own homes.[42] If the recession was a factor, however, its impact may also have been more profoundly felt because of the constitutional requirement of a balanced budget. This particular fiscal reality made more immediate the necessity for a cost-effective program.

Oregon was the first state to take advantage of the 1915 Medicaid waivers. Under a previous demonstration waiver, the Floxible Intergovernmental Grant, the state had conducted a three-county experiment in which one county had the discretion to fund all services, another featured intergovernmental cooperation to achieve services coordination, and a third acted as a control group. On the basis of the results of this experiment, the state concluded that a combination of coordination and financial discretion was required for cost-effective services delivery. The 1915 waiver opportunity thus appeared very attractive, as it allowed statewide replication of a demonstrably successful local experiment. The waiver has been maintained, in the face of federal vacillation, by the persistent efforts of Ladd, Deputy SDSD Administrator James C. Wilson, near unanimous state legislative support, the backing of the powerful Oregon congressional delegation, and support by the state's coalition of elderly advocates, United Seniors. Pressures from all these forces also led to Oregon's exemption from the "cold beds" rule.

Indeed, the advocacy can be viewed as the bedrock of Oregon's edifice of innovative aging policy. It was molded in a fashion not unlike the mobilization and crystallization of opinion that brought Medicare into existence. As Theodore Marmor and Judith Feder have described it, Medicare in the eye of one of its chief architects, Wilbur Cohen, then Secretary of Health, Education and Welfare, was the expected forerunner of a national health insurance program.[43] But there was no visible groundswell of public opinion behind Medicare; at least, there was not public support for a program that could be proposed and voted upon. The strategy pursued by Cohen, in concert with liberal Democratic congressmen and labor leaders, was to activate and channel latent opinion in support of such a program. The strategy worked; groups of elder advocates were formed across the country. The agents then could claim that their principals demanded action, despite the formidable opposition to Medicare by the American Medical Association.

In the formulation of aging policy in Oregon, one would have expected the state's nursing home industry to be the program's major antagonist. However, for reasons that are not entirely clear, the industry did not foresee the decline in their occupancy rates that was to occur. When nursing homes did experience the decline, it was too late: lower occupancy rates translated into decreased leverage over the major purchaser of services, now the State Senior Services Division (SSD). A coup de grace may have been the picketing by large numbers of United Seniors at the industry's 1989 annual convention.

There are two important features of the role of advocacy in explaining the Oregon experience, in addition to the fact that the voice of the movement obviously was speaking to public officials who were prepared to listen. First, that voice was articulate, informed, and politically sophisticated: the leadership of United Seniors included two ex-lobbyists who knew their way around the Capitol. Second, in recognition that a positive coherent voice would evoke the most satisfactory response, a "Negotiated Investment Strategy" has been pursued (see Figure 4.5) whereby semi-annual meetings of advocates, planners, policymakers and provider representatives are held to hammer out demands regarding legislation and its implementation. In essence, agents ask affected groups of principals to "tell them what they want" in light of budgetary realities and each group's competing demands. Agency theory thus not only describes the process and its outcomes in Oregon; the key elements of the theory are virtually imposed on the system so

Figure 4.5. **Negotiated Investment Strategy: AAA and Long-term Care**

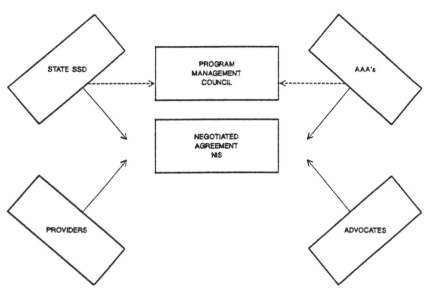

Source: Oregon Association of Area Agencies on Aging, 1990.

that the theory could not help but be descriptive.

North Carolina lawmakers and administrative officials have genuinely lamented the seeming lack of a well-formulated aging policy
mandate in their state similar to that which exists in Oregon. They
remark that the only credible bases upon which they can claim that
they are agents for their principals (our language, not theirs) in the
aging policy arena are episodic reactions to specific issues, such as
taxes, nursing home abuses, and the desirability of retaining Certificate-
of-Need.

The Exportability of the Oregon Model:
Political Cultures and Socioeconomic Constraints

Can the Oregon model work in North Carolina? One answer to the
question would be that the political cultures of the two states are too
dissimilar to allow for this possibility—the divergent policy ap-

proaches of the two states are "rooted in context." Such an answer is not only psychologically unsatisfactory, it likely is also unnecessarily pessimistic. But political culture does influence both political structures and processes as well as the shape and direction of public policy.

Political Culture

One now risks charges of banality more than inaccuracy in making the statement that understanding political cultures is important for understanding public policy and the relationship between political institutions and policies. This was not always the case. After enjoying the height of fashion in comparative politics in the 1960s,[44] the concept of political culture began to be discounted as a residual category or a "garbage can" for the unexplained variation in policy prediction equations that were constructed on the basis of socioeconomic variables.[45] Perhaps this view is a case of, to paraphrase Voltaire, the best driving out the good. That is, too much was expected of political culture; the concept was criticized for being posited as an "uncaused cause," or a deus ex machina.[46] Political culture now is having a renaissance, albeit with more subdued expectations regarding its explanatory power.[47]

Daniel Elazar has attempted to understand the relationship between state political culture and political institutions and behavior.[48] (Elazar does not typically focus directly on policy.) In examining subnational units, Elazar uses the term political "subcultures" to refer to shared sets of values, goals, and a view of the appropriateness of different types of individual and group political action for achieving these goals.

Elazar identifies three major political subcultural orientations: moralistic, individualistic, and traditional. These general categories represent shades of emphasis in values. And with increased communication, diffusion effects, and interstate mobility, Elazar's shades of emphasis probably have paled into tints since the writing of his seminal work on the subject.[49] Yet shades/tints remain quite visible.

We can dispense with the individualistic culture for present purposes since neither Oregon nor North Carolina fits into this category. In the ideal-typical individualistic culture, government is seen primarily as a tool for promoting economic development. The individualistic subculture is essentially materialist and, in Elazar's description, no state is singularly characterized by this type, the individualistic subculture is only a part of the mix in some states.

The moralistic orientation has strains of European conservatism (like "Toryism") with a collective, corporate, organic view of government responsibility for social policy. This orientation contrasts with the stress on individualism and distrust of government typical of the classic liberalism that pervades most of American political thought, behavior, institutional configurations, and attitudes toward policy.[50] As Henry Mahood puts it:

> In this view, the scope of governmental activity, though not unlimited, may be very broad indeed, embracing social and economic regulation in order to achieve the good society. For this reason, political competition tends to be issue-oriented, and highly programmatic, as parties and interest groups are organized to influence governmental policy in the public interest. Moreover, citizens bear a responsibility for participating in politics in order to achieve this end. And bureaucracy is viewed as an efficient nonpartisan institution for administering the public good.[51]

Elazar classifies Oregon, along with Utah, Colorado, North Dakota, Wisconsin, Michigan, Minnesota, and Maine, as more thoroughly moralistic than some other states in what he calls the "greater west." Elazar notes that in this region policymaking "often seems to be based on the assumption that there are no serious limits to people's ability to achieve their goals, except those they artificially impose upon themselves."[52]

Elazar depicts North Carolina as a hybrid traditionalistic-moralistic culture. As such, North Carolina has more in common with Arizona (the only other traditionalistic-moralistic state) than with most of its one-time confederates (South Carolina, Virginia, Tennessee, Georgia, Arkansas, Mississippi, Alabama, and Louisiana) which are characterized as "pure" traditionalistic subcultures. Traditionalistic subcultures have less impersonal bureaucracies, less competitive political milieus, and regard politics as the activity of an elite social stratum. V.O. Key presaged Elazar's categorization of North Carolina as traditionalistic-moralistic when he entitled the chapter on this state "Progressive Plutocracy" in his classic *Southern Politics in State and Nation*.[53] The continued aptness of Key's depiction has been underscored, with specific reference to Key's work, in Paul Luebke's recent book, *Tarheel Politics*.[54]

With respect to partisan competition and electoral participation rates, Oregon traditionally has been among the very highest in each category, North Carolina has been among the lowest, lending more credence to Elazar's classification.[55] Yet, one senses that the political subcultures of Oregon and North Carolina are less divergent than are their aging policies and programs, thus militating against a culturally deterministic view of their aging policy differences. Rather, the crucial link in the causal chain among cultural, political, institutional, and policy variables is that between culture and institutions. And the relationship is reciprocal: institutions affect as well as reflect subcultures.

Socioeconomic Differences

Figure 4.6 displays the types of variables commonly employed as predictors in models of policy outputs going back to the early work of Solomon Fabricant.[56] These aggregate indicators sometimes obscure more than they reveal. For example, the pronounced difference in the two states' population densities becomes less significant when one considers that almost all of Oregon's population is in the western part of the state. Still, it is clear that Oregonians' close proximity to one another cannot be held responsible for the relatively successful deployment of HCBS in their state.

Neither do the measures of state economic development presented in Figure 4.6 provide a ready explanation for the different degrees of success of Oregon and North Carolina aging policies. Economic development, following Wagner's law and its variants, has been viewed as an enabling factor in the production of progressive social policy. On the other hand, economic constriction could be viewed as a stimulus to the development and public acceptance of cost-effective programs. What the typical indicators in Figure 4.6 do not measure are economic dynamics such as Oregon's simple economy, with its heavy reliance on the lumber industry, which made more severe the already mentioned impact of the early 1980s recession on this state.[57]

In contrast, North Carolina's economy has been expanding rapidly. The growth in value added by the manufacturing industry from 1972 to 1986 was 283 percent versus a national average of 193 percent.[58] The state's gross state product (GSP) per capita increased 189 percent from 1975 to 1986, more than 20 percent higher than the corresponding figure for the United States.[59] Moreover, from 1981 to 1986 the rate of growth of the North Carolina GSP outstripped the national average by a considerable amount each year. The data on employment from 1975

Figure 4.6. **Socioeconomic Indicators: North Carolina, Oregon, United States**

	North Carolina	Oregon	United States
Population Density (Persons/Square Mile)	132.9	28.8	69.5
Average Disposal Personal Income (1988)	12,259	12,776	14,107
Percent Black (1988)	22.1	1.6	12.4
Percent of Population 65 Years of Age or Older (1988)	11.9	13.8	12.4
Percent Change in Proportion of Population 65 Years Old or Older: 1980–1990 (Projected)	2.1	1.9	3.3

Source: Statistical Abstract of the United States, 1990 U.S. Department of Commerce. Bureau of the Census.

to 1988 indicate similar trends. Unemployment decreased at a rate (58.1 percent) much faster than the national average (28.6 percent).[60]

But what matters is that Oregon's economy has become more complex since the last recession.[61] And of more immediate policy relevance, North Carolina's government is running a considerable deficit; Oregon cannot lawfully have a deficit and does not.[62] So the economic forces for change now being exerted on the policy process in North Carolina probably are not unlike those in Oregon in the early to mid 1980s. Another similarity between the two economies is that both have been reasonably successful in attracting "clean" high-tech industries.

With respect to differences in social indicators in North Carolina and Oregon, the relative racial homogeneity of the latter is striking. This difference is not an immediately obvious explanation for aging policy differences, but it undoubtedly affects the likelihood of the occurrence of the type of consistent advocacy that we have argued is requisite to coherent policy initiation, formulation, and monitoring. Racial complexity, however, is not the only reason for the relative ineffectiveness of advocacy, or else each race in North Carolina would have its own effective coalition, and neither does. In any event, as racial barriers break down, one could expect the same convergence in this characteristic of the Oregon and North Carolina environments as seems to be occurring in regard to their economies. Oregon also has an older population (13.8 percent sixty-five years of age or older) than does North Carolina (11.9 percent) but the growth in the elderly proportion of North Carolina's population exceeds the national rate. Therefore, the two states are converging with respect to this measure.

Conclusion

This chapter has compared aging policy in Oregon and North Carolina, starting with an overview of policy outputs and outcomes according to the often-used criteria of services quality, cost, and access. It appears that Oregon has lived up to its National Governors' Association—ascribed reputation as a model for long-term care reform. Reliance on nursing home care is decreasing in conformance with the expressed desires of elderly advocates for maximum independence. Hospital discharges are timely despite the shrinking size of the nursing home industry. This movement toward independence has occurred at bearable costs and without compromised quality of care.

We have described differences in the policy processes in the two states that might be responsible for the different outputs and outcomes. The key process difference noted was Oregon's more vigorous, sustained, informed, and effective advocacy. This difference is partly attributable to variations in the two states' dominant subcultures. Policy output and outcome differences as well as process differences, in turn, are partly due to the different socioeconomic complexions of the two states, differences that likely are waning, at least insofar as they may affect politics and policy.

Almost all the causal paths in the narrative have been treated as though they flow in one direction, from socioeconomic and cultural variations to politics to policy. That is, the discussion has implied that socioeconomic factors give rise to subcultural patterns which then predetermine how political affairs are handled. The political arrangements, in turn, largely prefigure the substance of policies for which they are responsible. This approach is not an unusual one in policy analysis. But as R.D. Masters, Robert Reich, Daniel Elazar, Elinor Ostrom and others recently have reminded us, political variables—institutions, structures and processes, funding mechanisms, ideas and leadership—themselves have causal power.[63] These variables are not mere epiphenomena; they do not just act as neutral agents for the translation of environmental stimuli into policy responses. And this is particularly true of the elusive concept of political leadership.[64]

Agency theory, which we touched on only briefly, highlights the leaders' roles as agents, but there is no reason to believe that these agents ought to be passive receptors of a cacophony of demands that they then convert into policies, programs, and practices. If ascribed leaders do behave in this manner, the policy response can only be expected to be as discordant as the stimuli. Rather, the public's agents—and, as the Oregon case vividly illustrates, these include dynamic visionary bureaucrats as well as legislators—who want to craft effective policy must orchestrate the sounds coming from their principals, namely, advocates for elderly independence. In Oregon, the waiver, the Negotiated Investment Strategy, the congressional support needed to keep the waiver in place are all instruments in this orchestration. The audience that judges the quality of the orchestration, of course, had to pay to get to hear it, in terms of the time and energy that sustained advocacy consumes. But they first had to be convinced that there was a high probability they would get their money's worth; they had to recognize the existence of responsive, effective leadership.

North Carolina has embarked on a strategy to establish some features of Oregon's structure and process for policymaking: a more consolidated budget for publicly funded aging services (albeit one that does not include Medicaid), and a "Plan" with clearly stated objectives, strategies, and tactics. And North Carolina is in the fortunate situation, at least from the perspective one acquires from a review of the Oregon case, of having a very limited nursing home supply. This state also is experiencing a constriction in the availability of public funding. All in all, the time appears propitious to launch major aging policy reform.

However, what does not augur well for such reform is the lack, at least up until now, of statewide sustained informed advocacy in North Carolina of the sort we have described in Oregon. In the dynamic combination of forces we have identified as influential in effecting such reform, that is a crucial shortcoming, and one that can be overcome only by effective leadership.

Notes

1. We resist using the more traditional label "long-term care policy" because that designation has a medical care connotation and because long-term care excludes many programs that chiefly target the elderly, such as rehabilitation. Also,

many long-term care services are provided to the nonelderly.

2. Diane Justice, Lynn Etheredge, John Leuhrs, and Brian Burwell, *State Long-term Care Reform: Development of Community Care Systems in Six States* (Washington, DC: National Governor's Association, 1988).

3. Mavis Mann Reeves, "The States as Polities: Reformed, Reinvigorated, Resourceful," *The Annals of the American Academy of Political and Social Science* (hereafter *The Annals*) 509 (1990): 83–93; Timothy J. Conlan, "Politics and Governance: Conflicting Trends in the 1990s?" *The Annals* 509 (1990): 128–138; Frank J. Thompson, "New Federalism and Health Care Policy," *Journal of Health Politics, Policy and Law* Tenth Anniversary Issue (1986): 647–666; Frank J. Thompson, "The Enduring Challenge of Health Policy Implementation," in *Health Politics and Policy*, 2d ed., eds. Theodore Littman and Leonard Robins (Albany, NY: Delmar Press, 1991); Daniel J. Elazar, "Opening the Third Century of American Federalism: Issues and Prospects," *The Annals* 509 (1990): 11–21.

4. "Washington Passes Paralysis on to the States," *The Economist*, 9 February 1991, 27–28.

5. Timothy J. Conlan, "Politics and Governance," 128–138; Mavis Mann Reeves, "The States as Polities."

6. Kenneth Manton, "The Interaction of Population Aging and Health Transitions at Later Ages: New Evidence and Insights," in *Health Care and Its Costs*, ed. Carl Schramm (New York: W.W. Norton, 1987).

7. James Fries, "The Sunny Side of Aging," *JAMA* 263 (1990): 2354–2355.

8. Charles Brecher and James Knickman, "A Reconsideration of Long-term Care Policy," *Journal of Health Politics, Policy and Law* 10 (1985): 245–273.

9. American Association of Retired Persons and the Villers Foundation, "The American Public Views Long-term Care" (Princeton, NJ: R.L. Associates, 1987).

10. Adam Przeworski and Henry Teune, *The Logic of Comparative Social Inquiry* (New York: Wiley, 1970).

11. Robert A. Kane, L. Illston, Rosalie L. Kane and John Nyman, *Meshing Service with Housing: Lessons from Adult Foster Care and Assisted Living in Oregon: Final Report to the John A. Hartford Foundation* (1990).

12. William Weissert, Cynthia Cready, and Jane Pawelak, "The Past and Future of Home and Community-based Long-term Care," *The Milbank Quarterly* 66 (1988): 309–388.

13. In fact, a representative of the Oregon Hospital Study Commission did not understand the question when asked if there was a hospital discharge delay problem in Oregon or if anyone had studied it.

14. U.S. Department of Health and Human Services (hereafter USDHHS), *Hospital Studies Program Hospital Cost and Utilization Project: Research Note* (Washington, DC: Government Printing Office, 1988).

15. David Falcone, Elise Bolda, and Sandra Crawford Leak, "Waiting for Placement: An Exploratory Analysis of Determinants of Delayed Discharges of Elderly Hospital Patients," *Health Services Research* (August 1991): in press; John Holahan and G. Keney, "The Nursing Home Market and Hospital Discharge Delays," *Inquiry* 27 (1990): 73–85.

16. This is evidenced by the fact that hospitals pay nursing homes to keep a nursing home patient's bed available so that discharge can be timely when the

acute-care portion of the patient's illness episode has ended. There is no generalizable model to estimate the financial effects of delayed hospital discharges. The Michigan Hospital Association study (1989) computed only "hotel" costs of the delayed discharge stay, and even these exceeded the reimbursement hospitals received for care of these patients. David Falcone, Elise Bolda, and Sandra Crawford Leak, "Waiting for Placement," in Michigan Hospital Association, *Study of Delayed Discharge* (Lansing, MI: 1989).

17. See Weissert, Cready, and Pawelak, "The Past and Future of Home and Community-based Long-term Care"; David Falcone and Boi Jon Jaeger, "Case Management of Health Services for the Elderly: Apologies and Promises," *Advances in Research* 12 (1988): 1–8.

18. *The Evaluation of the National Long-Term Care Demonstration: Final Report* (Princeton, NJ: Mathematica Policy Research, Inc., 1986).

19. Robert L. Kane and Rosalie A. Kane, *A Will and a Way: What the United States Can Learn from Canada About Caring for the Elderly* (New York: Columbia University Press, 1985).

20. Kane, Illston, Kane, and Nyman, *Meshing Service with Housing.*

21. Ibid.

22. Keren B. Wilson, "Assisted Living: The Merger of Housing and Long-Term Care Services," *Long-Term Care Advances* 1 (1990): 1–11.

23. We say "relatively new" because there have been other efforts based on similar concepts. For example, the Congregate Housing Services Program was a cost-effective federal demonstration project. See Donald Redfoot, "Dignity, Independence and Cost Effectiveness: The Success of the Congregate Housing Services Program," *A Report to the Subcommittee on Housing and Consumer Interests of the Select Committee on Aging of the U.S. House of Representatives* (Washington, DC: Government Printing Office, 1987). This program was based on the simple premise that services such as home health or choreworker could be delivered more efficiently to persons living close to one another.

24. USDHHS, Hospital Studies Program Hospital Cost and Utilization Project; and our calculations for Oregon based on data supplied by the Oregon Department of Human Resources, Office of Health Policy.

25. For example, more than forty areas are served by Community Alternative Programs (CAPs) under a Medicaid (2176) waiver. In these areas, a community's providers may receive Medicaid reimbursement for nonnursing home services (e.g., home health) if the services are rendered to persons who are nursing home eligible and if costs do not exceed what nursing home costs would be for care of the patient population covered.

26. Debra Lipson, *State Financing of Long-Term Care Services for the Elderly,* Volume 1, *Executive Report* (Washington, DC: Intergovernmental Health Policy Project, George Washington University, 1986).

27. Judith Feder, *Medicare: Politics and Policy* (Lexington, MA: D.C. Heath, 1977).

28. Falcone, Bolda, and Leak, "Waiting for Placement."

29. V. Tellis-Nayak and M. Tellis-Nayak, "An Alternative Level of Care: Retrospective Payment System and the Challenge of Extended Care," *Social Science and Medicine* 23 (1986): 655–671; Michael Mezy, "Transforming the American Hospital," in *The Role of Hospitals in Geriatric Care,* eds. C. Eisdorfer and

G. Maddox (New York: Springer, 1988); Edward W. Campion, Axel Bang, and Maurice I. May, "Why Acute Care Hospitals Must Undertake Long-Term Care," *New England Journal of Medicine* 308 (1983): 71–77; Jane E. Bowlyow, "Acute and Long-Term Care Linkages: A Literature Review," *Medical Care Review* 47 (1990): 75–101; Stanely J. Brody, "The Robert Wood Johnson Foundation Management Program on Hospital Initiatives," in *Long-Term Care: Economic Impacts and Financing Dilemmas*, ed. R. Wiltge (New York: National Health Council, 1990).

30. Falcone, Bolda, and Leak, "Waiting for Placement."

31. Michigan Hospital Association, "Study of Delayed Discharge."

32. USDHHS, *Hospital Studies Program Hospital Cost and Utilization Project.*

33. Michigan Hospital Association, "Study of Delayed Discharge."

34. Center for Research and Educational Services (CARES), *Aging in North Carolina* (Chapel Hill, NC: CARES, 1989).

35. C. Lambert and Bill Finger, "Targeting Older Persons for Services: An Overview of the Aging Network," *North Carolina Insight* 8 (1985): 9–31.

36. In Canadian provinces, albeit to varying degrees, governments are virtually the sole purchasers of long-term care services. See Kane, Illston, Kane, and Nyman, *Meshing Service with Housing.* As is typical of monopsonies, these governments largely determine what services are delivered and in what combination.

37. Oregon Association of Area Agencies on Aging, *Annual Report,* Portland, Oregon 1990.

38. Real relative price inflation refers to the expenditure growth in nursing home services in constant dollars over and above the constant dollar increase in the Consumer Price Index.

39. Margaret A. Mendleson, *Tender Loving Greed* (New York: Knopf, 1974).

40. Bruce Vladeck, *Unloving Care: The Nursing Home Tragedy* (New York: Basic Books, 1980).

41. Daniel J. Baum, *Warehouses for Death* (Toronto: Burns and MacEachern, 1977).

42. Kane, Illston, Kane, and Nyman, *Meshing Service with Housing.*

43. Theodore Marmor, *The Politics of Medicare* (Chicago: Aldine, 1973); Feder, *Medicare: Politics and Policy.*

44. Gabriel A. Almond, "The Intellectual History of the Civic Culture Concept," in *The Civic Culture Revisited,* eds. Gabriel A. Almond and Sydney Verba (Boston: Little Brown, 1980).

45. Michael Thompson, Richard E. Ellis, and Aaron Wildavsky, "Political Cultures," *Working Paper* 90–124 (Berkeley: Institute of Government Studies, 1990).

46. Peter A. Hall, *Governing the Economy: The Politics of State Intervention in Britain and France* (New York: Oxford University Press, 1986); Thompson, Ellis, and Wildavsky, "Political Cultures."

47. Ronald Inglehart, "The Renaissance of Political Culture," *American Political Science Review* 82 (1988): 1203–1230; Mildred Schwarz and Michael Thompson, *Divided We Stand: Redefining Politics, Technology and Social Choice* (Philadelphia: University of Pennsylvania Press, 1990); Thompson, Ellis, and Wildavsky, "Political Cultures."

48. Daniel J. Elazar, *American Federalism: A View from the States,* 2d ed.

(New York: Thomas Y. Crowell, 1972); Daniel J. Elazar and Joseph Zikmund II, *The Ecology of American Political Culture: Readings* (New York: Thomas Y. Crowell, 1975); Daniel J. Elazar, *The American Constitutional Tradition* (Lincoln, NE: University of Nebraska Press, 1988).

49. Daniel J. Elazar, *American Federalism.*

50. The moralistic orientation recently has been well articulated in a collection of essays edited by Robert E. Reich, *The Power of Public Ideas* (Cambridge, MA: Harvard University Press, 1990).

51. Henry R. Mahood, *Interest Group Politics in America: A New Intensity* (Englewood Cliffs, NJ: Prentice Hall, 1990), 30.

52. Elazar, *The American Constitutional Tradition,* 68.

53. V.O. Key, *Southern Politics in State and Nation* (New York: Vintage Books, 1951).

54. Paul Luebke, *Tarheel Politics: Myths and Realities* (Chapel Hill, NC: University of North Carolina Press, 1990).

55. S.M. Morehouse, *State Politics, Parties and Policy* (New York: Holt, Rinehart and Winston, 1983).

56. Solomon Fabricant, *The Trend of Government Activity in the U.S. since 1900* (New York: National Bureau of Economic Research, 1952).

57. W.H. Hedrick and L. Harmon Zeigler, "Oregon: The Politics of Power," in *Interest Group Politics in the American West,* eds. R.J. Hrebenar and C.S. Thomas (Salt Lake City: University of Utah Press, 1987).

58. U.S. Bureau of the Census, *City and County Data Book* (Washington, DC: Government Printing Office, 1988).

59. V. Renshaw, E. Trott and H. Friedenberg, "Gross State Product by Industry, 1963–1986," *Survey of Current Business* (May 1988).

60. U.S. Department of Labor, Bureau of Labor Statistics, *Geographic Profile of Employment and Unemployment: 1975–1988* (Washington, DC: Government Printing Office, 1988).

61. Hedrick and Zeigler, "Oregon: The Politics of Power."

62. *The Economist,* 9 February 1991.

63. R.D. Masters, *The Nature of Politics* (New Haven: Yale University Press, 1989); Reich, ed., *The Power of Public Ideas* (Cambridge, MA: Harvard University Press, 1990); Elazar, *The American Constitutional Tradition,* 68; Ostrom, *Governing the Commons: Evolution of Institutions for Collective Action* (New York: Cambridge University Press, 1990).

64. R. Heifetz and R. Sinder, "Political Leadership: Managing the Public's Problem Solving," in *The Power of Public Ideas,* ed. Reich (Cambridge, MA: Harvard University Press, 1990).

5

Deinstitutionalization of the Mentally Retarded in Texas: A Case of State Policy Innovation

Steven Laubacher and Malcolm L. Goggin

Studies of policy innovation in the American states have long recognized that some states are more innovative than others when it comes to adopting and implementing new public policies.[1] States, like New York, California, and Wisconsin, are usually early adopters, or "pioneers." Other states, such as Mississippi and Alabama, are frequently followers, or "laggards." A number of methodologically sophisticated aggregate statistical studies designed to explain differences in the nature and timing of policy innovation across the American states have identified several predictor variables, some internal and others external to the state.

These explanatory variables include: (1) the degree to which the state's electorate holds liberal views; (2) the level of resources available to the state; (3) the strength and composition of the state legislature; (4) the level of administrative capacity; (5) the degree of problem severity in the state; (6) the region of the country in which the state is located; and, (7) the extent to which neighboring states are early adopters.[2] While these studies can indicate central tendencies, they are not able to isolate, in any detail, some of the idiosyncrasies that might account for successful (or unsuccessful) innovation in particular states.

Empirical studies of intergovernmental policy implementation, either within or across states, also have attempted to shed light on the process of innovation.[3] These studies examined the relative importance of economic versus political variables and added additional "crucial" variables to explain differences in the timing of implementation from prompt, to delayed, to not at all. Whether a state is an early adopter, early majority, late majority, a laggard, or a hold-out,[4] or whether a state deliberately delays the timing of an innovation for strategic purposes[5] may be due to a number of factors beyond economic and political capability. These factors might include patterns of influence and communications, the nature and strength of advocacy coalitions in the state, or the will and skill of the program manager.

Our aim in this chapter is to move toward a better understanding of the nature of health policy innovation in the American states by first taking stock of the results of previous studies of state health policy innovation, representing a wide variety of approaches. Then, we report the results of original research on one case of successful innovation, namely, the deinstitutionalization of persons with mental retardation in Texas in the late 1980s. What we attempt to do in this case study is identify some of the unique policy design features of the Texas case that contributed to successful implementation and suggest lessons that can be transferred to other states.[6]

Review of the Literature

Studies that have contributed to our understanding of the underlying phenomenon have either compared one or more policies across several states or examined a single policy within a single state. One study has combined the single state study with a comparison of several states.[7]

Robert Rich's (1981) empirical investigation of differences in the implementation of mental health policy is a typical *cross-state* comparative study. In his comparison of the implementation of a program of deinstitutionalization in 18 states, he reached the conclusion that program discretion was usually in the hands of local service providers, with states themselves having little to do with either administration or service delivery until relatively recently.[8] As states began to operationalize a policy of deinstitutionalization across the country, "there seem to be few agenda items (issues), institutional structures, systems of reorganization, expenditure patterns, or belief systems that are particular to a state or region."[9] While acknowledging that cross-state differences do exist, Rich claims that they do not seem to be systematically related to the external and internal factors identified in the literature on innovation or intergovernmental implementation.

A different approach to the same research problem is Steven Laubacher's (1990) *within-state* statistical analysis of why some service delivery units did a better job than others in implementing a Prospective Payment Plan (PPP) in Texas in the late 1980s.

Laubacher's first cut at explanation was inclusive: Following a three-step "third-generation" approach to implementation research, he first developed a parsimonious model that incorporated several promising theoretically relevant explanatory variables.[10] He then used multiple regression analysis to identify which of these candidate variables were significantly related to successful implementation attempts. After identifying, through multivariate statistical analysis, three "crucial" variables that were related to successful implementation, he then employed qualitative methods of analysis to answer the question of why these particular factors might be statistically significant. Quantitative analysis of health policy innovation indicated that local providers were very interested in participating in the program, both because of ideological convictions of the superiority of community living and because of the monetary incentives offered by Texas.[11]

Now, in the final phase of this research project, the results of which are reported in this chapter, responses to a telephone interview schedule administered to 45 administrators are used to construct an argument as to why an innovative mental retardation program like the PPP was so successful in Texas. By examining a successful case of policy implementation intensively, one can develop a process theory that is not easily developed from *only* statistical analysis. But before reporting these findings, there is other research that helps us understand more fully what the editor of this volume has called "innovation from the states."

William Lammers' (1990) *cross-policy* study of state innovations as stimuli for federal action compared a certificate of need (CON) program with a strategy of hospital rate reduction. What Lammers found was that lessons can be learned from early adopter states. Organized interests serve as the channels of communications from early to late adopters and from early adopters to the federal government.

In looking for future policy debates over health policy issues, it also should be emphasized that the existence of experiments in some states can provide a lever for supporters of innovations who wish to promote greater use of a new policy approach than would likely occur with sole reliance upon state-level action.[12]

Lammers' research points to three conditions that favor a transfer effect from innovative states to the federal government: interest-group activity that builds on the experience of early adopters; publicizing the results of state-based experiments or demonstration projects; and building broad-based support among members of the state's congressional delegation who are generally favorably predisposed toward a larger role for the federal government.[13]

One study that *combines within-state and cross-state analysis* is Malcolm Goggin's (1987) investigation of the variability in the implementation of the Early and Periodic Screening, Diagnosis, and Treatment (EPSDT) program, an intergovernmental program of health screening, diagnosis, and treatment for poor children. Using a building-block approach to theory development, Goggin first attempted to sort out the many reasons why California chose to drag its feet at a time when other states were becoming innovators. Then he tested his findings from California in six states in the mid-South region of the United States and found that differences in the speed of adoption of this new program were due, in large part, to the design of the policy at stake, the capacities of the organizations responsible for program implementation, and the talents and attitudes of program managers.[14] There was considerable evidence from the comparative case studies that once design errors were detected and the program redesigned, state EPSDT programs were put in place at an accelerated pace.

In synthesizing the results of these statistical analyses across and within states, comparative case studies, and single-state studies, we have learned that states vary both with respect to whether or not they were early innovators and the extent to which they moved more or less quickly than their neighbors. But why study intensively one state's success effort to implement an innovation that is available to all states?

First, those who design public policy can learn from the efforts of others and incorporate the desirable qualities into their own public policies. Second, an examination of successful policy implementation can help identify the causal complexities of those relationships among variables that have been uncovered through more extensive studies, such as those reviewed in the preceding paragraphs. Both of these enterprises can be mutually reinforcing. This chapter will now turn to the examination of a successful effort by Texas to deinstitutionalize persons with mental retardation.

A Policy of Deinstitutionalization

Mental retardation is a condition that includes a limitation on intelligence coupled with problems in adapting behaviorally to the expectations of society. The American Association on Mental Retardation has adopted a definition of mental retardation that is universally accepted as the standard within the field of mental retardation: "Mental Retardation refers to significantly subaverage general intellectual functioning existing concurrently with deficits in adaptive behavior and manifested during the developmental period."[15]

It is estimated that approximately 3 percent of our population is mentally retarded. Of these people, approximately 90 percent are mildly retarded with an IQ of 52–67, 6 percent are moderately retarded with an IQ of 36–51, 3.5 percent are severely retarded with an IQ of 20–35, and 1.5 percent are profoundly retarded with an IQ of 19 or below.[16]

Such facts are startling to most people who have never stopped to realize either the magnitude of the problem or its profile. Most of us think of persons with mental retardation solely as being severely handicapped and fail to appreciate that most of these people are only mildly retarded. These individuals could, with limited support, live independently in the community. Nevertheless, United States policy during the first three-quarters of this century was to place any person with mental retardation into a state-operated institution. As recently as 1976, there were an estimated 176,000 persons with mental retardation living in approximately 235 publicly operated residential facilities.[17] The average per day cost for those residing in an institution in 1984 was $153.54.[18]

During the first half of the 20th century, the predominant locus of care for persons with mental retardation was institution-based. These mental hospitals or asylums were isolated from society and were designed to be "self-contained, autonomous communities."[19] Most of these institutions were funded in part by the federal government but operated without any federal mandate. It is surprising, but there is no federal or state mandate to care for persons with mental retardation.

Only state laws that are designed to protect any ordinary citizen from harm are applicable.

Throughout the 1950s and 1960s, however, serious questions began to be raised about the validity of the medical model and the concomitant institutional approach to the treatment of persons with mental retardation. These questions centered around the value of the care received[20] and the escalating costs associated with this type of care.[21] Civil rights fervor, public lawsuits, and increased public awareness fueled the development of a national consensus favoring a new direction in policy toward those with mental health problems. This new direction, which is known as deinstitutionalization, was the reverse of institutionalization.

Occurring after the attempt to deinstitutionalize those with mental illness, efforts to deinstitutionalize persons with mental retardation had a chance to prevent the mistakes that turned persons with mental illness into the homeless that inhabit all of our urban centers. In lieu of the medical model, it was widely agreed that persons with mental retardation could best be served in ordinary neighborhood community settings. This view was reflected in the report of President Kennedy's 1962 Panel on Mental Retardation and echoed by professionals. R. C. Scheerenberger, a frequent contributor to deinstitutionalization literature and an administrator of a state institution, reviewed the major criticisms leveled towards the quality of institutions. He evaluated empirical studies and examined: (1) separation from parents; (2) developmental characteristics of the individual such as intelligence, personality development, speech and language development; and (3) educational achievement. He concluded his review by stating that many institutions do not "foster maximum development."[22]

These feelings and convictions of Scheerenberger were adopted by many professionals within the field of mental retardation. They became so popular that it is reasonable to characterize deinstitutionalization as a new public policy. It should be noted, however, that the status of this policy was more informal than formal; there was no federal law or national referendum that mandated its execution. Instead, this policy could best be likened to a growing consensus echoed by an increasing number of professionals and advocates working in this field.

This preference for deinstitutionalization is strong and is clearly the prevailing sentiment operating in most states. Indeed, without federal prodding in most instances, state and local mental health professionals have acted on their preferences: during the ten years from 1977 to 1987, nearly 40 percent of those living in institutions (about 57,000 individuals) were released and returned to their communities.[23] Predictions are that this trend will continue at a rate of about 4 percent per year. Deinstitutionalization now has such a national impetus that it is likely to continue for the near future.

Each of the 50 states, however, is technically still free to decide whether to adopt this practice of deinstitutionalization, and if so to what degree. Some states like Nebraska and Michigan have closed all of their institutions. Other states, like Alabama, were opening up new institutions even as other states were closing theirs. Ultimately, even so-called "laggards" will be forced to adopt this innovation. They will be forced to participate by virtue of professional and public sentiment as well as litigation, with lobbyists who favor deinstitutionalization using the arguments of improved quality of care and reductions in the expense of care to support their positions.

The PPP Program in Texas

During the three year period between 1986 and 1989, Texas was involved directly in an attempt to return to community settings persons with mental retardation who were residing in institutions. This was prompted by litigation filed in federal court. Known as *Lelsz* v. *Kavanaugh*, the case was instrumental in prompting state officials to develop a concrete plan for deinstitutionalization.[24]

For ten years, the plaintiffs and defendants had parried over whether persons with mental retardation residing in institutions should be returned to the community. Other issues, such as how many residents should be involved, the amount of money that should be committed to this problem, and how the process should occur, were also problems that needed to be resolved. After ten years of negotiations, a resolution and settlement agreement required Texas to correct patient abuse and neglect, remedy the lack of appropriate training for institutional residents, remedy inappropriate institutionalization, and expand the availability of quality community services.[25]

Although participation rates varied across 45 different service organizations *within* Texas,[26] the Texas Prospective Payment Program (PPP) is treated here as a case of successful innovation *when compared to other states*. The PPP responded directly to the main complaints of the critics of institutionalization within the state. In the following section, we will argue that the program's success was due to its design. This design was characterized by creative financing arrangements, unique method of organization, and provisions for protecting client safety and fostering client well-being. These three design features will now be examined.

Financial Characteristics

Though set somewhat arbitrarily, the officials of the Texas Department of Mental Health and Mental Retardation established a return rate of $55.60 per day for every person with mental retardation who was returned to the community. This rate was fixed for all persons with mental retardation regardless of the degree of retardation or other accompanying secondary disabilities.

This money was not intended to meet the full cost of programming but instead to serve as an "incentive" to the local agency to match these resources with enough additional dollars to insure a quality program that could meet established, minimum program standards. The dollars also followed the client to the extent that they were needed to pay for services. If the client's need could be met for less than this amount, then the agency could use the difference either to add to the $55.60 of some other program participant, or to fund services for other clients in the area of mental retardation.

This "incentive" was a key feature of the Texas plan and set in motion a number of very powerful dynamics. First, the "incentive" plan allowed Texas to take a position on a matter of social policy that most other states ignore. This policy relates to the question of who is financially responsible for services to persons with mental retardation. In the 1950s, parents were free to refer their child with mental retardation to the state for care. If a child was accepted into a state institution, then, by paying for the initial costs the state was also implicitly agreeing to take financial responsibility for this care for the duration of that individual's life. Once a child under the care of the state became an adult, families were not required to contribute to the child's care, regardless of the financial means of the parents.

Currently, each state has thousands of individuals who require expensive care. Although states could eliminate or restrict future admissions into their systems, they still must pay for the current users. Texas attempted to share that burden with county authorities. It offered a fixed payment rate for every individual whom the local community agreed to serve. In some cases, that payment rate covered all costs, in some cases it exceeded costs, and in other cases it fell below required costs. However, by establishing a rigorous set of standards and enforcement procedures (to be discussed below) that could not be paid for with the "incentive" dollars alone, the state was also requiring local communities to share in the burden of the cost of care. With this simple incentive scheme, Texas was able to induce the private sector to respond to a generally stated policy objective, namely, to depopulate the Texas institutions.

Many complained that the amount of money was inadequate, and some seemed oblivious to the fact that the program was *intended* only to be an incentive. However, most providers understood that they were required to use other community dollars to complement the state portion. Unfortunately, this strategy was complicated by restrictive federal regulation that eventually put the program on hold. From the perspective of workability, however, the concept of "incentive" that Texas officials employed worked. If anything, the failed attempt to mix state, local, and federal dollars underscored the incompatibility and inability of the three levels of government to complement each other and work together for the benefit of persons with mental retardation.

The fiscal feature of the "incentive" that was implemented by state officials was bold, creative, and sound. The steady flow of state institutional residents into the community and the willingness of local agencies to participate were testimonials to the success of the approach. Other states would do well to emulate the Texas concept and develop an explicit state policy that calls for the sharing of costs to deinstitutionalize persons with mental retardation. Such an articulation of state fiscal policy is rare and demonstrated a courageous stand on the part of Texas state officials.

Organizational Characteristics

The most important organizational feature that characterized the Texas effort was the presence of sub-state structures. State law mandated the creation of "authorities" that were to be set up throughout the state. Each authority was required to be governed by a board of directors whose members were to be appointed by county commissioners. In cases where multiple counties were involved, the appointment power was shared by the commissioners from the various counties.

Each authority was responsible for planning and implementing programs for persons with mental retardation and mental illness throughout its geographical area. Required to raise a percentage of matching money, each authority entered into a unique and privileged contractual relationship with the state for the provision or contracting of services. In turn, state government was required to deal exclusively with that authority.

The advantage of this system was the clear identification of authority and responsibility. It is questionable if any state can successfully operate programs that cover the state through hundreds of different organizations. The Texas system resulted in the creation of relatively standard sub-state structures. If there was a problem with the provision of residential or vocational services in a given geographical area, then it was clear that one must turn to the authority. On the other hand, if little or no satisfaction was obtained, a person could turn to the state, which could then use its contractual leverage to influence the situation. Clear structures of accountability greatly enhanced the quality of services. Furthermore, by dividing services into manageable areas, the chance of successfully managing the services was greatly improved.

A second organizational characteristic was the appointment of a case manager to handle the details of the transfer from beginning to end. This service was guaranteed to last for as long as the service was needed; even for a lifetime, if necessary. The case manager was employed by the authority and served as the representative of the client relative to all client transactions, including those with the state institution and the community provider. This professional management insured that communication would be standardized and that quality services needed by the client would be in place.

The caseload of the case manager was low and consisted of no more than 30 active clients. The case manager was given considerable autonomy and was provided a budget to be used for the benefit of his or her clients in the event of an emergency. The case worker was solely responsible for the implementation of the service plan, as well as for insuring that such a plan, once implemented, was actually working. If the plan was not working, then the manager was expected either to implement procedures to change it or to remedy the problem(s). The case manager was required to visit each of his or her clients at least one time per month in order to observe the appropriateness of the setting and the quality of the program. In this way, it would be very difficult for clients to be living in substandard settings.

The third important organizational characteristic was related to the standards that every program had to meet. Each resident of an institution and participant in this program could only be placed in a program that met established, minimal standards. Every program option, and in particular, residential and vocational programs, was either required to meet standards created by recognized certifying bodies or standards created by the state. The advantage of this feature was that each program participant was guaranteed a placement that would meet a set of standards establishing minimal expectations in all areas of service. These areas included residential services, vocational services, and support services such as speech and physical therapy. No longer would there be a chance of a placement that could be characterized by being either substandard or nonexistent. At least the program goals and objectives would be clear and the intent of the program manifest.

All these organizational characteristics were built into the design of the Prospective Payment Program. They insured that at least minimal structural mechanisms were in place and would contribute to the achievement of the participants' program goals.

Client Safety Characteristics

The third cluster of variables of the Prospective Payment Program that apparently led to the program's successful implementation were features designed to protect the safety and well-being of the client. These features consisted of mandatory trial visits prior to placement, the requirement of program plans, frequent monitoring, and a guarantee made to each participant that he or she could return to the institution in which he or she had once resided.

The first safety feature involved the attempt to have every potential client of the Prospective Payment Program visit the proposed residential setting before a permanent placement was made. This step was an attempt to insure that the placement would be acceptable to the client. In this way, the placement could be pre-tested by the client and adjustments made if necessary before the placement became permanent.

Another safety feature was the requirement that detailed program plans be developed before any actual placement could be made. These plans were supposed to be based on comprehensive evaluations and were designed to meet the program participants' individual needs. The plans were not supposed to be developed in a vacuum. Instead, they were to be developed by professionals and shared with clients and their parents or advocates. By developing a detailed and intricate process, clients were theoretically assured that their own input would be respected. It should also be emphasized that the case manager and representatives from both the institution and the proposed setting were supposed to be present during the planning stages.

The placement was to be monitored by several individuals, including the institution, the Texas Department of Mental Health and Mental Retardation, the local mental retardation authority and/or a community provider (if the authority was contracting the service to another community agency), and the case manager. This level of monitoring might be considered excessive and was certainly redundant. However, considering the problems associated with deinstitutionalization, most professionals would agree that in terms of monitoring, more is better than less.

Finally, if for some reason none of these safety features worked, the client had one more remedy at his or her disposal. If the placement was either inadequate or unacceptable to the client or his or her family, the client could petition the mental retardation authority and could be returned to the originating institution. This right applied to every participating client and could be exercised for life. This right went a long way toward meeting the major objections of many parents, who could justifiably ask, "What would happen if the placement failed?" By assuring each client and parent the right to return to the institution in the event of program failure, the parent and client were undertaking only a minimal risk.

These safety features were incorporated in the program to prevent the horror stories that have taken place in many states. Persons with mental retardation would not become part of the urban homeless, living in the streets or under the bridges in Texas cities.

Conclusion

The Texas policy of deinstitutionalization in the late 1980s was implemented through a plan called the Prospective Payment Program. Was the program a success? In order to answer this question, the program needs to be examined both in terms of quantitative and qualitative criteria.

In terms of quantitative criteria, the program was a definite success. During the three-year period extending from 1986 to 1989, approximately 16 percent of the clients who were on the census of the state institutions were returned to their home communities. This percentage translates into 1,763 clients and exceeds the return rate of 4 percent predicted by White et al.[27] Considering that Texas officials had only spent three years implementing the policy, the reported rate of return seems to be quite good.

The program also rates high in terms of qualitative measures. The transfer operation took place with a minimum of negative outcome or harm experienced by program participants. Both the absence of negative news stories and the positive reports obtained through our own research indicates that the majority of placements made by this program enhanced the well-being of the participants. This is significant when compared to the efforts of some northern states that resulted in the displacement of thousands of former institutionalized residents. Many of these unfortunate individuals are now the homeless who wander the streets of our urban centers.

Whether measured in terms of the number of residents who actually moved back to the community or the qualitative degree of success of those placements, the Texas plan worked. It should also be noted that the achievement of Texas cost far less than the approximate $150 per diem associated with institutional care.

The reasons for this quantitative and qualitative success may be found within the program's design, namely the financial structure, organizational design, and the extraordinary measures taken to insure client safety. Advocates for persons with mental illness or mental retardation, or mental health and mental retardation officials in states who either are voluntarily becoming active in deinstitutionalization or are being coerced into becoming involved, would do well to consider modeling their plans after the Texas program. The lesson for researchers who are studying the more general phenomenon of health policy innovation in the American states is that reasons for the success or failure of policy implementation can frequently be found in the design of a policy.

Notes

1. Frances S. Berry and William D. Berry, "State Lottery Adoption as Policy Innovations: An Event History Analysis," *American Political Science Review* 84 (1990): 395–415; Virginia Gray, "Innovation in the States: A Diffusion Study," *American Political Science Review* 67 (1973): 1174–1185; Jack Walker, "Diffusion of Innovation," *American Political Science Review* 63 (1969): 880–899; Jack Walker, "Comment: Problems in Research on the Diffusion of Policy Innovations," *American Political Science Review* 67 (1973): 1186–1191.

2. Berry and Berry, "State Lottery Adoption as Policy Innovations," Robert S. Erikson, Gerald C. Wright, Jr., and John P. McIver, "Political Parties, Public Policy, and State Policy in the United States," *American Political Science Review* 83 (1989): 729–750; David Klingman, and William W. Lammers, "The 'General Policy Liberalism' Factor in American State Politics," *American Journal of Political Science* 28 (1984): 598–610; Gerald C. Wright Jr., Robert Erikson, and John P. McIver, "Public Opinion and Policy Liberalism in the American States," *American Journal of Political Science* 31 (1987): 980–1001; Gerald C., Wright Jr., Robert S. Erikson, and John McIver, "Measuring State Partisanship and Ideology of Survey Data," *Journal of Politics* 47 (1985): 469–489.

3. James P. Lester, J. L. Franke, Ann O'M. Bowman, and Kenneth W. Kramer, "Hazardous Wastes, Politics, and Public Policy: A Comparative State Analysis," *Western Political Quarterly* 36 (1983): 257–285; Malcolm L. Goggin, *Policy Design and the Politics of Implementation: The Case of Child Health Care in the United States* (Knoxville: University of Tennessee Press, 1987); Malcolm L. Goggin, Ann O'M. Bowman, James P. Lester, and Laurence J. O'Toole, Jr. *Implementation Theory and Practice: Toward a Third Generation* (Glenview, IL: Scott, Foresman/Little, Brown, 1990).

4. Robin Scott MacStravic, *Forecasting Use of Health Services: A Provider's Guide,* (Rockville, MD: Aspens Systems Corporation, 1984).

5. Malcolm L. Goggin, Ann O'M. Bowman, James P. Lester, and Laurence J. O'Toole, Jr., *Implementation Theory and Practice;* Malcolm L. Goggin and Steven Laubacher, "Administrative Initiative in Policy Implementation: Mental Retardation Deinstitutionalization Policy in Texas," Paper presented at the 1990 Annual Meeting of the Midwest Political Science Association.

6. Malcolm L. Goggin, *Policy Design and the Politics of Implementation.*

7. Ibid.

8. Robert Rich, "Implementing Mental Health Policy at the Federal and State Levels," Paper presented at the 1981 Annual Meeting of the American Political Science Association: 52.

9. Ibid., 53.

10. Malcolm L. Goggin, "The 'Too Few Cases/Too Many Variables' Problem in Implementation Research," *Western Political Quarterly* 38 (1986): 328–347; Malcolm L. Goggin, Ann O'M. Bowman, James P. Lester, and Laurence J. O'Toole, Jr., *Implementation Theory and Practice.*

11. Steven Laubacher, "Administrative Initiative in Policy Implementation: Mental Retardation Deinstitutionalization Policy in Texas," (Ph.D. diss., Univer-

sity of Houston, 1990); Goggin, and Laubacher, "Administrative Initiative in Policy Implementation."

12. William W. Lammers, "State Health Policy Innovations: A Stimulus for Federal Action?" Paper presented at the 1990 Annual Meeting of the American Political Science Association.

13. Ibid., 43.

14. Malcolm L. Goggin, *Policy Design and the Politics of Implementation.*

15. Grossman, cited in R.C. Scheerenberger, *Deinstitutionalization and Institutional Reform* (Springfield, IL: Charles C. Thomas, 1976).

16. Scheerenberger, *Deinstitutionalization and Institutional Reform.*

17. Ibid.

18. D. Braddock, R. Hemp, G. Fujiura, L. Bachelder, and D. Mitchell, *The State of the States in Developmental Disabilities* (Baltimore, MD: Paul Brookes, 1990).

19. The Senate Subcommittee on Health Services, *Interim Study on ICF–MR (Intermediate Care Facilities-Mental Retardation)* (Austin, TX: Texas Senate, 1989).

20. Gruenberg and Archer 1979, cited in Joel Warren Barna, *State Mental-Health Services: Change Under Pressure* (Austin, TX: House Study Group, Texas House of Representatives, 1984), 106.

21. Braddock et al., *The State of the States in Developmental Disabilities.*

22. Scheerenberger, *Deinstitutionalization and Institutional Reform,* 52.

23. White, Lakin, Hill, Wright, and Bruininks 1988 cited in S.A. Larson and K.C. Lakin, *Policy Research Brief* 1 no. 2 (Minneapolis, MN: Research and Training Center on Community Living in the University of Minnesota's Institute on Community Integration, 1989).

24. Lelsz v. Kavanagh, 807 F. 2D 1243.

25. Lelsz v. Kavanagh, *Implementation Agreement,* Civil Action No. 3–85–2462–H, 1987.

26. Steven Laubacher, "Administrative Initiative in Policy Implementation."

27. See Larson and Lakin, *Policy Research Brief.*

6

Rationing of Health Care: Oregon Comes Out of the Closet

Howard M. Leichter

In 1989 Oregon became the first state in the nation to adopt legislation that would explicitly ration health care for the poor. The Oregon Basic Health Services Act (OBHSA) guarantees health care to all those who fall below the federal poverty level but limits that care to what expert opinion, community sentiment, legislative judgment, and fiscal reality deem a "basic level of services." In the words of the law's chief architect, "Everyone will be in the health care lifeboat. Not everyone will eat steak, but at least everyone will eat." The fact that it will be primarily the poor who will be deprived of "steak" in the Oregon health care lifeboat is just one of many facets of the plan that troubles its opponents.

The Oregon rationing plan has left few observers neutral. It has been characterized as "bold," "pioneering," "rational," a "brave medical experiment," and "fundamentally flawed," "unfair," and "unethical."[1] What proponents and opponents of the Oregon law agree on is that the current "system" is seriously, and probably irreparably, flawed. Something must be done to control spiralling health care costs and to expand access to an estimated 32 to 37 million uninsured Americans. Where observers and participants disagree is over the question of whether or not the Oregon plan offers a fair, workable, and responsible solution. This chapter examines the origin, content, criticism, and implications of the Oregon rationing plan. It is not my intention to take a position on the legislative package that makes up the Oregon reform but rather to facilitate a better understanding of it.

The Oregon Basic Health Services Act

At the heart of the reform effort is Senate Bill (SB) 27, which explicitly confronts several of the most critical challenges facing the nation's health care system. Its purpose is to: (1) "provide access to health services for those in need"; (2) "contain rising health services costs through appropriate incentives to providers, payers and consumers"; (3) "reduce or eliminate cost shifting"; and (4) "promote the stability of the health services delivery system and the health and well-being of all Oregonians." To accomplish these ambitious and seemingly contradictory goals, the state will define a minimum entitlement to basic health services and apply it to those people who fall below the federal poverty level. (Persons covered under Old Age, Blind, and Disabled, Medically Needy, and Children in Foster Care programs were initially excluded from the program.) Leaders in the legislature ultimately want the entitlement to a basic level of health care to apply to all Oregonians.

By extending medical assistance to all those below the poverty level, Oregon is departing from prevailing national practices. Medicaid eligibility typically has been a function not merely of income but of gender, age, family status, and type of disease. For example, poor women without children, and low-income men are ineligible for Medicaid in Oregon and most other states. Moreover, each state sets an income eligibility requirement that is expressed in terms of a percentage of the federal poverty level. In the case of Oregon this has meant that only those who had incomes of 58 percent or below the federal poverty level were eligible for Medicaid. In 1991, for example, a family of three in Oregon earning more than $5,500 per year was "too rich" to qualify for Medicaid.

To bring all the poor into the Medicaid lifeboat, contain costs, and fairly compensate health providers for their costs, the state will ration the amount of money and therefore the range of services available to its Medicaid system. To insure the "social and political consensus" that the law's supporters felt was vital to the clinical and political success of the program, an elaborate mechanism has been designed to allocate health resources. The law creates an 11-member Health Services Commission that will conduct public hearings and encourage public involvement in preparation for recommending a prioritization of health services. The commission is required to seek testimony from health care providers and consumers, as well as social advocates. In addition, "the commission shall actively solicit public involvement in a community process to build a consensus on the values used to guide health resource allocation decisions." The commission will submit its recommended priorities to the governor and a Joint Legislative Committee on Health Care by July 1 of the year preceding each regular legislative session. Accompanying the list of priorities will be a report by an independent actuary on the rates for each of the services/treatments. The Joint Legislative Committee on Health Care will recommend to the full legislature whether to accept or reject the commission's report; it cannot change the priorities. Should the legislature accept the report, it must then decide how much it is willing to spend on health care for the next biennium. This money will then be used to buy a package of health services for each recipient from as far down the priority list as the legislative allocation will allow. The initial ranked list contained 709 condition/treatment pairs divided into 17 categories of care. (The 1991 legislature funded the program at a level that would allow for 587 of these to be covered in the basic health services package for the 1993 fiscal year.) To help contain costs, health services will be purchased primarily from managed care providers such as Health Maintenance Organizations (HMOs) and Physician Care Organizations (PCOs).

Should a revenue shortfall occur or should the number of persons below the poverty level increase, the state cannot drop people from the program, as it presently does, or reduce payments to providers below the cost of providing services "without compromising quality."[2] Instead, the legislature will retreat back up the list of priorities until it reaches the point where there is enough money to provide services for all those eligible under Medicaid.

In addition, two companion bills, Senate Bills 534 and 935, apply the principle of expanding access to two other groups of Oregonians. The first consists of about 10 to 20 thousand people who are considered "medically uninsurable" due to preexisting medical conditions. Senate Bill 534 created an insurance pool subsidized by the state and private insurers from which these people can purchase health insurance.

The more important of the two bills is SB 935. This is aimed at working Oregonians and their dependents who are above the federal poverty level but who have no health benefits and who do not qualify for medical assistance. The law affects about two-thirds of the un insured in Oregon (approximately 260,000 people). Under this legislation employers are encouraged, through tax credits, to provide health insurance for uninsured employees. To take advantage of the credits, however, they must participate in the program by December 30, 1995. After that date they must provide insurance but without the tax incentive. Significantly, the law provides that the benefits offered to these employees "must include substantially similar medical services as those recommended by the Health Services Commission [under SB 27]."

It is important to note here that initially there was some confusion and disagreement over the intended implications of the benefits package. Senator John Kitzhaber, the Oregon Senate president and the law's architect, has portrayed the package as a standard for a minimal level of health insurance coverage for all Oregonians. This view was not shared by other participants in the legislative hearings on SB 27. For example, when one witness in the early stages of consideration of the bill suggested that SB 27 "sets up a minimal acceptable level of health benefits and implies that all businesses in Oregon must provide at least that level of benefits," she was corrected by a committee member who said that he did not interpret the bill to mean that at all. The benefits that employers provide to their employees are the result of contract negotiations, he noted, not state policy.[3] As late as April 1989, after the bill had been approved by the Oregon Senate, another lobbyist argued before the House Committee on Human Resources that "when you develop the list [of health priorities] in Senate Bill 27, that list, as a result of other legislation [SB 935] also becomes potentially the definition for adequate health care for both your employed uninsured and your employed insured. *And this is not something that I think is widely known.* . . . "[4]

Whatever confusion or opposition there might have been to the broader implications of the Oregon experiment, one point seems clear: Despite Kitzhaber's early pronouncement on the issue, the potential applicability of the legislation to all Oregonians was not emphasized in the public debate on SB 27, although it may have been part of Kitzhaber's original intention. Only after the bill became law, and critics such as Congressman Henry Waxman (D–CA) and Senator Albert Gore (D–TN) began attacking it as "unfair" to the poor, did supporters begin emphasizing the not "widely known" point about its relevance to all Oregonians, and not just the poor.

However broadly or narrowly one chooses to define or understand the implications of Oregon's package of health insurance legislation, it is bold in both concept and prospect. How is it that Oregon took on the role of health policy innovator in this instance? The answer to the question lies in both a common malady that afflicts all the states and a particular expression of that problem in Oregon. I begin with the more general affliction.

"The Monster That Ate the States"

It has become virtually obligatory in writing about health policy in the United States to begin with the issue of cost. The litany is a familiar one: Between 1965 and 1990 health care costs in the United States increased from $41.9 billion a year, representing $206 per person and 5.9 percent of the gross national product, to an estimated $666.2 billion or $2,665 per person, or about 12 percent of the GNP. Furthermore, annual health cost increases in the last decade have been more than double that of other goods and services: overall inflation from 1980 to 1989 was 4.7 percent, while medical costs increased 10.4 percent. The increase in Medicaid costs for the federal government from fiscal year 1991 to fiscal year 1992 was the largest of any major national program. Explanations for the explosion in health care costs are similarly familiar. These include an aging population; overall inflation; costly advances in medical technology; a fee-for-service, third-party payer financing system; overdoctoring and defensive medical practices in response to a malpractice insurance crisis; and the failure of Americans to adopt more prudent lifestyles (use seat belts, not abuse alcohol or drugs, not smoke, and so on).

While no sector of the health care economy has been immune from the escalation of costs, the public sector has borne a considerable portion of the burden. To begin, public sector spending on health care services increased from about 25 percent of all spending in this area in 1965 to over 40 percent today. The reason for this substantial increase was the introduction in 1965 of Medicare and Medicaid. State general fund spending on Medicaid, the largest and costliest health program run by the states, is one of the fastest growing items in state budgets. When it was first introduced, Medicaid comprised about 5 percent of

state general fund expenditures. By 1990 it was up to around 11 percent and was predicted to go as high as 15 percent by 1995. Today
Medicaid is second only to education in terms of the percentage of
state budgets it consumes.

In the 1980s Medicaid became a target for social critics, who
pointed to the program's inadequate funding, the lack of uniformity
among states in eligibility criteria, and the decline in the proportion of
women and children covered by the program. In terms of eligibility,
for example, Medicaid is tied to two of the other major welfare programs in the nation, Aid to Families with Dependent Children (AFDC)
and Supplemental Security Income (SSI) for the aged, blind, and disabled. As Burwell and Rymer demonstrate, these two programs have
moved in opposite directions. Eligibility for AFDC has become more
restrictive, while SSI has become more expansive.[5] The tightening of
Medicaid eligibility occurred at both the state and federal level, either
through a failure of benefits to keep pace with inflation or, as in the
case of the 1981 Omnibus Budget Reconciliation Act (OBRA), by
deliberately tightening eligibility and, thereby, reducing recipients. As
a result, the number of children and single parents, mostly women,
eligible for Medicaid has declined. At the same time, SSI payments did
keep pace with, and in fact exceeded, inflation since they are by law
indexed to the cost of living. Between 1975 and 1985 overall benefit
levels for AFDC recipients declined 30 percent, while those for SSI
and state-provided supplementary income (SSP) recipients increased
10 percent.[6] The result of these trends has been the aging of the Medicaid population: In 1972, 18.1 percent of Medicaid expenditures went to
AFDC eligible children and 52.8 percent to people on SSI; by 1988
only 12.0 percent went to AFDC children and 73.4 percent went to SSI
recipients.[7]

In response to the growth in Medicaid spending, the states have
adopted one or more of three strategies. First, they have eliminated
benefits. Oregon did this in 1987 when it ended state funding of organ
transplants, a decision which set in motion the events that led to the
basic health services act. Second, states have redefined eligibility
and, consequently, thrown people off the Medicaid rolls. The
Children's Defense Fund has estimated that there were 200,000 fewer
children served by Medicaid in 1986 than there were in 1978, despite lower poverty rates in that earlier year.[8] In fact, the proportion
of poor people in general who are covered by Medicaid has declined

from a high of about 65 percent to less than 40 percent today.

Third, states have reduced reimbursements to providers, a strategy rendered more difficult by a June 1990 United States Supreme Court decision that upheld the right of hospitals and other health providers to sue the states for higher Medicaid reimbursements. In 1989, for example, Oregon's hospitals were reimbursed by the state for only 78 percent of the actual cost of providing services under Medicaid. Oregon was one of the states in which a lawsuit by providers seeking increased reimbursements was pending when the court issued its ruling. One consequence of underreimbursement to providers has been that physicians and hospitals have increased the fees they charge private patients or their insurance companies to cover their expenses.

The Medicaid problem facing the states—former Oregon governor Neil Goldschmidt called Medicaid "the monster that ate the states"—is in part the result of recent changes in the law that have mandated that additional health services be covered by the states.[9] Beginning in the mid 1980s, Congress made it easier for pregnant women and young children, and people who are making the transition from welfare to work, to qualify for Medicaid. It also increased the health services available to these groups. The Omnibus Budget and Reconciliation Act of 1989 extended certain mandatory benefits to children on Medicaid, including dental examinations, orthodontics, services for disabled children, *and* organ transplants. Ironically, it was a highly controversial and much publicized decision to stop Medicaid funding of transplants that started the process of reform in Oregon. It is to this story that I will now turn.

The Transplant Controversy

Oregon's road to prioritizing and rationing health services began in the 1987 legislative session when the state decided to eliminate funding of organ transplants for Medicaid recipients. This decision went all but unnoticed when it was made by the legislature. Oregon had first authorized funding of transplantation operations for the poor in the 1983–85 biennium legislative session. Between 1985 and 1987 the state paid for 19 transplants at a cost of about $1.2 million. The transplant program was covered by Medicaid, with the state absorbing 38 percent of the costs and the federal government the remaining 62 percent.

In the first two years of the program requests for transplant operations were approved on a case-by-case basis. The state could reject any transplant request and could stop the program when it had exhausted the allocated funds. In 1985, however, Congress required that states file a plan indicating which procedures they would fund; states were then obligated to fund *all* transplant requests that fell under the plan.

In 1987 the Oregon Department of Human Resources requested $2.2 million from the legislature to fund 34 transplant operations in the 1988–89 biennium, nearly double the cost of the previous two-year period. In a memorandum to the Oregon joint House and Senate Ways and Means Committee, the Adult and Family Services (AFS) Division suggested, "At some point AFS must face the question of continuing transplant coverage, or investing in more basic health care which could potentially benefit a much larger number of people. Such a decision would require the full support of the Legislature."[10]

A House and Senate Ways and Means subcommittee decided to take transplant funding out of the regular budget and place it on an optional priority list along with other requests for special social programs. The subcommittee had about $20 million at its disposal and requests that totaled about $48 million. Transplants had to compete with programs dealing with the mentally ill and disturbed, the deaf, head injury victims, juvenile delinquents, and senior citizens. The subcommittee ran out of money before it got to transplants. The decision to eliminate transplant funding was hardly noticed by the legislators; State Representative Mike Kopetski, who introduced the Human Resources budget in the House, called attention to the deletion of the transplant program twice in his speech. Not a single legislator questioned the decision.[11]

If the initial transplant decision went largely unnoticed, the next one did not; it brought the attention of the nation upon the state. On December 2, 1987, Coby Howard, a seven-year-old boy from Portland, died of leukemia. The boy had become a familiar personality across much of the state over the preceding two months as his family, school friends, and teachers tried to raise $100,000 for a bone marrow transplant. The highly publicized effort became necessary when Oregon officials informed Coby's unemployed and uninsured mother that the state no longer covered transplant operations under its Medicaid program and that they would not grant Coby an exemption from this new policy. The private fundraising campaign was $30,000 short of its goals when Coby Howard died.

In a January meeting of the Legislative Emergency Board, which acts on behalf of the full legislature during the interim period, Representative Tom Mason introduced a motion to appropriate $220,000 to the state's Medicaid program to fund five transplant operations for people whose requests for such procedures had already been denied. The proposal was opposed by the Oregon Senate President, John Kitzhaber, who presided over a subcommittee meeting on the proposal on January 28, 1988. He and House Speaker Vera Katz took the unusual step of attending the subcommittee meeting to vote on the funding request.[12]

Senator Kitzhaber said that the issue before the Emergency Board was not whether the state could find $220,000 to fund these five requests. Clearly it could. He argued, however, that the "basic issue is one of equity." There were thousands of working Oregonians who had no private insurance and still other nonworking Oregonians ineligible for Medicaid. Neither of these groups were eligible for these transplants.

> I think what this [transplant] policy does, is it gives to Medicaid recipients certain services that are not, in fact, available to a large number of other Oregonians and I think that there's a basic inequity involved there. What you're really doing is you're asking many taxpayers to buy services for people on public assistance that they can [not] even get for their own children.[13]

Another critical issue was one of priority. Since you cannot satisfy all demands, you have to make choices on how best to spend state dollars. "What we can do, with our limited money, is to reduce the number of deaths to the maximum. Save as many people as we can, because we can't save them all."[14] Despite an emotional plea by Representative Mason that Oregon not become "known as the state that lets children die," his motion failed on a tie vote. President Kitzhaber and Speaker Katz voted against the motion.[15] The next day, however, the full Emergency Board was scheduled to meet and Mason vowed to bring the issue before it.

That evening Ted Koppel featured the Oregon transplant decision, and Senator Kitzhaber on his "Nightline" show. He began the program with footage of Coby Howard and said, "When the State of Oregon decided to stop funding organ transplants, it allowed this boy to die." Koppel later asked: "Is the cost of modern medical technology forcing public officials to play God?"[16] It was in the rather heady atmosphere of national media attention, then, that the full Emergency Board met the next day. The arguments about equity, priorities, costs, and compassion were the same; and so were the results. The motion was defeated. In the course of the debate Senator Kitzhaber set the stage for the next act in this drama. "Now I guess I just want to close by saying that we are going to have to ration health care."

Rationing: The Oregon Trail

Although the decision to halt funding of transplants was not itself an exercise in health care rationing, it became the occasion for discussing one. That it did so can be attributed not only to the highly publicized specific tragedy of Coby Howard but to the political culture of Oregon and to John Kitzhaber himself.

Oregonians, who are ever mindful of the history of the Oregon Trail and of the courageous pioneers who blazed it, pride themselves in being social policy innovators. It was in Oregon, in the early part of this century, that the initiative and referendum were first introduced. That tradition of innovation has continued. "[T]his is a culturally liberal state on many issues, with many young and single voters, and one that is proud of being the first state to ban throwaway bottles and among the first to allow abortions."[17] The popular image that Oregonians have of themselves has been called a "moralistic" political subculture, in which "both the general public and politicians conceive of politics as a public activity centered on some notion of the public good and properly devoted to the advancement of the public interest."[18] (Falcone, Ensley, and Moore make this same point with regard to policy toward the aged. See Chapter Four.) Whether one relies on conventional wisdom and popular perception or scholarly artifice, many observers and participants were convinced that bold social experimentation, although not unique to Oregon, is certainly characteristic of the state. Also characteristic of the state is the tradition of participatory democracy in the policymaking process. This tradition is best exemplified in the use of the initiative and referendum but has manifested itself in SB 27 in the form of community meetings to aid in the formation of a popular consensus on what is an adequate level of health benefits.

Political circumstances also contributed to the ability of the state to tackle the difficult and complex policy issue of rationing. The Democrats controlled both houses of the legislature and the governorship, and the leaders of the two houses were close friends and political allies. But no political factor was as critical to the fate of health care reform in Oregon as the presence of John Kitzhaber.

John Kitzhaber, a liberal Democrat who was first elected to the Oregon House in 1978 and has been in the Senate since 1981, has served three terms as Senate president. His experience as an emergency room physician has added a good deal of credibility to his role as the premier legislative authority on the state's health policy system and aided him in gaining support within the medical community. Although Kitzhaber had been better known for his interest in environmental issues than in health ones, once he assumed the position of spokesperson in the transplant controversy, he pursued the issue of resource allocation with enthusiasm. Kitzhaber's articulateness and personal warmth has helped to create national celebrity status for him since Oregon first made the news with its decision on transplants. Consider, for example, the description of Kitzhaber, "the nation's leading exponent of health care rationing," in a 1990 *Boston Globe* interview with the senator in his hometown of Roseburg:

> The physician–senator exudes rugged health, confidence and authority, just as he had two weeks earlier in Boston, where he impressed leading politicians, policymakers and health care mavens with his standard speech on how Oregon is reordering health care priorities according to the greatest good for the greatest number.[19]

Kitzhaber remained the dominant force in formulating the new health policy partly because Governor Neil Goldschmidt decided that he had other priorities. In February 1988, at the time the Emergency Board was embroiled in the transplant controversy, the governor appointed an 18-member commission on health care that he charged "with identifying Oregonians who find it difficult to gain access to health care." In September 1988, the commission recommended encouraging business to use an existing voluntary tax credit program to cover uninsured employees; creating an insurance risk pool; and extending Medicaid benefits to pregnant women.[20]

Although some commission recommendations found their way into the Basic Health Services Act, the report had only a minor impact because the governor did not promote it.[21] Some have suggested that the governor was preoccupied with other policy interests, including prison finance and his "Children's Agenda," or that he was simply uninterested in health care reform. For whatever reason, Goldschmidt never played a very active role in the life of SB 27. This was, in every sense of the term, "Kitzhaber's Plan." He had the power, the allies, and the idea.

Senate Bill 27: The Legislative Route

Kitzhaber's dominance was both facilitated and symbolized by one of the first tactical steps he took in preparation for the legislative debate on his bill, namely, the creation of a new Senate Committee on Health Insurance and Bio-Ethics. This move enabled him to bypass the existing Human Resources Committee and its less congenial chairperson and deal instead with a sympathetic freshman senator. Kitzhaber submitted his health care reform bill to the legislature in January 1989. It was, by his own admission, a "mere skeleton," really just a "concept." As a result, even before the Committee on Health Insurance and Bio-Ethics met, Kitzhaber submitted several amendments to his own bill. These amendments were the first of many as the legislation evolved. The changes were not so much the result of controversy or fierce opposition but rather of the innovative and uncertain nature of the reform. Indeed, throughout the hearings conducted on the bill between February and June 1989, legislators heard little disagreement over the need for reform from health care providers and insurers, social advocacy groups, union leaders, and members of the public health and welfare bureaucracy. This is not to suggest that there were no differing views on how to accomplish the goals of increasing access and containing growing costs but merely to emphasize that virtually everyone agreed with the most fundamental assumption underlying the legislation, namely, that the current system was unsustainable.

Although there was agreement on principle, there was certainly disagreement on specifics. The most consequential concern, and the one that would become the rallying point for opponents both in the state and in Congress, was over the trade-off between access and benefit levels. Central to Kitzhaber's plan was the notion that not everyone would be able to get all the possible medical care he or she might need but that everyone should have some basic level of care. Under the existing system those covered by Medicaid effectively enjoyed the same full range of health services as those who had private insurance. Indeed social advocates wanted very much to protect the benefit level provided under Medicaid. The problem was that about 450,000 Oregonians neither qualified for Medicaid nor were covered by private insurance. SB 27 would pick up about 120,000 of these people when it was fully implemented by extending coverage to all those who fell below the federal poverty level. (SB 534 and SB 935 would cover the rest of the uninsured.)

However, achieving the goal of universal access would require rationing of benefits. The purpose of the prioritization process was to identify, through professional, social, and political consensus, those health services that constitute an adequate or basic level of care—and that the state could afford.

But here was the rub. Would the benefit package be adequate? What would be covered; what omitted? Unless you added a great deal of money to the Medicaid budget, something that did not appear likely, adding 120,000 people to the Medicaid pool would require reducing current benefit levels. Some who testified indicated that although they supported universal access, if presented with a choice between universal access with a "thin" package of benefits and something short of universal access with a more substantial package, they would prefer the latter.

Moreover, some charged that the plan would create a two-tier health care system: Guaranteed access to finite services for the poor, and virtually unlimited services for those who could afford to purchase insurance on their own. As a result of these concerns, opponents in both the social advocacy and health provider communities wanted some assurance that the basic benefits package would be rich enough to provide an adequate and acceptable level of health care. As a result, a House committee amended the Senate version of the bill to include a broad definition of basic health services. This included "so much of each of the following as are approved and funded by the Legislative Assembly: (1) provider services and supplies; (2) outpatient services; (3) inpatient hospital services; and (4) health promotion and disease prevention services." This rather general list apparently reduced some of the concerns about the bill.

Universal access to health care for the poor and basic level of services were at the heart of both the philosophy of the legislation and the concerns of the groups affected. But the politics of health care reform in Oregon produced other, more parochial, concerns. Who, for example, would be eligible to provide services, and which groups would be represented on the Health Services Commission and thus have a direct say in the prioritization process? In the first instance, there was predictable interest on the part of dentists, drug and alcohol counselors, mental health specialists, social workers, pharmacists, chiropractors and osteopaths, among others, that their services be included in the package authorized under the law.

Second, both provider and consumer groups wanted assurances that they would have an opportunity to influence the process through representation on the Health Services Commission. Advocates for children, the elderly, the disabled, the mentally ill, Medicaid recipients, persons with chemical dependencies, as well as all varieties of health care providers wanted to have a representative on the commission. Following intense lobbying, the bill that emerged provided for a commission of eleven members, five of whom would be physicians with clinical expertise in the areas of obstetrics, perinatal care, pediatrics, adult medicine, geriatrics, or public health. In addition, one of the physicians would be a doctor of osteopathy, and there would be a public health nurse, a social services worker, and four "consumers of health care."

Since not every interest could be accommodated by representation on the commission, the HSC was given the charge to "solicit testimony and information from advocates for seniors; handicapped persons; mental health services consumers; low-income Oregonians; and providers of health care, including but not limited to physicians licensed to practice medicine, dentists, oral surgeons, chiropractors, naturopaths, hospitals, clinics, pharmacists, nurses and allied health professionals." Clearly, the legislators were anxious to secure widespread support for the plan. Moreover, as Kitzhaber and his staff recall, it was "important to know what consumers wanted out of the system."

Following its odyssey through the three legislative committees, Senate Bill 27 was approved with overwhelming bipartisan support in both the Senate (19–3) and the House (58–2).

Coming Up with "The List"

Two very difficult tasks lay ahead before the state could implement the Oregon Basic Health Services Act. The first was to obtain a Medicaid waiver from the federal government. I will return to this part of the story shortly.[22] The second task was for the Health Services Commission to construct a list of health care priorities for the legislature. To accomplish this, the commission used three mechanisms. The first was a series of 11 public hearings held around the state, allowing interested parties to express their views. The second was authorizing Oregon Health Decisions (OHD), a highly respected citizens advocacy group, to conduct community meetings in every county of the state "to build a consensus on the values to be used to guide health resource allocation decisions." Ultimately 47 community forums were held, during which participants filled out a questionnaire soliciting their opinions on the relative importance of certain health situations, and engaged in group discussions. Like much else about the process, health care interest groups dominated this stage too. Although it was the hope and intention of OHD to have a cross section of Oregonians, this did not turn out to be the case. Of the slightly more than 1,000 people who attended the meetings, almost 70 percent were "mental health and health care workers."[23] Although the term "workers" is not defined, over one-third of the participants had incomes of $50,000 or more, and two-thirds were college graduates. Kitzhaber is convinced that the "discussions were wide-ranging and tended to deal primarily with broad issues and values rather than with narrow interests."

The third mechanism provided the most systematic solicitation and application of citizen values in the prioritization process. The commission authorized a state-wide, random-digit-dialed telephone survey of 1,000 Oregonians. To conform to the principle of incorporating community values in the ranking process and not simply rely on treatment-outcome data, the commission decided to use a modified version of the Quality of Well-Being Scale (QWB) developed by Robert M. Kaplan, M.D., of the University of California at San Diego. Respondents were asked to rate 31 health situations from 0 (a situation that "is as bad as death") to 100 (a situation that describes "good health"). Among the situations respondents were asked to rate were: "You cannot drive a car or use public transportation, you have to use a walker or wheelchair under your own control, and are limited in the recreational activities you may perform, but have no other health problems," and "You can go anywhere and have no limitations on physical or other activity, but you wear glasses or contact lenses."[24]

The results of the survey were then formally incorporated into a mathematical cost/utility or "net benefit value" formula that included data on expected outcomes of given treatments for hundreds of health conditions. The "Net Benefit Value" equation was in the form of a word formula where:

$$\text{Net Benefit Value} = \frac{\text{Net Benefits}}{\text{Net Costs}}$$

Benefits included the length of time the patient profits from a treatment, the public values regarding certain health states (such as death, return to asymptomatic state of health, and so on), and the probability that a health state will result from a particular treatment. Costs include "diagnosis, hospitalization, professional services, non-medical but prescribed services and ancillary services."

The formula produced a computer-generated prioritized list of 1,600 condition-treatment pairs. The first version of this list was released by the Health Services Commission on May 2, 1990 and received widespread national media attention.[25] Due to data collection and methodological problems, the list included some rather surprising priorities: crooked teeth received a higher ranking than early treatment for Hodgkins disease, and dealing with thumb sucking was ranked higher than hospitalization of a child for starvation.

Members of the commission insist that the initial prioritization was never intended to be anything more than a test of the methodology. Commission chair Harvey Klevit, M.D., told a reporter for *Science* in August that "I looked at the first two pages of that list and threw it in the trash can."[26] The HSC created an Alternative Methodology Subcommittee to rework and modify the original formula. The most significant change in the methodology was that "cost was eliminated as a systematic factor in the ordering of services on the final priority list" and emphasis was placed on the net benefit of the medical treatments.[27] On February 20, 1991, the HSC made public a completely revised "Prioritized Health Services List."

The new list contained 709 rather than the original 1,600 medical conditions and treatments. The scaling down of the list was largely accomplished by grouping related treatments (for example, open fractures of the toe, ankle, lower leg, became fractures of the lower extremities). The end result was a far more rational, and presumably medically and politically defensible product. There are seventeen major categories ranging from "Acute fatal, prevents death, full recovery," (for example, various forms of pneumonia) to "Fatal or nonfatal, minimal or no improvement in QWB" (for example, "terminal HIV disease with less than 10% survival rate at five years"). Reflecting both the current wisdom among the medical community and the values expressed in the community forums, preventive medicine was given high priority on the list. From the perspective of the history of SB 27, among the more interesting changes between the two lists was the relocation of organ transplants from near the bottom of the original list to various locations throughout the revised list, depending upon an assessment of potential outcome.

In April 1991, the Health Services Commission received the actuary's report on the priority list. The commission recommended to the legislature that it fund a benefit package that would include, at least, all "essential" services (that is, categories one through nine in the 17 category list) and most "very important services." On June 30, 1991, the Legislative Assembly approved a budget that included an additional $33 million for the Medicaid program. This would allow the state, in the first year of implementation, to add 78,000 new Medicaid recipients and extend health services to them through line 587 of the priority list—that is, through esophagitis, a painful swelling of the esophagus but not treatment of intervertebral disc disorders (line 588). The increased commitment of resources to the reform plan was particularly significant because it came in the first year in which Oregon operated under a property tax limitation that had strained the state's budget and various political alliances.

Where then does the Oregon rationing experiment stand as of this writing? The fate of the legislation depends largely on forces outside of the state. From the outset, state officials knew they would need a federal waiver to implement the program. Under Medicaid rules a state cannot drop any mandated services without federal approval, and the Oregon plan would not cover all services currently under mandate. In addition, the program would require an additional $110 million over five years from the federal government because of the additional 120,000 people brought into the program. State officials have followed, often simultaneously, two routes to securing the waiver. One has been to convince officials in the Health Care Financing Administration (HCFA), and ultimately the secretary of Health and Human Services, who, state officials are convinced, have the power to administratively grant the waiver.

The second route has been to get legislative authorization for the waiver. Republican U.S. Senator Bob Packwood and Democratic Congressman Ron Wyden have supported the state plan throughout the process, although Packwood has been the more enthusiastic player. At one point in 1989 the Senate Finance Committee, on which Packwood is the ranking Republican, voted to grant a waiver. However, forces opposed to the plan, including Senator Albert Gore (D–TN), Congressman Henry Waxman (D–CA), and Sara Rosenbaum of the Children's Defense Fund, began lobbying in earnest. The result was that when the proposed waiver reached the U.S. Senate Budget Committee, which is chaired by Gore's colleague from Tennessee, James Sasser, it was dropped from the budget bill.[28] Over the past two years the waiver has been kept alive by Packwood and Wyden despite considerable interest group and legislative opposition. Now that Oregon has "drawn the line," and committed additional resources to the plan, Congress or HCFA will have no alternative but to act. State officials were confident, in early 1992, that HCFA would grant the necessary Medicaid waivers by June. Furthermore, they believed that there was now sufficient support within Congress for health care reform so that any legislative effort to block the waivers would be defeated. This confidence was somewhat shaken in February 1992 with the leaking of the draft of a confidential report from the Congressional Office of Technology Assessment. In the draft, OTA indicated that it had "serious reservations" about the Oregon plan, principally because of what it saw as the highly subjective nature of the ranking system and the fact that some current Medicaid clients might be denied coverage. State officials hoped that they could address these concerns before the official release of the report later in the spring.

If Oregon receives its waiver, it will begin rationing Medicaid funded health services in July 1992—two years later than initially anticipated. Whether it ultimately does so or not, the state has begun a public policy debate that will be continued in virtually every state, and perhaps even the federal government, over the next several years. It is useful, then, to assess some of the implications of, and questions raised by, the proposed Oregon experiment and experience.

Discussion and Analysis

Coming Out of the Closet on Rationing

What is it about the Oregon plan that has stirred the interest, imagination, and, in many cases, the ire of so many opinion makers, leaders, and reporters in this country and abroad? One answer may simply be timing. Although there is no end to the candidates for "the most important domestic issue of the 1990s," health care seems to be on everyone's short list. After years of inaction by the federal government, the states have begun to respond to the problems of cost containment and access. The fact that Oregon was first out of the blocks—although folks in Hawaii and Massachusetts might disagree—and has been the only show in town for a long time may explain part of the national fascination with Oregon's experiment.

Novelty alone, however, cannot explain the attraction. What might explain it, in my judgment, is that Oregon has raised some of the most critical issues in the health care debate, namely access and cost restraint, and responded in a way that has thrown both liberals and conservatives off balance. Take, for example, the issue of access. Liberals have long argued that everyone in America should have access to health care and that the government has a responsibility to guarantee this. Proponents of the Oregon plan argue that the bundle of bills passed by the legislature will extend health care coverage to all Oregonians. However, and this is the shoe that pinches the liberal foot, universal access can only be bought, they argue, at the expense of limiting benefits. As Senator Kitzhaber remarked on the "Today Show" after the transplant decision, "We are not going to avoid rationing health care in this country. We can't afford to pay for everything for everybody."[29] Perhaps. But before looking at this assertion more closely, it is necessary to look at the notion of rationing.

Rationing is already a routine and integral part of the American health care system. It occurs when health care providers refuse to treat Medicaid patients, or when legislators redefine Medicaid eligibility and benefits so as to reduce coverage of persons or procedures, or when the poor but uninsured delay seeing a physician for a health problem. It is "stealth" rationing; virtually undetectable except by those who go without care. What Oregon has proposed is to allocate health resources in an explicit, public, consensual, and accountable fashion. The process of seeking citizen input has, as *JAMA* editorialized, "intuitive appeal."[30] It *is* an appealing process, but one that does not mask the ultimately troubling reality of rationing health care.

One of the questions that the rationing debate in Oregon has raised, both within the state and elsewhere, is whether the Basic Health Services Act should provide a model for rationing of health care for a broader population than simply those on medical assistance. I have already discussed the fact that there was considerable uncertainty during the debate over SB 27 over what populations would be covered by the minimum standard. This concern was based upon the proposed extension of the prioritization/rationing process to the populations covered under SB 935 and SB 534. The former, it will be recalled, require small businesses (25 or fewer employees) to extend health benefits to their uninsured employees. Employers who choose to participate will receive a tax credit. All employers, regardless of the size of their business, will be required to provide health care benefits to their employees and dependents by January 1995. The three measures are joined by the fact that SB 935 and SB 534 stipulate that the benefits provided under these laws "must include substantially similar medical services as those recommended by the Health Services Commission [under SB 27]." In other words, the prioritization will apply not only to Medicaid recipients under SB 27 but to working Oregonians under SB 935 and to the "medically uninsurable" under SB 534.

Potentially, however, health care rationing may extend to persons beyond those covered under these three laws, and this is where it may run into trouble as a national model. Oregon's universal access through benefit rationing could threaten the level of care for all Oregonians and, if followed elsewhere, other Americans as well. For working Oregonians the danger is that under the law it is possible for employers who currently provide health insurance to their employees to discontinue that coverage, wait two years, and then provide a reduced benefits package. Moreover, critics are concerned that the basic package of health benefits provided under SB 27, and by extension SB 935, will become the standard for *all* Oregonians, not, as Kitzhaber and others argue, as the *minimal* level of acceptable coverage, but rather as the *norm*. Thus the lobbyist for the National Association of Social Workers argued that his organization was committed to seeing health insurance extended to all uninsured Oregonians. "But, we don't want to see that [sic] 400,000 people insured at a minimum level of insurance, and see the other two and a half million people in this state see their benefits be dropped down to that minimum and admittedly inadequate level."[31]

On the Backs of the Poor?

The question of whether the Basic Health Services Act provides a model for a broader constituency raises another, highly charged, question:

Is Oregon using its poor population as a guinea pig to deal with the society-wide problem of runaway health care costs? Some critics, especially outside of Oregon, think that this is exactly what the state is doing. According to Arthur Caplan, a national authority on biomedical ethics, "It is wrong to make the poor, and only the poor, bear the burden of rationing."[32] More importantly, U.S. Senator Albert Gore, a member of the Senate Commerce, Science and Transportation Committee, also thinks the Oregon plan is unfair to the poor. Confronted with the problem of soaring health care costs, Gore says, "Oregon officials believe they have the answer: The weakest and most vulnerable groups in the state—poor women and children—should pay the bill."[33] Gore, and other congressional critics, including Henry Waxman, believe that the Oregon plan will give official sanction, indeed encouragement, to a two-tier system of health care in this country: one for the poor and one for everyone else. Furthermore, "Until recently, unequal access to health care was not tolerated. Oregon's decision to ration care to its poorest women and children is a declaration of unconditional surrender just as the first battles are being fought over the future of our health-care system."[34] The reference to women and children here refers to the fact that under the waiver sought from the national government, Oregon had excluded from the prioritization process persons covered under Old Age, Blind, and Disabled, Medically Needy, and Children in Foster Care programs. This meant that the majority of those remaining in the Medicaid pool, and affected by rationing under SB 27, would be women and children.

State officials defended the exclusion of these populations from the rationing process on the grounds that each represented a rather special problem not easily accommodated into the prioritization scheme. For example, about 90 percent of those in the Old Age program are covered by Medicare, and the state would have to seek a waiver from that program as well. In addition, because the disabled often face unique health problems, this group did not appear to be a good candidate for the formalized condition/treatment pairing approach that was applied to the nondisabled population. However, the charge that the state was only asking women and children to take reduced benefits consistently dogged state officials and threatened the prospects of securing a federal waiver. As a result, the law was amended in the 1991 legislative session to bring into the program, by October 1, 1993, the aged, blind, disabled, and foster children populations. Assurances were made to these groups that their special health care needs would be adequately protected.

Finally, it should be noted that in response to the criticism that women and children are being harmed by the Medicaid reform, state officials point out that over one-half of the 120,000 Oregonians living in poverty and without health insurance are women and children. It is this group that will be brought into the Medicaid program under SB 27.

Gore and others find Oregon's recourse to rationing particularly troublesome because the state has not put proportionally as much into its Medicaid program as other states: Oregon spends only 4 percent of its budget on Medicaid compared to the national average of about 11 percent. According to Gore: "If Oregon simply spent as much on Medicaid as comparable states do, it could add more than 120,000 patients to its program without rationing anyone's care."[35]

Defenders of the state's actions respond in two ways. First, they remind critics that SB 27 provides a standard for health services that will extend beyond the poor and include the "medically uninsurable" and persons working in businesses where there is no employer-sponsored health insurance. However, it must be noted that many of those who will be brought into the system under SB 935 will be among the most poorly paid of Oregon's working population. And, although the priority list may ultimately set a standard for all Oregonians, in fact it will only initially affect the poor and near poor in the state. It is hard to deny the charge that the law will create a situation in which some Oregonians will have virtually unlimited access to health care, as they do now, while others will have only limited, albeit "adequate," access. This, however, may be preferable and more humane than the current system, in the state and the nation, in which most have unlimited access, while others have none at all.

Second, with regard to the indictment against the state for its seemingly parsimonious policy toward Medicaid, defenders argue that while Oregon ranks low among the states in this regard—35th in terms of payments per recipient, and 42nd in payments per capita for the 1988 fiscal year—it is more generous in other areas of public assistance. For example, the state ranked 15th in the nation in terms of the maximum cash payment made to an AFDC–eligible family of three. Kitzhaber and others have repeatedly decried the tendency to equate health care with health. They argue, appropriately in my judgment, that helping a poor, pregnant mother get proper nutrition, prenatal information, and transportation to a health clinic is as important as any medical care she might receive. Moreover, state officials argue that Oregon spends less than other states on Medicaid in part because it spends more wisely. For example, 55 percent of those on AFDC are in managed health care programs that are far more economical than individual provider care. In an era of severe fiscal constraints, Oregon officials wonder, is spending less per capita necessarily bad?

The charge that the state is insensitive to the needs of the poor, or inadequately responds to those needs, may be unfair. It also may be largely beside the point. In the absence of a nonemployment-based, universal system of health insurance, the more fundamental issue at stake here is what principle should guide U.S. health policy for the poor: equity or equality? Specifically, should limits be placed on the level of medical services available to those on public assistance? Should we as a society say that fairness—equity—requires only as much health care as expert and popular consensus judges to be adequate? In the absence of unlimited resources, it may be that it is impossible to guarantee *equal* access for everyone to all available medical technology, service, and treatment that can be brought to bear on a particular condition. Although the legislative debates over transplants and rationing were not couched in terms of equity versus equality, in fact that is what those debates were largely about.

The debate is hardly a new one. Several years ago Charles Fried addressed this question and argued that, "To say there is a right to health care does not imply a right to equal access, a right that whatever is available to any shall be available to all."[36] In place of the notion of equality of care, Fried suggests a "dynamically defined" "decent standard of care." The question then becomes what constitutes the currently defined "decent standard?" Clearly, as Fried's operational directive suggests, such a standard must be a dynamic one, accommodating changing technology, available resources, as well as popular consensus and democratic values. The value of an adaptable standard of what is a decent minimum level of health care is also endorsed by Allen Buchanan. "So the first advantage of the idea of a decent minimum . . . is that it allows us to adjust the level of services to be provided as a matter of rights to relevant social conditions and also allows for the possibility that as a society becomes more affluent the floor provided by the decent minimum should be raised."[37] All this sounds remarkably like the Oregon Basic Health Services Act. The question is, of course, whether we as a society are willing to openly acknowledge that fairness, not equality, will and/or should govern health resource allocations.

Oregon has answered the question in the affirmative. Yet it has done so primarily for the more marginal elements of society. Moreover, I would argue that there was so little opposition to the program in the state, in part, because it was understood or perceived to affect primarily only the poorest segments of the state's population. The potentially broader implications of the law were not widely known or understood. However, should the debate over universal access to health care in other states or at the national level come down to the choice facing Oregon's poorest or most vulnerable populations, namely, buying universal access by accepting limitations on benefits, then the Oregon debate will be revisited. And the outcome may be quite different.

How Much Is "Too Much"?

As noted earlier in the chapter, soaring health care costs have been the fuel that has driven the health care debate over the last two decades. Kitzhaber's point, quoted above, that "we can't afford to pay everything for everybody" is a claim few would dispute. From a political perspective, there are two problems with this assertion. The first is that no one knows what "the traffic will bear" with regard to public spending on health care. While many public policy makers and economic analysts believe that 12 percent of the GNP is, or is very near to being, "too much," most Americans "do not seem to be overly troubled by the growing proportion of the economy devoted to health care."[38] Whether the ethic of "doing everything possible regardless of cost" that governs individual, private health care decisions will be applied to public spending is open to some question. Nevertheless, access to health care, even for the poor, continues to enjoy a rather special place in our value system even as Americans become increasingly troubled by the increased costs of their own health care bills.

In addition, Karen Hansen has suggested that relative to other major areas of public spending, health care may be a pretty good buy. She asks, "But is 11 cents out of every dollar too much to spend on an industry that doesn't wage war, doesn't pollute the environment, doesn't send money overseas, increases people's quality of life and employs ten million people?"[39] The point is that no one really knows if 12 percent or 15 percent is too much. Although it is true that health costs are rising more rapidly than other goods and services, that is not the same thing as saying we are spending too much on health care. As Alain Enthoven has conceded with regard to how much of the nation's resources should be spent on health care, "There is no magic number. The right number is what people want it to be."[40]

The second problem with the argument that we have reached the limits of spending on health care is that it assumes that people assign equal values to all areas of public spending. Yet public opinion polls and political and personal behavior—especially the extraordinary time and money spent on health—suggests that Americans attach a special importance to health and the means of maintaining and regaining good health.[41] The extraordinary social and individual value attached to good health and access to good health care suggests that the rules of efficiency and parsimony that may apply to other areas of public policy are more difficult to impose on the health policy process. As long as Americans give a "higher priority to the growth of medical investment than to expenditures for education, transportation, or urban problems," it is going to be as difficult to hold health care costs down by rationing as it was to hold them down by various cost containment mechanisms (such as DRGs, Certificates-of-Need, and the like).[42]

One implication, then, of health care rationing is that policymakers and the public must choose between health care and other services. Rationing is made difficult, in part, because health care typically enjoys a higher priority in the value system of most Americans than other services with which it competes. Furthermore, it must be noted that there are some who are unwilling to accept that any choice among public services must be made at all. Former State Representative, now U.S. Congressman Mike Kopetski, who appeared with Kitzhaber on "Nightline," asked on that program, "Why is it that there is this [sic] limited dollars for health care? I don't think that ought to be so in our state or on the federal level as well. There is plenty of money out there if we want to put it into human resources."[43]

Second, Oregon's experience over the last few years underscores another potential problem with efforts to ration health care. The outcome of any rationing debate will be determined, in part, by the nature of the procedures involved and of the groups affected. Although organ transplantation was in many ways a rather unique problem, the debate over its funding illustrated how the nature of specific populations, the patient-to-cost ratio of procedures, or the numbers who might benefit will raise questions of both equity and parsimony in public health spending. How receptive will the public be, for example, to placing high on a priority list funding for long-term and costly care to prolong—not save—the lives of AIDS victims, most of whom contracted the disease through what many consider irresponsible personal behavior? This issue will become especially hotly debated if public funding for, say, AZT for AIDS patients is seen as competing with prenatal care or childhood immunization programs. The Oregon transplant case suggests how easy it is for the media, legislators, and the public to pit one group (say, transplant candidates) against another group (low income pregnant women) in a battle over scarce resources for funding life-saving or life-enhancing medical procedures. This impression was reinforced by the parade of witnesses who appeared before Oregon legislative committees and the Health Services Commission on behalf of their groups' special health care needs.

Federalism and Health Care Reform

Although there were some in Washington who questioned their sincerity,[44] Oregon's leaders genuinely set out to craft what they thought was a reasonable and workable alternative to an inherently unfair and unworkable system. State legislative and administrative officials were determined to extend a basic level of health services to all Oregonians. No one, I think, would deny that compromises were necessary to ensure passage of the legislation. What frustrates state officials so much is that their efforts have been stymied by forces outside the state and, seemingly, beyond their control. And herein lies one final lesson from Oregon's experience.

Of all the factors involved in the nearly four years of intensive debate over health care policy reform in Oregon, none has loomed as large as the role of federalism. The thesis of this book, that innovative ideas in health care are now emanating largely from the states, does not alter the fact that the federal government continues to influence heavily the health policy agenda, the parameters of political debate, and the content of health care reform options. From the Medicaid mandates that precipitated the transplant decision and controversy to the two-year battle over the Medicaid waiver, state officials have had to contend with the "federal presence."

In this regard it is both ironic and instructive that while the chief architect of the Oregon experiment is a liberal Democrat, so too is its main opponent, Henry Waxman. Waxman, along with Gore and such liberal-oriented interest groups as the Children's Defense Fund and the Catholic Conference, not only opposes what he believes to be the creation of a two-tier health system but also apparently fears that the Oregon reform, which has received positive comment from the Bush administration, will divert attention from a national solution to the Medicaid mess and form a wholesale assault on the current health delivery system in this country. Backers of the Kitzhaber plan in Oregon would be delighted with a national health insurance plan, but argue that until the federal government adopts such a scheme, something about which they are not terribly sanguine, the states should be left to their own devices to deal with existing human hardships growing out of the current program. Among the obstacles facing health care reform in this country, none is more formidable than the fact that the states and the federal government share responsibility for health care but often have different agendas, serve different constituencies, and jealously guard their respective prerogatives. Those who oppose the Oregon experiment have found an ally in federalism, while proponents wring their hands in anguish.

Acknowledgments

The author would like to acknowledge the assistance of Mark Gibson, Oregon Senate President's Office; Ian Timm, Oregon Health Decisions; and, Jeane Thorne, Oregon Adult and Family Services Division. Portions of this article originally appeared in Daniel M. Fox and Howard M. Leichter, "Rationing Care in Oregon: The New Accountability," *Health Affairs* 10 (Summer 1991): 7–27. The author wishes to thank *Health Affairs* for permission to reprint that material.

Notes

1. Among the scores of newspaper articles written about the Oregon plan are William Raspberry, "A Question of Fairness," *Oregonian* (Portland), 24

October 1989; "Oregon's Brave Medical Experiment," *The New York Times,* 12 May 1990, editorial; Albert Gore, "Unfair Health-Care Plan Forces the Old and Poor to Pay the Bills," *Oregonian,* 5 June 1990; William B. Schwartz and Henry J. Aaron, "The Achilles Heel of Health Care Rationing," *New York Times,* 9 September 1990; Richard A. Knox, "Oregon Strips Its Medicaid Benefit Plan," *Boston Globe,* 9 July 1990; and Timothy Egan, "For Oregon's Health Care System, Triage by a Lawmaker with an M.D.," *New York Times,* 9 June 1991. The most comprehensive bibliography to date on the Oregon experiment is in Charles J. Dougherty, "Setting Health Care Priorities: Oregon's Next Step," *Hastings Center Report* 21 (May–June 1991): 9.

2. Memorandum from John Kitzhaber and Mark Gibson to the author, 26 December 1990. Hereafter cited as Memorandum.

3. Senate Committee on Health Insurance and Bio-Ethics, 16 February 1989.

4. Testimony of Mark Nelson, National Association of Social Workers, House Committee on Human Resources, 19 April 1989. Emphasis added.

5. See Brian O. Burwell and Marilyn P. Rymer, "Trends in Medicaid Eligibility: 1975 to 1985," *Health Affairs* 6 (Winter 1987): 30–45.

6. Ibid, 32–33.

7. National Center for Health Statistics, *Health, United States, 1989* (Hyattsville, MD: Public Health Service, 1990): 258.

8. See Julie Rovner, "Medicaid: A Safety Net Riddled With Holes," *CQ Weekly Report* 46 (20 February 1988), 366. Burwell and Rymer, "Trends in Medicaid Eligibility," similarly document the erosion of Medicaid coverage of poor children. Burwell and Rymer, 34–35.

9. For the Goldschmidt quote see Tony Hutchison, "The Medicaid Budget Tangle," *State Legislatures* 16 (March 1990): 17.

10. Adult and Family Services Division, "Organ Transplant Services," N.D.

11. Interview by author with Oregon State Represenative Mike Kopetski.

12. Kitzhaber and his staff claim that Kitzhaber presided only because the regular chair, Frank Roberts, was in the hospital. Other sources insist, however, that his attendance at the meeting was quite unusual. Memorandum, 28 November 1990.

13. Transcript of Oregon Legislature Emergency Board, Human Resources Subcommittee, 28 January 1988.

14. Ibid.

15. Kitzhaber and his staff insist that he had "moved [unsuccessfully] that funding the transplant program be restored *and* that the funding for prenatal care be increased as well." The effect of this motion was to persuade "influential members of the committee" that it was necessary to "concentrate on accomplishing the greatest possible good." Memorandum, 26 December 1990.

16. "Nightline," 28 January 1988.

17. Michael Barone and Grant Ujifusa, *The Almanac of American Politics* (Washington, DC: National Journal, 1990), 1001.

18. See Daniel J. Elazar, *American Federalism,* 3d ed. (New York: Harper & Row, 1984), 115–122.

19. Richard A. Knox, "Oregon Strips Its Medicaid Benefit Plan," *Boston Globe,* 9 July 1990.

20. See Governor's Commission On Health Care, "Report to Governor Neil Goldschmidt on Improving Access to Health Care For All Oregonians" (Salem, OR: Office of Health Policy, 1 September 1988).

21. See Office of Medical Assistance Programs, "Waiver Application for Oregon Medicaid Demonstration Project, Discussion Draft" (Salem, OR: Department of Human Resources, April 26, 1990).

22. For a detailed account of Oregon's efforts to secure a federal Medicaid waiver see Lawrence D. Brown, "The National Politics of Oregon's Rationing Plan," *Health Affairs* 10 (June 1991): 28–51.

23. See Romana Hasnain and Michael Garland, *Health Care in Common: Report of the Oregon Health Decisions Community Meeting Process* (Portland, OR: Oregon Health Decisions, 1990), 29.

24. For a copy of the complete questionnaire see Health Services Commission, "Preliminary Report," (Salem, OR: 1 March 1990), Exhibit 2. For a critical analysis of the technical aspects of the prioritization process, including the QWB, see David C. Hadorn, "The Oregon Priority-Setting Exercise: Quality of Life and Public Policy," *Hastings Center Report* 21 (May–June 1991): 11–16.

25. See *The New York Times,* 3, 6, 12, May 1990.

26. Virginia Morell, "Oregon Puts Bold Health Plan on Ice," *Science* 249 (3 August 1990): 468.

27. David C. Hadorn, "Setting Health Care Priorities in Oregon: Cost Effectiveness Meets the Rule of Rescue," *JAMA* 265 (1 May 1991): 2220. This is the most detailed discussion of the prioritization process to date.

28. See Brown, "The National Politics of Oregon's Rationing Plan"; and Merit C. Kimball, "Fluid Odds on Oregon's Medicaid Waiver," *Health Week* 11 (March 1991): 12.

29. Comments of Senator John Kitzhaber, "The Today Show," 15 February 1988.

30. William B. Stason, "Oregon's Bold Medicald Initiative," *JAMA* 265 (May 1, 1991): 2238.

31. Ibid.

32. *Oregonian,* 24 October 1989.

33. Albert Gore, "Unfair Health-Care Plan Forces the Old and Poor to Pay the Bills."

34. Ibid.

35. Ibid.

36. Charles Fried, "Equality and Rights in Medical Care," *Hastings Center Report* 6 (February 1976): 29.

37. Allen Buchanan, "The Right to a Decent Minimum of Health Care," *Philosophy and Public Affairs* 13 (Winter 1984): 58.

38. Robert Blank, *Rationing Medicine* (New York: Columbia University Press, 1988): 29.

39. Karen Hansen, "A Painful Prescription," *State Legislatures* (November–December 1988): 23.

40. Alain Enthoven, quoted in the *Congressional Record* (3 February 1981): 845.

41. See Gallup Poll, "Report no. 198" (March 1982); Carin Rubenstein, "Well-

ness Is All," *Psychology Today* 16 (October 1982): 28–37.

42. David Mechanic, "Some Dilemmas in Health Care Policy," *Health and Society* 59 (1981): 2.

43. Comments of Representative Mike Kopetski, "Nightline," 28 January 1988.

44. See Brown, "The National Politics of Oregon's Rationing Plan."

7

Hawaii: The Health State

Deane Neubauer

Public officials in Hawaii believe that their state has entered into a "new era of health care." This view is based on a series of recent innovations that are intended to reduce the proportion of the population without health insurance and create a health care environment that is conducive to and supportive of health promotion and disease prevention. This chapter chronicles these efforts and seeks to relate them to two critical political variables: the emergence of a "health culture" in the state and a new political leadership that is committed to pursuing an innovative health policy agenda.[1]

The chapter is organized in three parts. In the first I will briefly describe the setting of Hawaii, the health state. This idea emerges out of a political-economic context that is different from that of Hawaii's sister states and that owes much to the historical nexus in the state of agriculture and tourism. Hawaii has also produced a distinctive political culture in which the dynamics of politics in a small island state are readily identifiable. Central to these dynamics has been the development of the Democratic Party as the dominant political force during the statehood era. Imbued with a spirit of political liberalism, Democratic dominance has worked both to limit the effect of Reaganism on state policy and to provide a niche within which new political leaders have emerged. Health issues have proved a valuable currency in this emergence.

In the second part of this chapter I describe several recent health policy innovations, linking them to the political setting. Of these, the most important have been the Prepaid Health Care Act of 1974, the State of Hawaii Insurance Plan (SHIP), and a variety of environmental health initiatives designed to regulate biotechnology.

Finally, I return to the theme of the emerging health culture in Hawaii and suggest its likely role in the politics and economics of the state.

The Setting

The idea of Hawaii developing a special character as a health environment began to take form with the election of John Waihee as governor in November 1987. Many requisite ingredients were already in place, perhaps most importantly the fact that Hawaii is and looks to be a healthy place. The fortunes of geography and climate have spared it many of the indignities of industrial and "post-industrial" development. Its three major industries—tourism, government employment, and agriculture—are clean endeavors when compared with smokestack environments. And, whereas complex environmental issues continue to be associated with all three economic endeavors, such as continued high use of pesticides and herbicides in pineapple and sugar production, their visibility is minor compared with those associated with traditional industrial development.

Furthermore, the population of Hawaii is on the whole remarkably healthy when judged by conventional indicators: with the distinct and notable exceptions of Polynesians as a group (of which Hawaiians are the most numerous), the longevity of all major ethnic groups, such as Caucasians, Japanese, Chinese, Koreans, and Filipinos, exceeds that of their mainland counterparts.[2] (See Table 7.1.) Hawaii has also become an extremely attractive place to practice medicine. The ratio of physicians to the general population is among the highest in the nation, although it is unevenly distributed throughout the state. For example, the one-mile radius surrounding Queen's Medical Center, Honolulu's primary medical facility, is said to contain the highest concentration of physicians per population in the world. Local economic predictions hold that by the year 2010, health care will be the primary industry in the state, exceeding tourism.

"Hawaii, the Health State," then, builds from a convergent set of

Table 7.1

Estimated Life Expectancy by Birth of Ethnic Groups in Hawaii, 1980*

Caucasian	Chinese	Filipino	Hawaiian	Japanese	Other
76.38	80.24	78.78	74.01	79.66	76.58

Sources: East–West Center, Population Institute
* Both sexes.

environmental, economic, and social factors already in place: a benign climate and environment which in comparative terms is relatively free of "environmental insults"; a highly trained and plentiful health care workforce; a population that, while aging, has substantial resources to invest in health care, including the pursuit of healthy life-styles; and a tourist industry anxious to gain a competitive edge by packaging these health attributes as a new and relatively unique industry value.

This latter factor forms a significant, and perhaps one of the more interesting, ingredients of Governor Waihee's vision. As the health state, Hawaii would serve as a major destination for the residents of less attractive physical and social environments. As people become more concerned with health issues, the argument goes, Hawaii gains in relative value through its ability to provide an alternative environment. "Recreation" under this formula would focus on its literal meaning: recreating the individual in settings designed to reverse the effects of those stresses. Simple and conventional tourism would be restructured to include all that was/is necessary to recreate the individual under stress: a completely healthy physical environment emphasizing out-door activities of all types, supplemented by the full range of medical services and convalescent needs. All of these would be effectively advertised by the obvious good health of the resident population.

Steps toward achieving these early 21st century goals are already underway. For example, a major Japanese-financed resort community on leeward Oahu has already entered the land acquisition, planning, and development stage, organized around the concept of supplying the complete outdoor life, complimented by requisite health facilities. For its part, the state has underwritten attempts to acquire major sporting events that would advertise Hawaii as a healthy environment, including blue water events like the America's and Kennwood Cups. A "corporate games" festival, inaugurated in October 1990, featuring teams representing transnational corporations competing in a wide variety of events is meant to symbolize the commonplace unification of corporate goals with the norm of fitness/health. The annual Aloha State Games, featuring competition in 45 sports from arm wrestling to canoeing to the decathlon and horseshoe pitching, have become a vehicle for eliciting mass participation from both residents and visitors at all skill levels. The volunteer labor force alone for these games numbers in the thousands, and corporate sponsorship is both visible and strong. These activities join an already long list of more conventional running, biking, swimming, canoeing, and walking events featured almost weekly, all of which celebrate as a norm extensive physical activity in an attractive setting.

Steps such as these to produce a value-added "health" component to tourism are but one aspect of a broader commitment the state has made to its conception of health, which extends from an activist concern with the mechanics of health insurance coverage to the core dynamics of its political economy. Increasingly, state economic planners are looking to the health care industry as an alternative to both traditional tourism and a declining agricultural sector. That health care should be perceived as an industry and a social service, both capable of being developed under the aegis of state planning, is consistent with the liberal political culture that has emerged in Hawaii since statehood.

For most of continental America, statehood is but a dim aspect of its received history. For those living in Hawaii, it is a recent and important experience. Historically, statehood has been associated with a commitment to a tradition of political liberalism as new political forces moved into government imbued with the spirit of reform. Since 1959 Hawaii has been sensitive to the ideological tides sweeping across the United States while at the same time remaining loyally identified with the commitments formed within the political coalition responsible for achieving statehood. This coalition, located within the Democratic Party, was anchored by Japanese-Americans emerging for the first time as a political force and led by highly decorated and recognized war heroes, who in the immediate postwar period added legal educations to their military accomplishments. As a group they represented a newly developed middle-class faction that had grown out of a prewar history of virulent plantation labor struggles.

The period dating from the overthrow of the Hawaiian monarchy in 1892 until the onset of World War II was one of unrelieved Republican

Party dominance. It was also a period characterized by self-conscious social, economic, and political domination by a narrow Caucasian elite. For those struggling to gain the right to full and effective political participation, the Democratic Party was the obvious vehicle. When these emerging ethnic groups achieved legislative power in 1954, the political program from which they took their cues was mainland reform liberalism. The central organizing principle for this reform-minded coalition was the application and extension of political rights to ensure the place of its constituent, newly emerging groups.

The first ten years of statehood witnessed a significant boom in real estate and tourist industry development, attenuated by infusions of federal spending for the war in Vietnam. A prosperous and growing economy provided ample means to extend strong public commitments across the range of social services. One important example was greatly increased spending on public education at all levels, including the building of a state-wide system of higher education that was perceived as a channel for upward mobility for "local" students unable to follow the career path of their more prosperous peers who traditionally attended mainland institutions. Another dimension included the development of relatively generous state support for public welfare, worker's compensation, and unemployment compensation. The International Longshore Workers Union (ILWU) had been a major vehicle for the unionization of plantation agriculture in Hawaii. With statehood it enjoyed great political standing and served to establish a climate within which the unionization of the entire public sector was achieved, thereby institutionalizing a form of "liberalism" that would in later years continue to inform legislative agendas, especially on social welfare issues. This has remained the case, as the relative decline of the ILWU in political influence has been compensated for by the growing importance of government service unions. Another aspect of this programmatic liberalism was the promotion of an active planning mechanism within state government. Thus, much to the dismay of many business groups who would prefer solely market-oriented solutions to development and social issues, Hawaiian state government has followed an activist and interventionist model in which state planning plays a large role.

By the 1970s Hawaii had earned the label in some business circles of having an "undesirable" business climate, by which was meant a continuing penchant for supporting labor values and structuring new economic ventures through state mechanisms.[3] But, tellingly, these rhetorical assaults were most strident within the small-business community. In macro political and economic terms, a compromise appears to have been engineered during these decades that provided for the shift of big-business support from the Republican to the Democratic Party within a broad understanding that the latter would embrace a program of continued economic development, essentially through tourism. Like all such "policy stories" this one is far more complex than suggested by this telling.[4] The "compromise" has been itself a developmental undertaking without conscious articulation so much as the working-out of the structural dynamics that inform the political economy. For example, during the administrations of George Ariyoshi (1973–86) efforts were made through governmental planning mechanisms to slow growth. Although some of these actions did provoke complaints from "big" business that the state was overregulated and fostered an "anti-business" climate, the large firms in the economy at the same time accepted the fact that electoral fortunes had shifted decisively to the Democratic Party, and their financial support followed accordingly. In turn the Democratic political leadership has provided a development agenda essentially congenial to those interests. The result has been to deny the Republican Party access to its traditional source of electoral funding.[5]

Ironically, the vicissitudes of local versus state politics have in recent years provided the four Hawaii counties (Kauai, Maui—which includes the islands of Lanai and Molokai—Hawaii, and the city and county of Honolulu with 85 percent of the state's population), with several Republican mayors. This, however, speaks far more to the ability of local politicians to utilize the Republican Party label as a passport into the general election, therein bypassing the dominant Democratic Party coalition's influence in the primary process, than to significant ideological differences between the parties. For all practical purposes, virtually all Hawaiian politicians are indistinguishable "liberals" who differ only moderately on particulars.

Since 1959, then, Hawaii has been effectively a one-party state, displaying unbroken Democratic dominance in both houses of the state legislature and the executive. Correspondingly, the Republican Party has grown proportionately weaker: in the 1990 legislative elections Republicans won only six seats in the 45-member House and three in the 25-seat Senate. This one-party dominance within the context of the grand political economic compromise has meant that all major effective political disputes take place within and between the various factions of the dominant Democratic Party. On social welfare issues this has had the effect of relatively isolating the small-business community, which has seen itself most relatively disadvantaged by progressive social welfare legislation.[6] Overall these dynamics accounted for the general continuation of Hawaii's liberal politics during the 1970s and, more interestingly, during the Reagan years.[7]

One last point remains to be made before turning directly to innovations within the health sector. The events of the past five years have involved a rather unique confluence of factors involving both the structure of the political economy and the role of new political actors. Structurally, as suggested above, the Democratic Party became the repository of a "traditional" liberalism and through its dominance "protected" the local environment from those features of Reaganism that took hold in many other states. Moreover, the economic environment during the Ariyoshi administration was one of generally sustained, if moderate, growth that provided a generally supportive climate for continued governmental action.[8] This was followed during the first term of Governor Waihee (1987–90) by rather extraordinary budgetary surpluses, brought about by a booming tourist industry and striking real estate inflation initiated in large part by Japanese investment.[9]

The personality of major actors in the health sector has also made a difference. The election of John Waihee in 1986 brought to office a young, dynamic native Hawaiian governor bent on making a name for himself through exceptional governmental programs. As his health director, Waihee appointed John Lewin, an equally young and dynamic physician with a background of political activism and a commitment to expanding the boundaries of health promotion activities. In contrast to his predecessors, and like Waihee, Lewin's dynamism is focused on an activist role for government in addressing social problems, an attitude he has worked to instill in his rather large and unwieldy department.[10]

During these critical years the health committees in both houses of the Hawaii state legislature were chaired by individuals keenly interested in health questions and not themselves representatives of any portion of the provider industry. In the House, Representative James Shon, a full-time legislator with a background in curriculum development at the University of Hawaii, was entering his second term.[11] In the Senate, Andrew Levin, a young attorney from the island of Hawaii, was widely viewed as "enlightened" with respect to social welfare issues. Although in no way constituting a group, Waihee, Lewin, Shon, and Levin were ideologically sympathetic toward the policy initiatives that were to occur.

The emergence of these actors within the arena of health politics in Hawaii is due in part, as I have argued, to the structural politics Hawaii provides. It also, however, seems akin to two related developments occurring during the same period in the broader context of American politics. One is the role the states have played generally in governmental innovation; the other is the attraction health care politics has provided for political leadership talent. With regard to the first, David Osborne has pointed to a tendency under the Reagan administration for various issues, especially social welfare issues, to be "pushed down" to the state level. One outcome of the budgetary struggles between Reagan and the Congress was to transform existing budget levels into strategic targets, which the Congress was then forced into defending against proposed administration cuts. Lessened federal revenues led both to the Reagan budget deficits and a narrowed federal social welfare responsibility with very few new programs. Of necessity the states have come to be, in Osborne's phrase, "laboratories of democracy," as they have sought novel solutions to the riddle of providing new solutions within very limited budgets to structural changes in the economy and society. This process has scrambled traditional policy positions of Democrats and Republicans, liberals and conservatives at the state level, and drawn new figures into the political arena. Save for the fact of Democratic Party dominance described above, Hawaii would seem no exception to this process.[12]

Where many policy arenas have shrunk in relative importance with the budget constraints of the 1980s, health care has proved just the opposite. The persistent growth in health care expenditures throughout the nation has rendered it a particular source of attention within federal politics, where Lawrence D. Brown asserts it has become the site of a "new activism." The enormous stakes in this particular game are evident to all, and the endemic crises of the health care system have served to draw to the fore both talented and committed policy participants as it becomes clear that in a literal sense health care policy is "where the action is." As Brown comments:

Payment System and catastrophic provisions are the most salient departures from expectations, ideology, and past practice but they are only promontories in an impressive range of expansionist legislative and regulatory measures adopted during the Reagan years. Indeed, some sizable extension of the federal role in health care has become almost an annual event.[13]

A parallel dynamic is at work in the states where the problems arising from the incomplete nature of federal health initiatives have combined with budgetary stringency to produce repeated crises of care and coverage. These issues have very much been a part of the emergence of new leadership in Hawaii determined to address and resolve them and by so doing become a model for both other states and the federal government.[14]

Health Policy Innovations

In the eyes of its creators, the State of Hawaii Health Insurance Plan (SHIP) has been the keystone to the emergence of Hawaii as the health state. To most health professionals, the ability to develop SHIP was entirely dependent on the prior success of the Prepaid Health Care Act.

The Prepaid Health Care Act

Passed in 1974, the Prepaid Health Care Act mandates an employer-based insurance coverage system for all employees not covered by collective bargaining. It operates through the existing insurance system, which is dominated by two major providers, the Hawaii Medical Services Association, covering approximately 80 percent of the insured, and Kaiser, the state's dominant health maintenance organization (HMO). The law stipulates that "the plan must provide health care benefits equal to or medically substitutable for benefits provided by plans having the largest number of subscribers in the state," thereby guaranteeing this relationship to the primary providers and ensuring that employees covered under this plan would not receive a lesser form of coverage. The legislation has also provided the opportunity for the periodic negotiation with providers of mandated benefits, services which must be provided in the basic universal package.

Financing for the system is shared equally by employees and employers with the exception that the employee in no case contributes more than 1.5 percent of total wages. Employees are not permitted to refuse coverage, and coverage is universal within the category of non-unionized employees, with a few designated exceptions, such as real estate sales agents who receive all of their income from commissions. Business sector opposition to early drafts of the plan was resolved with the inclusion of two key provisions. One permits employees covered by two plans—through, for example, spousal membership or multiple employment—to choose the coverage they wish to apply. The more important provision was designed to meet the opposition of small-business owners upon whom the additional costs of providing care would fall most heavily. The act created a special premium supplementation fund for such marginal small employers. Supplementation is available only to employers of fewer than eight employees if the employees' share of coverage exceeds 1.5 percent of total payroll and if the amount of excess is greater than 5 percent of pre-tax income. In the first year of the act, the legislature appropriated $166,000 for supplementation. In practice, small employers have found it difficult to apply for supplementation and tend not to do so. Of far greater significance has been the fact that by requiring all employers to provide coverage, health care contractors have been able to create a community risk pool that provides rates for small employers comparable to large employers.

It is instructive to note that a major motivation for the development of the Prepaid Health Care Act was the belief that other states and the federal government were also moving in the direction of mandating compulsory health insurance. The 1974 act was the concluding piece to a 1967 legislative request (Act 198, Session Laws of Hawaii, 1967) that the state's Legislative Reference Bureau study jointly the issues of temporary disability insurance, covered by legislation in 1969, and prepaid health care. The author of the 1971 study that formed the basis of the 1974 legislation cites as the context for prepaid health insurance both the repeated federal efforts to produce a compulsory health care act and the passage of Medicare and Medicaid in 1965.[15] In fact, these were the very grounds on which the Chamber of Commerce opposed the bill during its 1973–74 legislative gestation: that it was unnecessary because it would soon become subject to federal preemption. Advocates of the bill saw themselves not so much as bold innovators but as anxious to join what they viewed as an impending national development.

It is of equal interest to note that both the author of the original report and its legislative sponsors believed this legislation would eliminate the "gap group." At the time people without hospital insurance constituted almost 12 percent of the population, while those without physician insurance coverage amounted to more than 17 percent. In promoting the bill, its conference committee manager, Democratic Representative Hiroshi Kato, claimed that, "[T]his bill establishes the concept that every resident of this state has the right to good health care."[16] A decade and a half later Jack Lewin said of SHIP that it is but a step toward a more important goal. "We haven't admitted the obvious, that health care should be a right of citizenship—a promise through government."[17]

SHIP

The creation of SHIP in 1989 is, therefore, unique not so much for its presumed universality, since that is precisely what the Prepaid Health Care Act sponsors thought they were achieving in 1974, but rather for its combination of the elements of universality, comprehensive care, and attention to prevention. The latter is, in Lewin's mind, the critical element of the three, for it is here that the larger idea of Hawaii as the health state begins to gain substance. In this view health insurance itself is a lever for social change. The first task is to convince people to choose healthy life-styles; the second is to sell the argument to business that including health values in business makes good economic sense; and the third is to move to a broader social agenda of creating a healthy society. As Lewin wrote in an in-house communication to Department of Health personnel shortly after SHIP's announcement, "Every health professional and citizen in our state may take pride in the fact that Hawaii is about to make history by implementing the most ambitious health insurance program in the United States."[18]

Like the Prepaid Health Care Act, the political strength of SHIP lay in the fact that it would operate through existing provider organizations, thereby being institutionally positioned among market forces that would act to control costs. A major selling point of the program was its presumed ability to effect overall utilization patterns, especially the common tendency of noninsured people to utilize emergency room facilities in lieu of primary care and other more effective preventive mechanisms. One predicted benefit that sweetened its political palatability among providers was a reduction in the bad debt/uncollectables pool.

The enabling legislation, which was adopted on April 28, 1989, and signed into law in June, provided $4 million for the first 16 months of operation and $10 million for the second full year. It was vital to the passage of the act that the Department of Health could persuade legislative committees that these limited amounts would be sufficient to fund the act and that it would not become a vehicle for slippage from private and Medicaid coverage into SHIP. State spokespersons have been careful to bill SHIP as, in Lewin's words, "a partnership between government, individuals and families, and the private sector. Government subsidizes insurance coverage for those unable to pay. Insurance companies provide the coverage and the already existing health care providers deliver direct care."[19]

The gap group addressed by SHIP does not encompass the entire uninsured population. Rather, SHIP is targeted to those "who have been uninsured by public or private health care coverage programs and who are at a low enough income level where they cannot access current health care coverage."[20] At the time of SHIP's passage, the size of this group was estimated at 30,000 to 35,000 people. In retrospect it is clear that the creation of this gap group has been caused in part by structural changes in the economy that have increased the percentage of the working population not covered by collective bargaining, the original concern of the Prepaid Health Care Act, and below the fully employed threshold. These structural dynamics are equally prevalent within the economy of the continental United States and contribute significantly to the gap group throughout the nation. The particular contribution of the Prepaid Health Care Act has been to winnow the overall gap group to roughly 5 percent of the population by removing all fully employed individuals. A 1988 survey found this remaining gap group to be composed primarily of the unemployed (30 percent of the uninsured), dependents of low-income workers (particularly children), part-time workers, off-Oahu residents, immigrants, seasonal workers and students.

SHIP is, therefore, conceived of as a vehicle to subsidize affordable health care coverage that builds on both the Prepaid Health Care Act and Medicaid. Initially, only Hawaii residents who had no previous health insurance in the preceding three months were eligible for the program. SHIP establishes a sliding fee schedule. Individuals under the stipulated poverty level (the defined poverty level is termed, 100 percent of poverty) pay nothing. Payments rise with income so that between 251 and 300 percent of the federal poverty standard, adults pay for the entire cost of insurance, while health care for children is still somewhat subsidized. Only those below 300 percent of the federal poverty standard are eligible, which for Hawaii in 1989 amounted to $41,759 for a family of four.[21] To be eligible for SHIP the applicant would need to prove ineligibility for Medicare, Medicaid, CHAMPUS, and VA benefits.[22]

The logic that underlies SHIP makes one important assumption and contains another fundamental philosophical premise. First, it is a temporary service, a "hand up" for those in need, "most of whom will be fitting into the Prepaid Health Care system soon"; and second, the emphasis in SHIP is on preventive and primary care, "health" insurance instead of "sickness" insurance.[23] To accomplish the latter, SHIP focuses on services such as health appraisals, of which well-baby, well-child care, and age-appropriate health screenings are typical; and a package of basic primary care items, such as 12 physician visits a year with a $5 co-payment per visit, laboratory and X-ray services, immunizations, and the like. Larger cost items are deemphasized and where possible shifted over to Medicaid, where spend-downs render the individual eligible for Medicaid. Hospitalization is limited to five days with a dollar limit of $2,500. Two days are allowed for maternity care. Exclusions include elective surgery and high-cost tertiary care. Costly care and procedures such as neonatal intensive care, end-stage renal disease care, and open-heart surgery are shifted, where possible, to Medicaid.

Enrollment costs for the program are shared between individuals and the state. In its first full year of operation $1.7 million was obtained from individual payments. The first year projection of total coverage was 150,000 enrollee months and a year-end enrollment of 20,000 persons. As indicated below, this target figure has not been reached.[24] Contracts for the first year's service were signed by Kaiser (limited to 1,000 Oahu residents) and the Hawaii Medical Services Association (HMSA).

A key feature of the program is its implementation structure, which was designed to identify and enroll people unaccustomed to participation in a medical insurance scheme and put off by bureaucratic mechanisms; people who are often viewed as "outside the system." Implementation, begun on April 16, 1990, was statewide and organized to eliminate barriers to entry. Forms were shortened to collect only the most basic information; asset data were not collected. A statewide toll-free number is available for those wishing to call for information. Certain persons, such as those dropping off Medicaid rolls, have instant access to the program, as do pregnant women and children. A broadly based community outreach program, assisted by over 200 volunteers trained to help applicants fill out the necessary forms, has also been developed. Close cooperation between the Departments of Labor and Industrial Relations and Human Services provides a referral service for SHIP.

One year after initiation SHIP has enrolled approximately one-third of the gap group in its programs. Less than 2 percent of enrollees are in the 251–300 percent of poverty range; 56 percent are below 100 percent of poverty, which in Hawaii is equivalent to $7,608 per annum for a single person and $15,408 for a family of four. These figures lead some to see the program as a distinct success. Lewin, for example, continues to see SHIP as a model for other states that can thread the gap between a concern for providing coverage and the attendant fear of uncontrolled costs. The key for him, as suggested above, is the emphasis within SHIP on prevention and primary care. Admittedly the program does not provide all the benefits of private medical care, or even Medicaid, but by placing emphasis on primary care it works to constrain demand for the health system as a whole, and it organizes recipients toward the more efficient allocation of services.

The first full evaluation of SHIP, released in March 1992, was generally positive, although it pointed to substantial problems within the program's initial implementation and current operation. The report recognized numerous administrative problems in the initial implementation of the program that were "brute forced" through to bring it on stream but which remain to be resolved on a more efficient, long-term basis. The initial marketing of the plan was apparently insufficiently focused, as SHIP administrators demonstrated their lack of a sure sense of where it might best be marketed. An additional concern has been the relatively smaller-than-expected number of participating primary care clinics. This has complicated the outreach features of the plan because these clinics serve important target populations, such as recently arrived immigrant groups, and thereby limit program effectiveness. A similar problem existed early in the program with a relative shortfall in the number of physicians, and especially primary care physicians, participating through HMSA. Through that organization's efforts to increase enrollments, however, this deficit has now been corrected. Currently 65 percent of the SHIP participating physicians are primary care physicians, as opposed to 55 percent in the normal HMSA physician mix.

SHIP has surprised its evaluators by being more cost effective than predicted. HMSA utilization rates, for example, have been one-half those of its general program subscribers. This compares with a utilization rate of 10 percent above normal for Kaiser subscribers. The presumed explanation for this unusual finding is that HMSA SHIP subscribers have not yet fully figured out how to use the somewhat more administratively complicated HMSA system compared with Kaiser's flat token fee HMO approach. These cost savings have permitted HMSA to return funds to the plan fund and build surpluses against catastrophic care expenditures. As a bottom line, the report concluded that a "big population" of potential SHIP beneficiaries still exists which the program has yet to reach. A second evaluational volume, due in 1992, will assess this population and efforts to reach it.[25]

Other voices in the health care community such as Jim Shon, are more skeptical that SHIP is meeting the real needs of the community. Shon points out that initial funding for the program owed more to the convenient budget surpluses enjoyed during the legislative session when it was approved than to a careful assessment of the genuine requirements of the system. It may also be the case that from the perspective of the overall health needs of the community, SHIP may have displaced a major initiative to provide long-term care insurance for the entire population that would have benefited from the same set of propitious political forces. SHIP proved a more popular issue, he argues, in part because it fit well with the interests of the local insurance providers.[26] From his perspective, SHIP is something less than the major innovation it is held to be. It is, rather, more a stop-gap measure made reasonable in Hawaii's circumstances by the existence of prepaid health care. If other states are to replicate SHIP, he sees it imperative that they begin with some form of prepaid health care. Not to lay down this preliminary step is to court the experience of Massachusetts which he predicts will develop into a cost disaster. (See Chapter Eight.) Shon believes the optimum model for the development of state-based health care systems is social security, which spreads payment across generations in a life-time accrual process.

SHIP has also displaced attention from other important elements within the local health care cost environment. One of these is the cost of delivering outpatient care, which is growing at a more rapid rate than hospital costs. The latter are controlled to some degree by the Certificate-of-Need process, whereas the former are not. Outside the regulatory loop, the explosive growth of high-technology equipment situated in the offices of private physicians contributes significantly both to overall cost and to safety issues with their related cost consequences.[27]

Other Areas of Concern

The concern that SHIP will leave too many loose ends dangling and that effective public policy management of health care is only possible within an overall integrated system of care was the basis for a companion measure adopted by the 1990 legislature that calls for an extensive study of Hawaii's health care delivery system. Specifically the legislation requests the governor to organize a blue-ribbon panel to study the system and prepare recommendations for the legislature's consideration and action. The panel is instructed to develop a more comprehensive understanding of the health care system through widespread community consultation and to develop recommendations to facilitate more effective cost control and the more effective application of health care. While acknowledging the key role played by the Prepaid Health Care Act and the combination of coverage established by SHIP, Medicaid, the Community Health Nursing Program, and the Certificate-of-Need process, legislators underscored those problems not yet addressed by state legislation. These include the burgeoning elderly population, a growing shortage of certain health care professionals, acute and long-term care bed shortages, and dramatically increasing health care costs. This point of view indicates far less enthusiasm for the image of Hawaii as the health state than those held by Lewin and the governor.[28]

Not mentioned in this context but of continuing concern to health care advocates in Hawaii, are the persistent problems with state health and mental health care programs for native Hawaiians. The generally poor health of native Hawaiians stands in stark contrast to the generally good health of the rest of the population. The reasons for this poor health profile are numerous and are subject to considerable and contentious differences of emphasis and interpretation. Where many see the issue as one of improving access to medical care for Hawaiians, others, including many activists within the native Hawaiian community, see the issue in the broader perspective of cultural conflict between Hawaiian and "modern" life-styles. These issues have been addressed in part through the Native Hawaiian Health Care Act passed by Congress in 1988. As the law is currently in the early stages of implementation, it is too early to assess its likely impact on overall Hawaiian health.[29]

Hawaii has had the indignity of having its mental health facilities ranked fiftieth of the states for several years running since the mid 1980s. Lewin, with the cooperation of his legislative allies, has struggled to overcome this situation, one that owes much to the existence of an antiquated facility and an organizational climate mired in traditional bureaucracy. A new state mental health hospital opened in October 1991. To deal with the organizational issues, Lewin, early in his first term, appointed Henry Foley, an extremely able health care manager with considerable experience in a variety of mainland health care settings, to head the state mental health division. Foley has gained small but persistent successes in transforming the mental health climate in Hawaii, but it has remained an area of contention.[30]

In the news release announcing the composition of the blue-ribbon panel on December 7, 1990, the governor stressed that the panel "represents a cross section of Hawaii's economic and social leaders including representatives of business, insurance providers, unions, academia, consumers, government agencies and healthcare providers."[31] The actual appointment of the panel proved an act of delicate political maneuvering for the governor's office as it struggled to represent those constituencies in a manner that balanced the reality of existing vested interests with the prospect that the panel might actually break new ground. As finally constituted, the panel presents a pattern very similar to that noted by Robert Alford in his well-known study of health care reform efforts in New York City. These he found to be more notable for their success in symbolically legitimizing the major players in their previously established roles than for producing reforms.[32] It is, of course, impossible at this juncture to predict the fate of this newly constituted panel, but one does want to acknowledge it as a classic instance in which the same group of players that is charged with the seemingly "neutral" task of "gathering information" about the system supported the growth of that very system within its existing configuration.

Not unexpectedly, the governor did not emphasize these aspects of the panel in his statement. Rather, his language closely reproduces that identified with SHIP. "Hawaii's health care delivery system," he asserted,

> like those everywhere in the nation, is changing dramatically. We must get out in front of that change and decide our own future. . . . The panel will give us a clear understanding of our health care delivery system and will provide recommendations to strengthen it. A healthy system means a healthy people.

Jack Lewin added,

> The panel's job is critical to Hawaii's health and economic well-being. The federal government is not willing to make the difficult decisions necessary to control health care costs as we strive for quality care for all. This is a really tough job, but we are the state that can set the national health agenda . . . This historic work will be a vital component in our efforts to make Hawaii truly the 'Health State.'[33]

These innovations in health care proceed from an implicit model that essentially equates medical care and health. Within this frame the major policy issues revolve around access to care and its associated costs. One effort to enlarge this frame is to include within it a concern for the demand for medical care and to work to limit that demand. That has been both national policy since the Surgeon General's 1978 Report *Healthy People* and state policy as all 50 states have adopted some version of a program for disease prevention and health promotion. As I have detailed, it is SHIP's guiding principle. These efforts to reduce medical care demand by focusing on the role of the individual in health matters and to give emphasis to access to primary medical care compete with broader views of health that view control of environmental factors as essential to establishing conditions that affect the health of populations as a whole.[34] Within the arena of health care politics, those concerned with medical care issues are often not those concerned with these broader environmental issues.

In Hawaii a distinct exception has been Jim Shon. He has used his position as chair of the Health Committee in the House of Representatives to bring attention to the possible dangers of bioengineered agents being introduced into the Hawaiian environment and to regulate those agents when and where appropriate. On this issue, Shon's liberalism is consistent: he advocates a strong state interventionist role both in expanding access to health care to the uninsured and in regulating the overall health of the population to ensure freedom from environmental toxins. He has publicly been labeled a conservative by the state's agricultural lobby, which includes strong representation from University of Hawaii's agricultural and biological scientists, who portray him as obstructing the march of scientific and technological progress.

Hawaii agriculture is, and has been for at least two decades, a declining sector of the economy. Pineapple and sugar production, the two historic mainstays of the plantation economy, have been kept alive over this period primarily through political intervention: subsidies for sugar at both the federal and state level are made necessary because Hawaii sugar is simply not viable at world prices; and exceptions from federal environmental regulation to permit pesticides for both crops to be used in Hawaii long after they have been banned on the mainland United States. The results have been controversial in Hawaii. In 1981 Heptaclor, a substance then banned on the continental United States but used in Hawaii to control ants that destroy pineapple plants, found its way into the state's milk supply, posing a particular danger to children and nursing mothers. (The chemical was used on the pineapple plant, which was then converted to "green chop" and fed to cows.) Within two years of this event several drinking wells on the center of Oahu were found to be contaminated with other organic pesticides that had leached through the fields into the water table. At one point contamination of the underlying "cap lens" that supplies virtually all Oahu's water was feared.

These events pointed both to the relative political strength of the old plantation sector to gain regulatory exceptions that redounded to its economic benefit and to the relative weakness of the Department of Health to intervene effectively.

Under the Waihee administration, and as a direct result of the legislative/administration coalition discussed above, efforts have been made to deal with water issues that seek to redress the result if not entirely to address the cause of the problem. These have included a significant ten-fold increase in the number of tests of drinking water, creating an environmental superfund to protect the environment from oil and hazardous material spills, a $50 million wastewater revolving fund, and building a new $35 million laboratory that will permit increased technological sophistication in the treatment of water.

Shon's efforts to push the state past this conventional response mode to anticipate new up-stream health problems has been far more controversial. Of central concern has been the introduction of legislation to monitor and control the introduction of bioengineered organisms in Hawaii. The 1988 legislature passed Act 193, a notification provision, that requires companies intending the release into the environment of such agents to send an application to the state as well as the federal government. This notification activity provides at least three advantages to the state. First, it permits the state to receive the application early, giving it 120 days to respond, rather than the normal 30 days or less required by the federal government. In these latter circumstances the environmental assessments previously have often been completed before the state could affect the process. Second, the advisory opinion of the attorney general requires firms making such application to supply the state with confidential product information. In the opinion of one state official, "they can no longer hide information from us. Before they did it routinely."[35] Third, the state can stipulate conditions to proposed environmental impacts that it feels will more effectively protect the environment from migration of the bioengineered organism, such as overhead rather than drip irrigation to promote more complete germination of seeds. These risk assessment activities are viewed as critical to the state's efforts to control such technology and, thereby, enhance the health of citizens.

The response of the state's agriculture lobby to these efforts has been both intense and extensive. Again citing an involved state official, "this notification bill has got the whole state scared." This legislation, of relative insignificance in and of itself, draws strong reaction from the agricultural industry in part because it threatens to shift the regulatory site from the federal level, where the well-placed Hawaii congressional delegation can serve the industry through effective intervention, to the state level, where the play of other interests is less predictable. It would, as this official puts it, "keep the USDA from controlling this technology."[36] The fact that Hawaii's politics historically and preeminently are land politics, coupled with the decline of sugar and pineapple agriculture and the desire of agricultural interests to discover new products, for which bioengineering is the most likely channel, ensures that this turf will be highly contested and that efforts to control it through public health policy will evoke controversy.

Discussion and Analysis

The efforts of one segment of Hawaii's political leadership to promote the growth of a "health culture" in the state may be viewed as one state's attempted solution to the vexing economic questions that attend the transition to a "postindustrial" service economy. In Hawaii the transition is rendered somewhat simpler since the state lacked a genuine industrial period, although plantation agriculture performed that role historically in the consolidation of its dominant wealth structure. Tourism came to the fore in the years following World War II by "democratizing" what had been a prewar pleasure of the rich; the storied vacation to the islands. Tourism, however, has become an increasingly competitive market and efforts to distinguish local settings are common to most popular tourist destinations. "Hawaii the Health State" becomes a vehicle for enshrining the value of health in the state's politics and making it a part of its political/social structure.

Just how much this value should be centered in the state's politics remains open to dispute. Characteristically, Jack Lewin is eager to extend the image and the vision. One begins, he argues, with the notion of the value added tourist dimension; "rejuvenating excursions," he calls them. One then moves beyond this logical extension of the existing environment to utilize Hawaii as the model of a future society, in which all elements of the community are viewed with respect to their health implications. Transportation, for example, is a source of continued stress in urban environments. Thus, new settlements have to be designed specifically to reduce those stresses. This may involve taking the service economy back to where the industrial economy began, locating people and their work in proximity, and then ensuring that the quality of those settlements, unlike their industrial precursors, is equal to the demands of health promotion. A primary feature of this strategy is a campaign to restore the quality of public space.[37] Since mid 1991 Lewin has promoted this vision, with SHIP and health promotion activities as the cornerstones, as "Hawaii's seamless Health Care Plan." To the extent that in some respects politics is always about the contested terrain between what should be regarded as part of the public sphere and what is private, Lewin's vision situates health squarely in the center of forthcoming political debate in Hawaii.

Hawaii's health care leaders also have been very conscious of the state's possible leadership in national health care matters. Both Lewin and Waihee have taken advantage of their roles as heads of their respective national organizations to promote Hawaii's accomplishments in health care. These appear particularly strong when compared with recently announced plans by other states or national groups to address gap group issues. Hawaii already has in place many of the provisions of the more promising plans such as UNY*Care or the proposals of the Pepper Commission.[38] Discussions are currently underway among Hawaii's key health care participants to explore further modifications of the system to include features of these other programs, such as full coverage of dependents, further extension of medical and hospital benefits, operation of the system under a global budget with a single payer authority, and a system-wide reform of billing and information practices to recoup savings from program administration. Such a unified proposal is currently being submitted to the governor's blue-ribbon commission for consideration.

Hawaii is frequently held to be an ideal laboratory for social research. Its isolation, complex ethnic population, and relatively small size make it suitable for social experimentation. From that perspective its efforts to develop innovations such as Prepaid Health Care, health promotion through environmental protection, and SHIP can stand as "virtual experiments" for other states to study and model. On the other hand, Hawaii as a whole is socially much like the isolated valleys on the north side of Maui that, cut off from other portions of the island, develop their own miniecosystems with flora and fauna unique to that place alone. Hawaii is the only island state; the only state to have been a kingdom; and the only state to develop its particular form of plantation agriculture. From these have come a political culture and climate that render it different in important respects from its sister states.

What it holds in common with these states are its ties through the federal system to the range of national programs that impact health issues at the local level. It has experienced the dynamics of Reaganomics that have increased the obligation on all states to significantly expand their involvement in the financing and provisioning of health care services. The Prepaid Health Care Act of 1974 has proved an excellent vehicle for this purpose. Through its mechanisms, significant extensions of care in the form of mental health benefits, assistance for alcohol and drug treatment, and mammography examinations have all been channeled in recent years. This act has also served as a platform upon which to construct a community-wide effort to address issues of cost control at the state level. All told, this act, amply antedating Reaganomics, has proved an effective liberal bulwark against policies that would contract public sector involvement in health care.

Notes

1. I wish to thank Robert Grossman of the Hawaii Department of Health for his assistance in providing documents for the preparation of this chapter. I would also like to acknowledge the Social Science Research Institute at the University of Hawaii for its release-time support during the period in which this chapter was written.

2. The overall death rate of native Hawaiians is 34 percent higher than that of the total U.S. population. This group also experiences distinctly higher rates for diseases of the heart, cancer, cerebrovascular disease, and diabetes mellitus. Eldon Wegner, "A Framework for Assessing Health Needs," *Social Process in Hawaii* 32 (1989).

3. This language recycles over the decades. In April 1991 a leading local attorney specializing in facilitating Japanese investment in Hawaii cited the identical objections, warning that such an unfavorable business climate will "kill the golden goose." *Honolulu Advertiser,* 24 April 1991.

4. For the notion of policy stories see Deborah Stone, *Policy, Paradox, and Political Reason* (Glenview, IL: Scott, Foresman and Company, 1988).

5. In the 1990 gubernatorial election the incumbent Democratic candidate outspent the Republican by a ratio of four to one and won decisively.

6. In part this is because the larger firms have been relatively more successful in passing on the costs of these programs to consumers, whereas, typically, smaller businesses tend to exist in a more competitive price environment wherein such cost distributions are less easy to accomplish.

7. Consistent with the premise that "real" political issues take place within the Democratic Party, it is important to note that George Ariyoshi, who became governor in 1973 upon the death of John A. Burns (the "architect" of the grand coalition), was a fiscal conservative to match most mainland Republican governors. His brand of fiscal conservatism was, however, more gradualist than Reagan's.

8. Many would dispute this on the grounds of two significant "down" economic periods, one occurring at the end of the Burns administration, spanning the period 1972–75 and the other at the end of the Ariyoshi administration, 1983–85. Each was accompanied by various "budget crises" and cutbacks in state governmental services. The argument I am making here is that these were in effect "normal" cyclical phases of the Hawaii economy, albeit they owed something to larger U.S. economic system dynamics. As this is being written, the state is approaching another "crisis," this one caused by a decline in the extraordinary revenues available to the state over the past several years. An underlying text in all this is that tourist-based economies are highly sensitive to macro changes in disposable income.

9. Recessionary slowdowns to the tourist industry have induced the governor to call for restrictions in the fiscal 1991 operating budget and for a cut of $150

million in the previously announced executive budget for the 1991–93 biennium.

10. John (Jack) Lewin's role in this administration is worth a separate piece on the capabilities and limitations of individual actors within state government. The department that he inherited was widely seen as a disaster. It is the largest department in the state government with a budget of $300 million. Among other tasks it is charged with running the state hospitals on the neighbor islands, which lack the density of private facilities and physicians characteristic of Oahu, and the state mental health facility on Oahu. Its immediate two past directors had been appointees with long ties to the controlling faction of the Democratic Party who could be counted on to do little more than preside over what had become a very large and ineffective bureaucratic organization.

Lewin is a person who describes himself as an activist first and foremost, to whom medicine has been almost incidental. He sees himself committed to an ever increasing understanding of the human condition and the diversity of human experience. The various crises that currently beset medical and health care are, for him, opportunities to invest government with these values. It is often the case that when such self-identified activists find themselves in governmental roles, they find themselves "in front" of their key constituencies on various issues. This has certainly been true of Lewin, who is frequently described both admiringly and derisively as an "idealist" and a "dreamer."

11. James Shon is an equally interesting political story. Although Hawaii politics has very little of what an outsider would recognize as a conventional "left/right, liberal/conservative" dimension, Shon has become something of a "radical," at least within the perceptions of the local medical community which has worked assiduously for his defeat in the last two political campaigns. His "sins" against the establishment are of two kinds: one is a committed interest in environmental issues that have direct, or strongly probable, public health consequences. Typical of these has been the issue of biogenetic testing in the agricultural sector. A more recent interest and concern has been the issue of the health effects of nonionizing radiation, especially that associated with several very large military antennas located on Oahu, and the pathways of high voltage transmission wires.

The second major source of "complaint" has been his support for two legislative proposals that, under certain circumstances, would extend to nurses and clinical psychologists the physician's privilege of prescribing medication. In the 1990 legislative election the local medical establishment strongly supported his primary election opponent, one effect of which was to mobilize nurses to their most public level of political action ever. Shon won by about eight hundred votes. In the general election he defeated his conservative Republican opponent for the second time, winning by less than 300 votes in a race in which health and abortion issues figured strongly. That an election would be contested so explicitly on issues is rare in Hawaii politics. Immediately following the election, Shon was drawn into an intense battle within the Democratic Party between incumbent and contesting factions for control of the House. He sided with the incumbent leadership and retained control of his Health Committee chairmanship. His House seat has been abolished in the 1991 reapportionment of the state legislature.

12. David Osborne, *Laboratories of Democracy* (Cambridge: Harvard University Press, 1988).

13. Lawrence D. Brown, "The New Activism: Federal Health Politics

Revisited," *Bulletin of the New York Academy of Medicine* 66 (July–August, 1990): 293.

14. Lewin has been sensitive to bringing new voices into the statewide discourse. He has surrounded himself with a set of deputies who are amenable to his vision of health care and the role the department may play in that, and who themselves are relatively young, talented professionals. The result is a group quite willing, as Brown suggests, to turn its back on conventional wisdom in the search for novel solutions.

15. Stefan A. Riesenfeld, "Prepaid Health Care in Hawaii," University of Hawaii, Legislative Reference Bureau, Report No. 2, 1971. The imminent nature of such coverage in the minds of the author and affected legislators can be gained from this paragraph that completes the contextual narrative preceding the outline of a model bill's provisions: "The newest development in the field of compulsory health insurance is the President's announcement of his Family Health Insurance Plan for children. . . . Legislative proposals are promised for January 1971. . . . Finally, it should be noted that the general desirability of prepayment plan protection against medical cost was again strongly stressed in June 1970." *Recommendations of the United States Department of Health, Education and Welfare, Task Force on Medicaid and Related Programs," 9.*

16. State of Hawaii, House Reports, 1974.

17. Interview by author with John Lewin, 29 October 1990.

18. John Lewin, "From Vision to Reality: Insurance Plan Establishes Hawaii as the Health State," *Hawaii Health Messenger*, State Department of Health, 52, no. 2, 1989.

19. John Lewin, "Hawaii's System of Universal Access to Health Care Coverage," address to the Advisory Council on Social Security, Department of Health and Human Services, 27 July 1990: 3.

20. Lewin, "Hawaii's System of Universal Access to Health Care Coverage," 3.

21. There is no discernable compelling logic for this figure. Apparently Lewin and his Health Department colleagues felt that level would both sell politically and was a realistic assessment of living costs in Hawaii, which typically has the highest cost of living in the nation.

22. Lewin, "From Vision to Reality."

23. Hawaii Department of Health document, 21 April 1990.

24. Ibid.

25. SHIP Evaluation Report, Center for Health Research, Portland, Oregon, contracted through University of Hawaii, School of Public Health, Mark Hornbrook, P.I. March 26, 1992.

26. Another legislative player, Senator Bert Kobayashi, who at the time of SHIP's formulation was the outgoing chair of the Senate Health Committee, suggests that insurance interests were drawn into the program more through the Department of Health's inability to formulate funding and implementation procedures clearly than through the industry's intense concerns to dominate the program. Interview by author, 13 February 1991.

27. Interview by author, 17 January 1991. On the cost side of this situation see John M. Eisenbert, *Doctor's Decisions and the Cost of Medical Care* (Ann Arbor: Health Administration Press, 1986), Chapter 2.

28. Hawaii, Department of Health, "Study of Hawaii's Health Care Delivery System," (Draft memo, 17 December 1990).

29. For a recounting of the process leading to the passage of the Native Hawaiian Health Care Act and a statement of the broader cultural argument, see KeKuni Blaisdell, "Historical and Cultural Aspects of Native Hawaiian Health," in *Social Process in Hawaii* 23 (1989).

30. Foley resigned in late spring 1991 to accept a position with the University of Houston.

31. News Release from the Executive Chambers of the Governor, 7 (December 1990): 1. (Hereafter News Release.)

32. Robert Alford, *Health Care Politics* (Chicago: University of Chicago Press, 1975).

33. News Release: 1–2.

34. Meredith Turshen has called this a focus on the "social production of disease" and outlines the politics that typify it. See her *The Politics of Public Health* (New Brunswick: Rutgers University Press, 1990).

35. Interview by author, 12 February 1991.

36. Attributions of this sort are always difficult to measure, but Lewin's reappointment for a second term as health director was opposed in the Hawaii Senate. The unhappiness of segments of the agriculture industry with expansion of the state's regulatory role in this area played a large part. After a highly public set of hearings, Lewin was reaffirmed by a relatively comfortable majority.

37. Interview by author, 29 October 1990.

38. Dan E. Beauchamp and Ronald L. Rouse, "Universal New York Health Care, A Single-Payer Strategy Linking Cost Control and Universal Access," *The New England Journal of Medicine* 323 (6 September 1990): 640–644. A brief but excellent review of the Pepper Commission report (actually it is the U.S. Bipartisan Commission on Comprehensive Health Care) can be found in "Special Report: The Pepper Commission Report on Comprehensive Health Care," *New England Journal of Medicine* 323 (4 October 1990): 1005–1007.

8

Universal Health Care in Massachusetts: Lessons for the Future

Camille Ascuaga

The story of universal health care in Massachusetts attests to the inherent vulnerability and fragility of state policy reforms. Once the favorite child of a Democratic governor and his administration, the universal health care law fell into disfavor when a new governor and a different party came to power in Massachusetts. On January 1, 1991, William Weld, a Republican, was sworn in as governor, capping an election campaign that promised the downsizing of state government and the repeal of the universal health care law. To the new administration, the controversial law symbolized all that was ill-fated and short-sighted about government solutions to human problems. Charging that the law would destroy small business and draw the uninsured from across state borders, the administration repeatedly and, as yet, unsuccessfully sought the law's repeal. Despite the fact that the law remains on the books, its promise has been stifled by political leadership that no longer supports it. Most of the law's earlier supporters and implementers have found other causes or jobs on which to focus their energies. The law has become a shadow of its earlier self; its demise appears certain.

In this chapter, I will chronicle the development and apparent demise of the Massachusetts Universal Health Care Law. Beginning with a description of the bill's passage and the politics of the process that led to its enactment, I will proceed to explore the content and guiding principles of the law. In the final sections, I will tell the story of how the law was implemented and attempt to draw conclusions from the experience.

I intend to show that the law's most significant contribution to health care reform lay in enlisting the aid of the small business community in addressing the problem of the uninsured in Massachusetts. However, this achievement was threatened with failure by two ungovernable forces: mounting health care costs and questionable political support. The universal health care law sailed against a powerful tide of rising health care costs from its very inception. At the same time as the state was charged with demonstrating new ways to make health insurance affordable for small businesses and individuals, coverage was becoming less affordable for everyone, threatening to swell the ranks of the uninsured even further. The trends were clear: from the first quarter of 1988 to the first quarter of 1989, average large group family premiums for Blue Cross Master Medical coverage went up 27 percent; the same premium rose 28 percent for Master Health Plus. Bay State Health Care and Harvard Community Health Plan, the State's largest health maintenance organizations (HMOs) hiked comparable rates by 26 and 20 percent respectively. Finally, as Blue Cross non-group coverage rose beyond the reach of more and more people, the number of these subscribers dropped from 163,000 to 147,000 between 1987 and 1989.[1]

Apart from the threat of rising health care costs, the law ran the risk of running aground on political shoals. Riding on the tails of a failed presidential campaign, the universal health care law passed with narrow support in the state legislature. As one writer for *The Boston Globe* observed: "The hot potato legislation passed by only nine votes in the House and four in the Senate—and that was undoubtedly the high-water mark of its political support."[2] Indeed, the budget crisis that followed threw state initiatives on the defensive everywhere, a particularly ominous development for the fledgling law, unquestionably the state's most high-profile new program.

The Nature of the Problem

Despite the political and financial obstacles mentioned above, state political leaders and advocates sought to address with the law's enactment at least three major problems.

First, close to one million Massachusetts residents lacked adequate financial protection against medical costs. A household survey of Massachusetts residents found that in 1989 roughly 15 percent of the population lacked adequate financial protection against illness;[3] 8 percent had no health insurance at all, whether from a private source or government program; and 7 percent were underinsured.[4]

Second, the lack of health insurance created strong barriers to medical care. Uninsured Massachusetts residents tend to be in poorer health than their insured counterparts. Eleven percent of the uninsured versus only 6 percent of the insured reported being in poor or fair health.[5] Moreover, while only 7 percent of the insured said they had a disability which limited their activities, 16 percent of the uninsured reported having such a disability.

But despite being in poorer health, the uninsured use substantially fewer health care services than the insured. According to the survey just cited, 47 percent of uninsured individuals with chronic or serious illnesses did not see a physician for their problem at least once during the year prior to the survey, compared with only 18 percent of insured people with these illnesses. Similarly, only 29 percent of uninsured people who over the previous 30 days had experienced a serious medical problem sought medical attention in comparison with 51 percent of insured people. Overall, uninsured adults saw physicians 29 percent less frequently and were hospitalized 13 percent less often than insured adults. Uninsured children, who were found to have a similar rate of ill health as insured children, saw doctors 50 percent less frequently than children with insurance.[6]

Third, the hospital uncompensated care pool, although providing an important safety net for the uninsured and underinsured, was not by itself adequate to meet the needs of these groups. The pool was created in 1985 as a mechanism for ensuring access to hospital care for those who cannot afford to pay and for spreading the burden of uncompensated care equitably across hospitals in the commonwealth. Uncompensated care includes both free care to people with limited incomes and reimbursement for bad debts for which the hospitals have not been able to collect the full amount owed. Prior to the universal health care law, the uncompensated care pool was the primary mechanism for paying for health care for the uninsured and underinsured in Massachusetts.

The uncompensated care pool provides an important safety net for people with inadequate insurance protection but by itself cannot act as a substitute for universal health care. It falls short in at least three ways. First, by entitling institutions to reimbursement rather than individuals to care, it does not solve the access problems of uninsured residents. As described above, uninsured residents go without needed medical care. Second, the financing of the pool places an unfair burden on employers who offer health insurance to their workers. The pool, funded through a surcharge on private insurance, translates into a penalty on employers already insuring their workers. In other words, these employers are not only paying for their own employees' health insurance but also that of their competitors who do not offer insurance and whose workers therefore rely on the pool when they get sick. More than 10 percent of every hospital bill paid goes for the cost of such care. Finally, hospitals are often expensive and inappropriate settings for such medical care. When the pool serves as the major point of access for health care for the uninsured, it forces people to go to hospitals for care that may better be delivered in physicians' offices or other nonhospital locations—for example, by having strep throat infections treated in local hospital emergency rooms. With private sector costs to the uncompensated care pool approaching $400 million, the interests of the business community and public officials coalesced around the desire for a solution.

The Role of the Business Community
in the Passage of Universal Health Care

Early efforts by Governor Michael Dukakis and the House of Representatives to pass a health care reform bill came to an impasse in mid October 1987. Beginning with the governor's legislation (House 6000), an attempt to marry support for the concept of universal health care with provisions for hospital financing took shape. A slightly modified version of the governor's proposal (House 6068) was reported out of the House Ways and Means Committee onto the floor of the full House where it soon became apparent that it lacked the support to pass. On October 14, 1987, upon recommendation of the House Ways and Means, the House passed a bill (House 6090) that merely extended or "rolled-over" the expiring hospital financing system for six months. Not long after, it passed another bill (House 6100) that allowed for an immediate increase in revenues of approximately $120 million to 43 "underfinanced" hospitals. Both bills were referred to the Senate Committee on Ways and Means; the promise of an access bill appeared dead.

The Senate committee faced the choice of concurring with the House action or attempting to reconstruct a comprehensive hospital financing and health care access bill. The first option posed serious problems for the hospital industry. Enactment of House 6100 would have significantly increased revenues to 40 percent of the industry, while further restricting revenues to the remaining hospitals. More important still, enactment of House 6090 would have created six months of uncertainty for hospitals, rendering the simplest management decisions impossible. Furthermore, it heightened the unlikelihood that access to health care would ever be addressed.

The Senate committee clearly preferred the second option: a comprehensive hospital financing and health care access bill. However, the scenario played out in the House revealed little support for universal health insurance as conceived in House 6068. With the exception of the advocacy community, other interests—including hospitals, small business, large business, and insurers—expressed dismay at specific provisions of the bill and lobbied members of the House of Representatives to vote against its passage. Major health legislation had been enacted in the past only with broad support. Senate leaders realized that reconstituting a coalition of support for the health care reform legislation held the key to its passage.

For the first time, state political leaders, through the Senate committee, sought the involvement of small-business leaders in building a health care coalition. Earlier health care coalitions in Massachusetts rarely touched on small-business interests. National data indicated that small businesses were less likely to contribute toward the health insurance costs of their employees than large business. As a result, political leaders largely ignored them in the debate over health care financing. Whereas the lobbying group for large businesses, known as the Associated Industries of Massachusetts (AIM), played a strong role in previous negotiations, small-business groups were virtually absent from the debate.

This exclusion from the negotiation process may have made sense in the past when small-business possessed little financial stake in the outcome. However, with the advent of House 6000 and its obligation on all employers—large and small—to subsidize the health care costs of their employees, the policy arena shifted, and small businesses demanded a voice. In addition to AIM, the Senate committee invited several small business groups to join the coalition, most notably the National Federation of Independent Business and the Smaller Business Association of New England.

Small-business interests shaped these negotiations and the legislation that emerged in several important ways. First, small business argued forcefully for the creation of voluntary incentives for small businesses. By stating that many small firms wanted to provide health benefits to their employees but were prevented from doing so by exclusionary insurance practices and high cost, they sought to change the perception of the problem. Citing costs that range well above those charged to large businesses and underwriting techniques that screen elderly and "high risk" employees from coverage, small business demanded that government assure equity in a marketplace that essentially failed.

Second, they pushed for a careful, phased-in approach to the provision of universal health care. While the coalition unanimously agreed that everyone in the commonwealth ought to have access to reasonably priced health insurance, they did not agree on the ability and capability of the state to establish it. Small business fought for, and won, a concession that allowed for phase-in initiatives, and statewide pilot programs for providing health insurance to small businesses and individuals were to be established.

Third, they fought for elimination of the health care mandate for employers. The health insurance mandate was the provision of the bill most. vehemently opposed by the business community, particularly small business. The governor's initial bill proposed that each business be required to provide a minimum level of health insurance benefits to its employees. In large part because of pressure from the small-business community, the coalition decided to eliminate the mandate, instead making the state responsible for providing affordable health insurance to all the uninsured in the commonwealth, including uninsured workers and their families. Under this alternative scheme, employers would constitute an important source of funding for the state insurance plan through a surcharge on their unemployment insurance (UI) contributions. Against this surcharge liability, employers could deduct their costs of providing health insurance for their employees. This move divided the business community, with larger employers generally supporting the move and small business continuing to oppose it.

By the middle of December, the revised bill had gained the near-unanimous support of the members of the coalition and other interested health care factions, with only the National Federation of Independent Business formally opposing it. However, when Governor Dukakis signed the bill on April 21, 1988, business support remained nonetheless shaky.

Universal Health Care in Massachusetts

Five fundamental principles guided implementation of the Massachusetts universal health care law.

Expansion of the Employer-based System

Most Americans—and most Massachusetts residents—obtain their health insurance through their employers. Yet not all employers offer health insurance to their workers: fully 84 percent of the uninsured are working people and their families. Chapter 23 (the Massachusetts Universal Health Care Law) is based on the premise that the most practical way to close the uninsured gap problem in the state is to extend the employer-based system.

The Massachusetts Universal Health Care Law initially encourages, and later requires, employers to contribute to health insurance for their workers. Beginning in 1992, most employers not insuring their employees will be subject to an annual surcharge of 12 percent on the first $14,000 of each employee's wages for a maximum contribution of $1,680 per employee. These monies would fund health insurance for the uninsured through state-sponsored plans. Employers are not required to contribute toward the health insurance of employees who have other health insurance coverage, work less than 20 hours per week, or work in temporary or seasonal jobs. Employees not receiving coverage through their workplace could purchase it through the Department of Medical Security (DMS), the agency established to implement the law.

Employers who *do* offer health insurance would be able to deduct the cost from the required surcharge. As a result, most employers offering health insurance to their workers would not have to contribute to the state.

Equitable Access to Health Care Services and a Reduction of the Burden on Businesses Already Providing Health Insurance

As mentioned earlier, the hospital uncompensated care pool continues to play an important role for the uninsured and underinsured in Massachusetts by providing a safety net of care and minimizing hospital practices of turning away people without health insurance. But the pool does not fully solve the access problems, it encourages medical care to be provided in expensive hospital settings, and it places an unfair burden on businesses that do provide insurance.

The Massachusetts Universal Health Care Law is designed to reduce the reliance on the uncompensated care pool by increasing the number of people with insurance. For the uninsured, this means full and equal access to medical care. For businesses, it means a more equitable spreading of the burden of coverage for the uninsured. More specifically, the law capped the private sector's liability to the pool and gradually reduced it from $375 million in fiscal 1988 to $312 million in fiscal 1990. At the same time as the law capped the business community's liability, it transferred management of the pool to the new DMS. With this provision, state leaders effectively secured the support of the business community—particularly large business—in the law's passage.

Comprehensive Insurance Reform

For many employers, health insurance is a necessary means of attracting and retaining a competent work force. As health care costs escalate, however, providing health insurance becomes increasingly problematic for many employers. Small employers, particularly those with 25 or fewer workers, feel threatened. On average, these businesses pay 20 to 30 percent more than their larger counterparts for health insurance. In addition, if any of their employees are deemed "at risk" of illness, they may find it difficult to insure individual employees or the entire group. And if one of their employees actually becomes ill, small employers typically face dramatic rate increases. Even small businesses that currently offer this benefit to their employees find it increasingly difficult to do so.

While insurance reform is not an explicit requirement under Chapter

23, universal employer-based health care mandates will not succeed if employers cannot obtain adequate and affordable health insurance. To require employer participation in an insurance system that is inequitable and unavailable to those who need it most would be unfair at best and politically unfeasible, at worst. As a result, reform of the small-business insurance market framed much of the policy agenda for the DMS during its first two years.

Recognition of the Uninsured as a Heterogeneous Group

Expanding employer-sponsored health insurance takes the state a long way toward universal health care. Nonetheless, some residents will still not have access to insurance through an employer-based system. Chapter 23 recognizes the wide variety of people included under the label "uninsured" by targeting special groups. It also gives special emphasis to these groups by establishing programs for them beginning earlier than the employer mandate.

Specifically, the law targeted:

- pregnant women and young children, by expanding Medicaid coverage in 1988;
- people moving from welfare to work, working disabled adults, and disabled children, by providing them with coverage through the CommonHealth program;
- college and university students, by requiring them to purchase health insurance through their schools beginning in September of 1989;
- unemployed workers collecting unemployment benefits, by providing them with medical coverage beginning in July 1990;
- general relief recipients by covering acute hospital care, where possible, through managed care plans in 1991.

Under the original law, by 1992 all Massachusetts residents who could not obtain insurance through their employer—or the employer of a family member—were to purchase coverage through the DMS. The plans offered by the department would be financed through a combination of employer contributions, state subsidies, and individual premiums based on income.

Incremental Change

Under the universal health care law, implementation of universal health care was to proceed over a four-year period, running from

1988 through 1992. It was by design incremental in four ways.

First, the law calls for different programs to be implemented at different times. As described above, programs for special populations have been introduced each year since the law passed in 1988. Second, the universal health care law directs the DMS to establish phase-in initiatives to test alternative methods of providing health insurance to small businesses and individuals. Third, the law calls for studies on the small-business insurance market and the uninsured to structure learning to provide an informed basis for full implementation. Finally, the law contains requirements for evaluations and checkpoints to ensure that implementation is moving in the right direction.

The Business Community as Partners in Implementation

With the law's passage and Governor Dukakis' subsequent presidential defeat, opposition to the universal health care law mounted. The tenuous alliance of small- and large-business interests that guaranteed passage of the law began to unravel, as small employers voiced their growing opposition to employer mandates contained in the law. For large employers, the uncompensated care pool offered the key to their support; to the extent that the state met its commitment to cap the private sector's liability to the pool, large business remained at least passively supportive of the law. Within the small-business community, however, the issue of employer mandates rose as a lightning rod of controversy. From both a philosophical and financial point of view, this feature of the universal health care law came to be viewed as excessively costly to the small-business community.

At the same time, then-Governor Dukakis appointed a commissioner to head the Department of Medical Security, the new agency charged with implementing universal health care. A community organizer and health center director by training, James Hooley brought unique skills and perspective to the task of building the controversial agency. Immediately, he sought the active participation of all elements of the business community, with a special emphasis on the small-business community. His guiding principle was that only by working with all elements of the employer community, including those opposed to the law, could the state fashion policy responses to the uninsured problem that were both practical and fair. In addition, by grappling with the problems facing small employers in the health insurance market-place, the state could potentially win the support of this important constituency.

Almost immediately, the commissioner and his staff held meetings across the state with leaders and members of the small-business community. These meetings were well attended, with attendance ranging from 150 to 200 participants. Sentiment against the employer mandates ran high at these meetings, yet the degree of understanding reached by the two sides was clearly promising. Not uncommonly, small employers expressed surprise and satisfaction that "this was the first time the state had consulted them on anything." For DMS staff, the meetings provided an important testing ground of how well the law stood up to challenge and where likely implementation problems lay. These encounters set an early precedent for the department's efforts to involve small employers in seeking solutions to the uninsured problem in Massachusetts.

The next step involved establishment of the Small Business Advisory Board. Required under the universal health care law, the Small Business Advisory Board was established to "advise the department relative to small business access to affordable health care . . . and on all matters concerning small business for which the department is authorized to establish programs."[7] According to statute, the board was comprised of representatives from the small-business, broker, and insurance communities. In part because they held a clear majority, small-business interests largely dominated the agenda of the board and the department during its first two years of existence. In fact, virtually no major policy initiatives emerged from the DMS that did not have the explicit or tacit approval of the Small Business Advisory Board.

Small Business Insurance Reform

Undoubtedly, the most important legacy of the advisory board was the creation of a report to the legislature on the small-business insurance market and subsequent insurance reform legislation. Early in the law's passage, advocates for small-business argued the need for a systematic analysis of the small business health insurance market. According to their view, unique problems plagued this market which, if unremedied, made employer mandates untenable. In response to these concerns, drafters of the universal health care law included language requiring the DMS to conduct:

> . . . a study of the insurance market and the practices of insurance companies, hospital service corporations, medical service corporations and health maintenance organizations, to determine the causes of the relative unavailability of health insurance plans for small business and of disproportionate health insurance premium costs for small business, and to recommend and develop initiatives and strategies to improve the availability and reduce the relative cost of health insurance for small business.[8]

This analysis, entitled "Report to the Legislature: Status of the Small Business Insurance Market," was approved unanimously by the Small Business Advisory Board and submitted to the legislature in January 1990.

In essence, the report provided the first systematic analysis of the barriers to coverage in this market. It identified three principal areas of "market failure" in the small-business insurance market:

Rating. Small businesses pay 20 to 30 percent more on average than large firms for health coverage. Increased use of demographic, experience, and durational rating means that older and sicker groups must pay substantially more for health coverage than other small businesses. A single event for one individual in a group can lead to dramatic increases in insurance premiums for the entire group.

Availability. Medical underwriting in the small group market generally prevents individuals with a history of medical problems from obtaining health insurance from any carrier other than Blue Cross/Blue Shield and some health maintenance organizations. Even those joining Blue Cross/Blue Shield may be subject to waiting periods and coverage limitations. Much of the competition within the small-business insurance market is based upon avoiding high-risk groups rather than controlling the costs of providing care to those groups.

Stability. Small groups with good health histories receive favorable rates when they decide to purchase insurance. Over time, these same groups experience large unanticipated rate increases that send them searching for lower-cost coverage through another carrier. This "churning" in the market increases administrative expenses and drives up costs.

A series of public hearings followed the release of the report; representatives of the small-business, insurer, and broker groups were invited to attend. Based on testimony delivered at these hearings, the board reconvened to develop specific proposals for reform of the small-business health insurance market.

The final proposal, adopted by the full board, sought to address concerns that have been voiced by small businesses and insurers alike. All parties agreed that the current market structure led to unstable insurance rates and inefficient switching of carriers while insurance remained unavailable to many of those with the greatest health care needs. The goal of the two groups was to create greater stability in the market and improve access to insurance while controlling costs. The final proposal adopted by the board guaranteed all small businesses access to the carrier of their choice and established rating "bands" on how much insurers could charge individual small businesses for their coverage. Having gained the support of the HMOs and Blue Cross/Blue Shield, as well as the small-business community, the proposal is under serious consideration by the state legislature.

Phase-In Initiatives

The second major area of partnership between the DMS and the small-business community centered on the phase-in initiatives, regional demonstration insurance programs for small businesses and individuals. The phase-in initiatives were established as part of the universal health care law in response to the demands of the small-business community. Small employers and their representatives argued that they would purchase health insurance at the same rate as large employers if products were available to them at comparable rates and without the restrictions that small groups face. At the same time, they argued that voluntary incentives, such as the phase-in initiatives, would alleviate the need for government mandates. Once the barriers of cost and access were removed, small businesses would begin to purchase insurance for their workers at the same rate as large businesses currently do.

In setting up the phase-in programs, the department ensured that these conditions were met: by subsidizing premiums and sharing risk, it guaranteed premiums that were comparable to those available to large businesses and access to coverage without regard to health status. In essence, the phase-in programs replicated the market in which large employers purchased their health insurance—that is, less expensive products with no restrictions—and tested small-business willingness to buy under these circumstances.

Nonetheless, enrollment proceeded slowly, and the phase-in programs faced elimination with the new Republican administration's first round of budget cuts. As part of its fiscal 1991 budget, the Weld administration cut the phase-in budget from approximately $12 million to $3 million and halted new enrollment in the programs. Notice went out to all insurers participating in the programs that the phase-ins would be formally terminated on March 31, 1992. The net impact of this change is that approximately 1000 insured individuals and families will lose subsidized access to these health insurance products. At the option of the carrier, individuals may have access to nongroup conversion options. However, in all cases this will translate into significantly higher premiums, and in all but one case only individuals passing a health screen will be eligible to join.

In retrospect, several reasons may account for the initial slow pace of enrollment even before the Weld administration decisions.

Definition of "Affordability" for Small Business

Under the universal health care law, the standard of affordability for small businesses was measured against what large groups pay. Specifically, a product was affordable to small businesses to the extent its rates approximated those charged to large businesses. This definition may have needed refinement given the slow enrollment in these programs. The department intended to develop low-cost products for small businesses that would have provided a useful point of comparison in gauging the level of price sensitivity in this market. However, it was never able to do so given the short lifespan of the program.

Perceived Viability of the Programs by Different Insurers

The relative success of certain phase-in programs, most notably the one administered by John Hancock Mutual Life Insurance Company in Essex County, demonstrated the importance of commitment to these programs on the part of individual insurers. Clearly, where commitment ran high, enrollment proceeded steadily and even strongly, marketing strategies were creative, and employers seemed satisfied with the programs. Where commitment was less strong on the part of insurers, marketing was not vigorous and enrollment results were weak.

Condition of the Economy

In fiscal 1991–92, Massachusetts faced a dire economic and fiscal crisis. The state's 1991 unemployment rate of 9.0 percent was well above the national average of 6.9 percent, and its BB bond rating was the lowest of any state in the nation. In addition, the state legislature faced the rather daunting task of cutting nearly $2 billion from the budget to avoid a deficit. The instability of the state's economy over the past year and a half affected small-business decisions to control costs and to assume new ones. This undoubtedly affected decisions to purchase health insurance.

New Programs Need Time

New products, whether they are public or private in nature, require an adequate amount of time to become saturated in the market, to become part of the public's consciousness. The phase-in programs were only on the market for six months before they were closed down. It may simply be a matter of giving them sufficient time to begin selling.

Lessons from the Massachusetts Experiment

Immediately after his inauguration as governor, William Weld acted on his promise to downsize state government and seek repeal of the universal health care law. A budget reduction package totaling roughly one-half billion dollars in cuts, largely in the area of human services, was released. As part of the same package, the administration eliminated the Department of Medical Security and slashed funding of the phase-in programs to $3 million. To date, efforts to overturn the law have proven unsuccessful. However, the administration successfully obtained a delay in the 1992 "pay or play" mandate, pushing back to 1993 the date by which employers are required to provide health insurance to their workers or pay a surcharge to the state. The governor vows to continue his efforts to seek full repeal of the law.

Clearly universal health care is dying a premature death in Massachusetts. Important programs to provide health insurance to the unemployed, small businesses, and low-income individuals came into place only to face elimination before they could be seriously evaluated. In retrospect, several lessons seem apparent.

The heavy dependence of states on federal funding, combined with balanced budget requirements, reduces the flexibility of state government to sustain policy reform in hard times. The Massachusetts Universal Health Care Law did not rely on federal monies for support; it relied on a combination of state, employer, and individual contributions. However, Massachusetts does depend heavily on federal support for much of the financing of its public programs. In addition, it does not have the luxury of engaging in deficit financing when times are hard the way the federal government does. This situation leaves states with little flexibility to sustain policy reforms initiated in more prosperous times. As a result, the universal health care experiment would undoubtedly have encountered barriers to continued implementation even if Governor Dukakis had remained in office. This is a structural problem that is generic to our system of fiscal federalism and that makes new policy departures highly vulnerable.

The lack of institutional support, nurtured over time, may facilitate policy reversal. Another reason for the apparent premature demise of the law is that it lacked sufficient time to build vested interests, both within the state bureaucracy and from consumer and advocacy groups. Had the Massachusetts law been in existence longer, it may have attracted a constituency that sought to protect it both in hard fiscal times and from a hostile new governor.

Policy initiatives undertaken at the state and local level are highly vulnerable to the vagaries of local politics. At the time of its passage, the Massachusetts experiment was widely touted as the most comprehensive effort undertaken to date in this country to address the needs of the uninsured. The law established an aggressive schedule of implementation that had largely been met. Important programs were established that provided coverage to groups of people either neglected or rejected by the existing health care system. And yet these programs could not sustain the pressure that a new Republican administration brought to bear on them.

The move to dismantle universal health care in Massachusetts represented a vote against the previous administration and its policies, rather than a prudent response to the state's fiscal problems. The Department of Medical Security operated on an administrative budget of less than $1 million annually, a miniscule amount compared to other state agencies. Moreover, its programs were largely financed through a combination of public, employer, and individual contributions, making universal health care a relatively small cost to the state. Nonetheless, the state's fiscal crisis, combined with a new and very different ideology about the role and value of government contributed to its almost certain demise.

Partnerships between public and private sector leaders can yield valuable insights and solutions to social problems. For the first time in Massachusetts' history, the state actively sought the involvement of the small-business community in solving a very real social problem. Opposition to the mandates contained in the law at once obscured and made possible an alliance between the state and small business that aimed to unravel the health insurance morass that threatened them. As the largest consumers of health care in this country, government and business came together to address the problems of cost and access to health care.

Gradually, the state and small employers began to learn the business of insurance. It allowed them to navigate successfully a package of insurance reforms through the powerful vested interests of the insurance community, and it fostered the phase-in initiatives, which if allowed to continue, would have taught us important lessons about how costly universal access really is. Taken together, they would have taught us whether the exclusion of 35 to 38 million people nationally from our health care system, many on the grounds that they are too sick, too old, or happen to be in the wrong job to merit coverage, is a policy we, as a nation, can justify. Nonetheless, as this nation is forced to grapple with the worsening plight of a growing number of working and sick Americans who are left with no means of paying for their care, the Massachusetts story hopefully will provide insight into the benefits of constructing a solution to this problem.

Notes

1. Massachusetts State Division of Insurance, Executive Office of Consumer Affairs, quarterly rate filings submitted by all HMOs and Blue Cross/Blue Shield.

2. Richard Knox, "Now—Universal Health," *Boston Globe*, Business Extra, 21 February 1989, 39.

3. *A Household Survey of the Health Status of Massachusetts Residents*, A Report of the Harvard School of Public Health, Louis Harris and Associates and the Department of Medical Security of the Commonwealth of Massachusetts, October 1990.

4. Ibid. A respondent was deemed "underinsured" in the context of this survey

when he reported having health insurance but nonetheless had to pay more than 10 percent of his annual income on medical bills in the previous year.

5. Ibid.

6. Ibid.

7. *An Act to Make Health Security Available to All Citizens of the Commonwealth and to Improve Hospital Financing,* Massachusetts General Laws, Chapter 23, 22 April 1988, 64.

8. Ibid.

9

Democratic Values and Health Policy Reform

Bruce Jennings

Throughout the 20th century, in roughly 20-year intervals, the vision of a universal health care system has risen to the national public policy agenda and has been defeated by a powerful coalition of groups with a vested interest in maintaining the status quo.[1] Today fundamental reform in health care service delivery and financing is back in the policy arena once again, but there are signs that the historic coalition preventing such reform is no longer in place. The American Medical Association, traditionally a leading opponent of systemic change, has officially sponsored a plan to achieve universal coverage that departs in many, if not all, respects from positions organized medicine has taken in the past.[2] Large corporations find their health care insurance costs rising rapidly and have begun to press for cost-containment measures and for controls that will restrict the cost shifting that has traditionally occurred to enable hospitals to support indigent care. The hospital industry, in turn, finds its own interests compromised by uncompensated care. Insured workers find their out-of-pocket costs increasing as their employers impose large deductibles and copayments and increase the cost of family coverage.[3] The elderly also find their medical expenses increasing as a financially strapped Medicare program increases their share of costs and as the cost of such items as prescription drugs rises.

In this rather unstable constellation of forces, the status quo finds few defenders, and inertia rather than principled support seems to be what is keeping the system going at the moment. That, and the inability of the various groups and interests that are dissatisfied with the present system to agree on a particular direction or strategy for reform. Thus far the short-term calculus of self-interest has led to attempts by practically all sides to shift their costs and liabilities to some other player in the system; less effort has been made to address common interests and to find viable institutional and financial mechanisms to realize those interests. The atmosphere in the health care system, therefore, is somewhat eerie, like a calm before the storm. Change seems almost inevitable, but it is not clear exactly when or how it will come about. No one seems to know what shape the system will finally take, what basic values it will serve, or what process might lead to reaching some consensus on the values and priorities the system ought to serve. Policymakers are like builders who understand the owners' dissatisfaction with the present house but who do not have a set of remodeling plans. The Bush administration's plan, which relies on tax credits and deductions to subsidize the purchase of private insurance coverage, is a limited and inadequate response to the problem. Its proposed cutbacks on federal Medicare and Medicaid expenditures would increase the fiscal problems of the states. It is most unlikely that this White House initiative, as it stands in early 1992, will provide the catalyst to break the current impasse and stalemate in federal health policy.

The most radical and fundamental reform proposals call for a single payer, universal public system, such as Canada's, or for an abandonment of employer-based health insurance in favor of a few large community risk pools or funds that centrally negotiate rates and annual budgets with providers, such as the German system.[4] Reform proposals modeled along Canadian lines have been debated in Ohio, Oregon, and Michigan but have little prospect of becoming law at the moment.[5]

More typically, as the chapters in this book suggest, states have worked within the existing parameters of the mixed public/private arrangement of health insurance, with competition among providers and insurers undergirding the system. Pursuing the goal of universal access for those now excluded from health insurance coverage, several state governments have proposed or undertaken experiments to restructure coverage publicly provided under the Medicaid program, and to leverage change in the private employer-based health insurance sector as well, by mandating basic coverage by almost all employers, establishing coverage pools for uninsurable individuals and for uncompensated care, and the like. This approach, pioneered in Hawaii several years ago and discussed by Deane Neubauer in Chapter Seven, has been seriously proposed in states such as Colorado, California, Vermont, and New York and has been enacted in Massachusetts (see Chapter Eight) and Oregon (see Chapter Six), where the most systematic and far-reaching legislation to date has been passed.[6]

It is interesting that, at least in the late 1980s, the most innovative ideas for reform and redistribution were coming from the state governments rather than from federal policymakers or national opinion leaders. The basic lesson in social policy since the 1960s has been that marginalized and disenfranchised constituencies can get a fairer, more effective hearing in Washington than in the capitals of the states where they live and that welfare problems cannot be tackled at the state level anyway. However valid these lessons may still be in other policy areas, it is not obvious that thinking at the federal level about health care access and cost containment is more progressive and responsive to the needs of the least well-off than thinking at the state level. National proposals for reform, such as the Pepper Commission, have continued the traditional call for vastly expanded access for the underserved— primary care for poor women and children, long-term care for the elderly—but only by making sizable net increases in medical care spending.[7] Debates at the state level, by and large, have been more prone to link the problem of expanding access with the problem of setting priorities among health care services. One reason for this may be that at the moment tax increases to pay for expanded benefits are even more politically taboo at the state level than they are at the federal level. Another reason is that business groups have been focusing their arguments for cost containment at the state governmental level since that is where insurance and provider regulation is centered.

This is a complex drama, and the denouement is not yet in sight. There are many political and economic forces at work driving these policy debates and experiments. In this chapter I wish to focus on one special, but I think not marginal or irrelevant, factor in this complex equation, namely, the ethical and normative discourse that informs and to some extent underlies the health policy reform momentum now evident at the state level.

The dozens of health policy reform plans now being debated

throughout the country compel us to consider innovative political, economic, and institutional arrangements. In one way or another, most of these plans call for many changes in the way health care is delivered as well as the way it is financed. New modes of managed care, quality assurance, utilization review, and technology assessment are just some of the factors that will ultimately determine what kinds of services reach which patients, when, and at whose expense. We are still struggling to figure out how to manage and to govern these innovations.

No less important, these health policy reforms are forcing us into new and relatively uncharted ethical terrain, a terrain that challenges many of the core liberal and individualistic notions in our political morality and public philosophy. These challenges come primarily as we move from the question of justice in access to health care to the question of justification and process for setting priorities in health care. In the past health policy has largely been guided, I believe, by a constellation of values associated with the notions of individual rights, equality of opportunity, and pluralistic interest-group politics. In the future, it will become necessary to explore the meaning and practice of a somewhat different cluster of values related to communal solidarity, societal obligation, and democratic participation. To look at the current scene in health policy reform in the United States today, especially at the state level, is to see a confrontation building between liberal individualism and a democratic, communal emphasis. In what follows I explore the roots and implications of that confrontation, with special attention to the problem of establishing a legitimate basis for setting health care priorities in a pluralistic society.

From Access to Priority Setting

In 1983 the President's Commission for the Study of Ethical Problems in Medicine and Biomedical and Behavioral Research issued its report, *Securing Access to Health Care*. This document marks a significant watershed in the discussion of justice and equality in the social distribution of benefits offered by the American health care system. At that time the extent of the problem—the sheer numbers of persons medically uninsured or underinsured, estimated today at approximately 50 million people—was not widely appreciated. The impressive compilation of data marshalled by the President's commission helped to define the access problem and to place it squarely on the national health policy agenda.

Equally important, the report summarized a kind of normative consensus about what distributive justice requires of society in providing access to health care. Given the massive facts of inequitable access, and given the fundamental importance of health care as a basic social good that plays a key role in the overall scheme of equality of opportunity, the moral foundations of the medical marketplace and the prevailing health insurance system were thrown into question.[8] From an ethical point of view, health care rationing based on ability to pay could muster little convincing support, and the issue ceased to be *whether* the status quo should be changed and became *whither* change should lead: what directions should a new health policy take and what basic purposes should it serve?

The President's commission finally concluded that an "adequate" level of care should be universally available and that the costs should be borne equitably by society as a whole. The commission's formulation is worth considering in some detail:

> [S]ociety has an ethical obligation to ensure equitable access to health care for all. . . . Equitable access to health care requires that all citizens be able to secure an adequate level of care without excessive burdens. Discussions of a right to health care have frequently been premised on offering patients access to all beneficial care, to all care that others are receiving, or to all that they need—or want. By creating impossible demands on society's resources for health care, such formulations have risked negating the entire notion of a moral obligation to secure care for those who lack it. In their place, the Commission proposes a standard of "an adequate level of care," which should be thought of as a floor below which no one ought to fall, not a ceiling above which no one may rise.
>
> A determination of this level will take into account the value of various types of health care in relation to each other as well as the value of health care in relation to other important goods for which societal resources are needed. Consequently, changes in the availability of resources, in the effectiveness of different forms of health care, or in society's priorities may result in a revision of what is considered "adequate."[9]

The main shortcoming of the commission's work, and indeed of most writing on this topic in the 1980s, was the failure to pursue the question of setting health care priorities and of reflecting those priorities in the type of social provision for health care that we make universally available, either through a single payer public system or a mixed public/private health insurance system. There still is great resistance to change, to be sure, because a great deal of money and powerful vested interests are at stake. But the situation today seems to be that the philosophical argument about the justice or rightness of equitable access to basic health care for all has pretty much been won. If, as I argued above, no major social group is economically or politically satisfied with the status quo, neither is it morally comfortable with the glaring gaps and inequities of the American health care system. America offers state-of-the-art acute medical care to those well-insured or supported by government benefits but virtually excludes approximately 35 to 38 million who are without insurance and millions more who have only partial or intermittent coverage. These marginal citizens in our health care system are largely the working poor and their families, or those who make too much to qualify for Medicaid in their state even though their income is well below the federal poverty line. One in four children under the age of eighteen lack adequate insurance coverage, a state of affairs that hampers their getting preventive and timely care. Nearly 30 percent of black Americans are uninsured, as are 41 percent of Hispanic Americans.[10]

As striking and disturbing as these figures are, however, it has become clear in the past decade that it is no longer sufficient to argue the case for universal access as a matter of justice and rights per se. We must also address the content of the social obligation and entitlement that equitable and universal access constitutes—what I propose to call here the "priority-setting problem." Nor is it enough to speak in vague and general terms of a "floor below which no one is permitted to fall," a "basic package of benefits," or a "decent minimum." Theoretical questions of social justice in health care have now become very concrete questions about the process and results of differentiating among the different kinds of needs patients bring to their encounter with medicine, and the value of the different kinds of benefits that medical care can offer them.

Part of the reason why the priority-setting problem has come to the fore is political and economic. Since 1983 the problem of controlling the rate of increase of rising health care costs has become much more salient and urgent for policymakers. Market-inspired solutions, such as fostering competition and providing positive financial incentives for health care providers to limit utilization (for example, the DRG-based system of hospital payment under Medicare), have not worked and health care costs are now almost universally perceived as being out of control. In 1990 Americans spent $666.2 billion (about 12 percent of GNP) on health care, a figure that had more than doubled in real terms in the past decade.[11] It is expected that by the year 2000 health care costs may climb to a staggering $1.5 trillion—15 percent of GNP and around $5,500 per person/per year.[12] It is not politically realistic to expect that we will move to a system of universal coverage and access, without at the same time setting some priorities and limits on the social entitlement a universal system would create. Both public officials and private payers will demand assurance that they are not being asked to write a blank check.

In addition, there is a moral and philosophical reason why the problem of priority setting must be addressed in tandem with the problem of access. As the President's commission recognized, ethical principles of justice and equity do not require unlimited access for all to every medical treatment or service everyone might want—or even might objectively benefit from, if that benefit is marginal. Until the problem of priority setting is addressed, the ethical case for fundamental reform in the health care system remains fundamentally incomplete. Until we define what just priorities are—what needs are to be met as a matter of general societal obligation, we will have little to say that has a direct bearing on specific public policy initiatives. In particular, it will be difficult to sort out the respective obligations of the public and the private sectors, and it will be difficult to make the case for a specific share of limited social resources that ought to be channeled into health services, as opposed to other social programs in housing, education, public health, the environment, and employment, which also have an effect—perhaps even a larger effect than medicine—on the overall health status of the population.

Priority Setting and the Human Good

Priority setting in health care is a cultural construction of value superimposed on the social use of medical technology and medical practice. The limits of medical science at any given time and the natural constraints of human biology merely set the outside parameters within which cultural, value-laden priorities must be set and choices must be made. When medicine could in fact do very little, priorities were relatively straightforward in the sense that those treatments that did work and provide medical benefit were given precedence over those that did not. Much more difficult is the choice between the relative worth of different treatments that do work and provide benefit to some extent, in different degrees to different patients. Similarly, it makes little sense to place a high priority on a goal that defies the facts of human biology. If there is a natural upper limit to the human life-span, for example, then giving priority to research designed to increase the life expectancy past 110 years of age, say, is simply foolish; it is more like a visionary quest than rational public policy. Still, one of the devilish—as well as magnificent—aspects of modern medicine is that natural givens and limits seem increasingly to yield and to recede in the face of biomedical science. Advances in genetic medicine, for example, may fundamentally transform our expectations about what is chronic illness and what is curable disease for many widespread disorders from schizophrenia to diabetes, Alzheimer's, and many more.

The ethical problem of setting priorities only begins, therefore, when the "fat" has been eliminated from the system, when unnecessary, ineffective, and nonbeneficial treatments have been set aside. That in itself would be no mean accomplishment and could certainly ease the cost-containment problem enormously. But it is an ironic testimony to the very success and power of medicine that it can always beneficially and rationally manage to consume as many resources as society chooses to allocate to it. Define benefit broadly enough, and give a social carte blanche to individual perceptions of need and want in a society as risk averse and as health conscious as ours, and one more incremental utilization of health care services can always be justified. And it will always be demanded by someone. Thus at some point a value-laden social limit must be placed on the use of medicine, a limit that will constrain the unbridled calculus of individual medical self-interest and demand. That, I suggest, is what the problem of priority setting in health care really amounts to.

One of the reasons this is so difficult is that it is empirically so complex. Gains no doubt will be made in the next few years from technology assessment, and certain procedures now thought to be beneficial will be abandoned. This sort of natural selection process happens in medicine all the time. But again, cost-benefit and cost-effectiveness analysis alone will take us only so far, and then they will have to give way to—or, more likely, become disguised forms of—a more self-conscious kind of normative priority-setting exercise.

A more telling reason why priority setting is so difficult lies in the fact that it is conceptually complex and always prone to what philosophers refer to as a condition of "essential contestability." That is, not only do we find it difficult to say what the actual priorities should be, we find it difficult as well to say what the right criteria or standards for defining priorities should be. The problem is not that priority setting, in Oregon or elsewhere, will be debatable—debate, after all, is the medium of democratic public life. No, the problem is that we apparently lack a common language, a common idiom of publicly available meanings and concepts, within which to conduct a truly communicative debate in the first place. Lacking that common normative language we do not debate, we accuse; and we talk past and through one another.

I believe this situation is especially serious in the United States because our political discourse, and especially our policy analytic discourse, is framed essentially by the notions of individual rights and aggregative social utility. The process of setting health care priorities raises questions that do not lend themselves very well to these categories and this moral language. In the first place, health care priorities are not about priorities among individuals (as in "this person and his needs are more important to society than that person"). They are about the relative value of the individual and common benefits that accrue from particular modalities of medical care for particular medical conditions. This means that behind any particular pattern of priorities that is established it will be possible to interpret an explicit or implicit conception of the human good, a conception of human flourishing related to a particular notion of what constitutes health.

Part of the task of bioethics or normative policy analysis is to throw into relief conceptions of the good that are embedded in a set of health policy priorities and to subject them to critical scrutiny and debate. Policymakers may also be made somewhat more perspicacious about the latent values and ideals their own decisions embody, even if those policy decisions seem explicitly to be driven by economic or political considerations seemingly far removed from philosophical notions of the good. This is important because finally the legitimacy of the priorities policy will stand or fall on the moral acceptability of the notion of the good that the policy furthers.

Second, thinking about health care priorities involves thinking about the ends of medicine itself in a way that is communally oriented and not simply individualistic, and in a way that sees medical knowledge and technology as a public resource of common value and not simply as an instrument for the realization of individual self-interest.

Constructing (or discovering) a socially legitimate and defensible conception of human flourishing that is the basis of—and is furthered by—public policy, and understanding medicine as a social enterprise that serves the common good as well as individual interests are the conceptual prerequisites of priority setting in health policy. They challenge and defy the mainstream political languages of individual rights and social utility in our liberal tradition of political morality. If this is the case, then what Howard Leichter describes in Chapter Six as taking place in Oregon is a quest for a new language for public deliberation and debate as well as an attempt to set priorities for the benefits package offered to Medicaid recipients and ultimately others as well. It is a language of "we need" more than a language of "I want" or "they [the poor, minorities, the Other] will be given." From a democratic point of view and from the perspective of its future implications for our society, the process of forging this alternative language of public discourse is actually the most important aspect of what is being attempted in Oregon.

The basic elements of the Oregon reform plan, discussed in detail by Leichter—expanding Medicaid eligibility, the "play or pay" approach to expanding private employer-based health insurance coverage, a politically representative commission to determine the basic benefits package, and a risk pool for uninsurables—are neither new nor unique to Oregon. Two elements in particular, however, do make the Oregon experiment stand out. The first is the explicitness and publicity with which it has approached the priority-setting problem. The second unique aspect of the Oregon experiment is the limited but important and concerted effort that has been made to supplement the normal channels of representative democracy and bring grassroots participation to bear on the process.

The three laws that comprise the Oregon Basic Health Services Act established the Health Services Commission (HSC) and charged it with creating a prioritized list of medical services. This priority list will define the basic benefits package, the floor beneath which no one in Oregon would be allowed to fall. How generous it will be depends on cost projections and on how much the legislature decides to allocate to the Medicaid program overall. The law stipulates that the HSC must "actively solicit public involvement in a community meeting process to build a consensus on the values to be used to guide health resource allocation decisions." Behind that requirement and that language of participatory involvement stands the state's private grass roots bio-ethics organization, Oregon Health Decisions (OHD).

Since its founding in 1982, Oregon Health Decisions has promoted community forums to discuss health decisions and values, on topics ranging from the termination of life-sustaining treatment to personal responsibility for health status. In 1988 a multiyear OHD project on allocation of health care resources culminated with a statewide citizen's parliament that adopted recommendations calling for allocation decisions to be made explicitly and openly and with special attention to promoting health and preserving quality of life. This grass-roots activity helped to stimulate a discussion in the state that paved the way for the passage of the Basic Health Services Act. The prior experience with grass roots consensus building on health values gave policymakers a model to turn to when seeking to anchor the work of the HSC in a community-oriented perspective. This presented an interesting marriage between the usual representative mechanism for ensuring accountability and responsiveness (namely, the appointment of lay members and consumers on the commission itself) and more direct public input through public hearings, a public opinion survey, and the grass roots town meeting approach of OHD. Ultimately, the commissioners did factor the results of the OHD organized meetings into the final adjustments and rank orderings of the priority list and recommendations released in February 1991.[13]

A Role for Democracy?

The Oregon experience, no matter how incomplete and imperfect, should stimulate us to raise the following question: What is the special contribution that democratic values and processes can make to the health policy reform process now taking place at the state level, and why is it important? It is all too easy to affirm in ritualistic fashion a commitment to democratic values. More difficult, and much more important, is to explore a role for democracy that would take us in some new intellectual directions and would respond to a serious limitation in mainstream political processes. In my estimation the ongoing debate over health care priorities is perhaps the most promising venue for a genuinely democratic, grass-roots turn in social policy today.

To explore further why this might be the case, it is essential to distinguish between the liberal, pluralist conception of "representative democracy" and the participatory, or civic, conception of democracy. Partly the difference between these two understandings of democracy has to do with the role and involvement undertaken by ordinary citizens at the grass-roots level. In representative democracy ordinary citizens are asked mainly to vote and to make a judgment about which candidate will best represent and serve the voter's private interests. In civic democracy, the practice of citizenship is more active and involves direct involvement in a process of deliberation and decisionmaking at the local level, as well as voting and communicating with elected representatives at higher levels of the system.

More fundamental than this difference between voting and participating, however, is the difference between the way these two conceptions of democracy understand the moral consciousness and perspective that the citizen must bring to—or derive from—political life.[14] For representative democracy in the tradition of James Madison and James Mill, for example, the public interest is an aggregation of private interest. It grows out of a pluralistic and procedurally fair competition of organized interests that reflect natural or voluntary clusters of individual interest in the society. In the civic conception of democracy, by way of contrast, the common good is defined and constituted by a process of active, common deliberation in which each citizen self-consciously attempts to grasp the shared needs and aspirations at work in his or her community of co-equals and fellow citizens. In the civic tradition of democratic theory, stretching from Jean-Jacques Rousseau to John Dewey, the promise of participatory democracy has always been that it can provide a space for the transformation of private perspectives into public vision; from the voice of "I want" into the voice of "we, together, need" that I referred to earlier.

The question to ask about democracy and health policy, then, is whether the policy problem of priority setting requires (or at least lends itself to) a revival of democratic values and practices in the civic sense of democracy? Here the Oregon experience so far gives us quite mixed signals.

Certainly one of the defining features of the Oregon approach has been its commitment to openness and accountability. Much of the strategy rests on the moral proposition that explicit, public priority setting is superior to the covert, invisible priority setting that goes on now in the health care system. It also rests on the political proposition that by making hard choices more visible and public, legislators will not be so prone to neglect the needs and interests of the least well off, as they now do when they protect state revenues by lowering Medicaid eligibility requirements ever further below the federal poverty level. Or as they do by reducing provider reimbursement rates, which has the effect of making it more difficult for some Medicaid recipients to find a provider willing to take care of them or to accept assignment.

Moreover, as Leichter indicates, the involvement of grass roots civic education groups, such as Oregon Health Decisions, in the official priority-setting process is indicative of the desire of Oregon policymakers to have the priority system be reflective of, and supported by, some measure of community dialogue and consensus at least in terms of general values and directions policymakers might follow.

There is one striking feature of the Oregon plan, however, that goes beyond its openness or its unusual solicitation of grass-roots input. This is its emphasis on "rationalizing" the process of making health policy by insulating the process from the ordinary play of interest-group politics and by altering the process of policy choice in the legislature so that legislators will be subject to a different array of pressures and political incentives. For years state health policy and budgeting has been shaped by an incremental process of interest-group health advocacy for targeted populations and special conditions. The result was a complex scheme of health insurance mandates as well as a growing number of special requirements coming from the federal government. The recent Oregon legislation seeks to wipe most of that slate clean and to replace this incrementally built up patchwork "system" with a more systematic and unified health policy approach. A linchpin in this strategy is the autonomy of the Health Services Commission, the body responsible for devising the priority list of health care services. The legislature will determine how much money to allocate to the state health care program in a given budget cycle, and so it falls to the legislature to decide how far down the priority list to fund, but it may not reorder the priority list itself.

This arrangement will certainly alter the outcomes of bargaining, lobbying, and coalition building in the legislative process. But how well it may serve the values of civic democracy remains to be seen. It is possible that a kind of technocratic elitism could step into the policymaking role normally performed by representative, interest-group democracy, and no great advance for democratic values and processes would be registered there.

In the end, much will depend on whether this entire priority-setting process, which is to be repeated every two years, will continue to elicit significant public attention and involvement, as more and more citizens come to believe that their deliberations and their voices on health values do matter. The same is true for the other states where community health decisions groups similar to Oregon Health Decisions have conducted or are conducting a series of grass-roots forums on access and health care priorities.[15] There are community health decisions groups now active in 20 states, including California, Colorado, Georgia, Ohio, New Jersey, New Mexico, and Vermont, where grass-roots education on health policy is underway.

What if grass-roots democratic involvement actually increases and catches on in the health policy arena? There are risks as well as benefits in moving from liberal democracy to civic democracy. Will there be a conflict between the liberal ideals of justice and the rights of the least well-off, on the one hand, and the democratic tendency toward middle-class consensus and majority rule, on the other? I do not think an unequivocal answer to this question can be given. The answer depends on whether we are able to combine democratic processes (similar to but even more inclusive than Oregon has tried to attain) with the civic democratic outlook or spirit I mentioned earlier. Grass-roots democracy is dangerous when it only fosters a discussion, mainly held among middle-class citizens, about what the least advantaged should be given. It must foster instead a conversation about what we owe and should provide for one another. If the former happens, an important opportunity will be lost, and the health care priorities that will be set will probably not be very equitable. Nor for that matter will they be a true expression of democracy.

The conventional wisdom about American politics and society at the present time would certainly have us be pessimistic in this regard. But the community health decisions projects may yet prove the conventional wisdom wrong, and they may reveal that the transformation from a private to a civic outlook is easier and more urgently desired among the American people than we thought.

Notes

1. Paul Starr, *The Social Transformation of American Medicine* (New York: Basic Books, 1982).

2. James S. Todd, S.V. Seekins, J. A. Krichbaum, and L. K. Harvey, "Health Access America—Strengthening the U.S. Health Care System," *JAMA* 265 (15 May 1991): 2503–2506.

3. National Conference of State Legislatures [NCSL], *Medical Indigency Project Notes* 1 (February 1990).

4. K. Grumbach, T. Bodenheimer, D.U. Himmelstein, and S. Woolhandler, "Liberal Benefits, Conservative Spending: The Physicians for a National Health Program Proposal," *JAMA* 265 (15 May 1991): 2549–2554; and B.L. Kirkman-Liff, "Health Insurance Values and Implementation in the Netherlands and the Federal Republic of Germany: An Alternative Path to Universal Coverage," *JAMA* 265 (15 May 1991): 2496–2502.

5. New York State Department of Health, *Universal Health Care: Voices from the States* (Albany: New York State Department of Health, 1990); and Courtney S. Campbell, "Laboratory of Reform? Setting Health Priorities in Oregon," *BioLaw* 2 (May 1991): S549–S563.

6. New York State Department of Health, *Universal Health Care*; and Alpha Center, "State Initiatives to Expand Health Insurance Coverage" (Washington, DC: Alpha Center, 1990).

7. J.D. Rockefeller, "A Call for Action: The Pepper Commission's Blueprint for Health Care Reform," *JAMA* 265 (15 May 1991): 2507–2510.

8. Norman Daniels, *Just Health Care* (Cambridge: Cambridge University Press, 1985).

9. President's Commission for the Study of Ethical Problems in Medicine and Biomedical and Behavioral Research, *Securing Access to Health Care*, Vol. I (Washington, D.C.: Government Printing Office, 1983).

10. Emily Friedman, "The Uninsured: From Dilemma to Crisis," *JAMA* 265 (15 May 1991): 2491–2495.

11. Ibid., 2493.

12. Health Care Financing Administration, "National Health Expenditures, 1986–2000," *Health Care Financing Review* 8 (Summer 1987): 1–36.

13. Courtney S. Campbell, "Laboratory of Reform?"; Charles J. Dougherty, "Setting Health Care Priorities: Oregon's Next Steps," *Hastings Center Report* 21 (May/June 1991); and David Hadorn, "Setting Health Care Priorities in Oregon: Cost-Effectiveness Meets the Rule of Rescue," *JAMA* 265 (1 May 1991): 2218–2225.

14. Benjamin Barber, *Strong Democracy: Participatory Politics For a New Age* (Berkeley: University of California Press, 1984).

15. Bruce Jennings, "A Grassroots Movement in Bioethics: Community Health Decisions," 18 *Hastings Center Report*, Special Supplement (June–July 1988): 1–16.

Selected Bibliography

Alford, Robert. *Health Care Politics.* Chicago: University of Chicago Press, 1975.

Almond, Gabriel A. "The Intellectual History of the Civic Culture Concept." In *The Civic Culture Revisited,* edited by G.A. Almond and S. Verba. Boston: Little, Brown, 1980.

American Association of Retired Persons and the Villers Foundation. "The American Public Views Long Term Care." Princeton, NJ: R.L. Associates, 1987.

Andrulis, Dennis P., Virginia B. Weslowski, and Larry S. Gage. "The 1987 U.S. Hospital AIDS Survey." *Journal of Medicine* 262 (1989): 1598–1603.

Arkansas Department of Human Services. "Expanded Services for Pregnant Women and Infants." Little Rock, AR: Arkansas Department of Human Services, 1987.

Barber, Benjamin. *Strong Democracy: Participatory Politics for a New Age.* Berkeley: University of California Press, 1984.

Barna, Joel Warren. *State Mental-Health Services: Change under Pressure* (Report No. 106). Austin, TX: House Study Group, Texas House of Representatives, 1984.

Barone, Michael, and Grant Ujifusa. *The Almanac of American Politics.* Washington, DC: National Journal, 1990.

Baum, Daniel J. *Warehouses for Death.* Toronto: Burns and MacEachern, 1977.

Beauchamp, Dan E., and Ronald L. Rouse. "Universal New York Health Care, A Single-Payer Strategy Linking Cost Control and Universal Access." *The New England Journal of Medicine* 323 (6 September 1990): 640–644.

Benjamin, A.E. "Long Term Care and AIDS: Perspectives from Experience with the Elderly." *Milbank Quarterly* 66 (1988): 415–443.

Benjamin, A.E., Philip R. Lee, and E. Solkowitz. "Case Management of Persons with Acquired Immunodeficiency Syndrome in San Francisco." *Health Care Financing Review* (Annual Supplement 1986): 69–73.

Bennet, T. *Enhancing the Scope of Prenatal Services: Strategies for Improving State Perinatal Programs.* Washington, DC: National Governors' Association, 1990.

Berry, Frances S., and William D. Berry. "State Lottery Adoption as Policy Innovations: An Event History Analysis." *American Political Science Review* 84 (1990): 395–415.

Blaisdell, Kekuni. "Historical and Cultural Aspects of Native Hawaiian Health." *Social Process in Hawaii* 23 (1989).

Blank, Robert. *Rationing Medicine*. New York: Columbia University Press, 1988.

Bloom, B. "Health Insurance and Medical Care: Health of Our Nation's Children, United States, 1988." *Advance Data From Vital and Health Statistics* 188 (1 October): 1–8.

Bovbjerg, Randall R., and John Holahan. *Medicaid In the Reagan Era: Federal Policy and State Choices*. Washington, DC: The Urban Institute Press, 1982.

Bowlyow, Jane E. "Acute and Long-Term Care Linkages: A Literature Review." *Medical Care Review* 47 (1990): 75–101.

Bowman, Ann O'M., and Richard Kearney. *The Resurgence of the States*. Englewood Cliffs, NJ: Prentice Hall, 1986.

Braddock, D., R. Hemp, G. Fujiura, L. Bachelder, and D. Mitchell. *The State of the States in Developmental Disabilities*. Baltimore, MD: Paul Brookes, 1990.

Brecher, Charles, and James Knickman. "A Reconsideration of Long Term Care Policy." *Journal of Health Politics, Policy and Law* 10 (1985): 245–273.

Breyel, J. *Coordinating Prenatal Care: Strategies for Improving State Perinatal Programs*. Washington, DC: National Governors' Association.

Brody, Stanley J. "The Robert Wood Johnson Foundation Management Program on Hospital Initiatives." In *Long-Term Care: Economic Impacts and Financing Dilemmas*, edited by R. Wiltge. New York: National Health Council, 1990.

Brown, Lawrence D. "The National Politics of Oregon's Rationing Plan," *Health Affairs* 10 (June 1991): 28–51.

———. "The New Activism: Federal Health Politics Revisited." *Bulletin of the New York Academy of Medicine* 66 (July-August 1990): 293–318.

Buchanan, Allen. "The Right to a Decent Minimum of Health Care." *Philosophy and Public Affairs* 13 (Winter 1984): 58–78.

Burwell, Brian O., and Marilyn P. Rymer. "Trends in Medicaid Eligibility: 1975 to 1985." *Health Affairs* 6 (Winter 1987): 30–45.

Campbell, Courtney S. "Laboratory of Reform? Setting Health Priorities in Oregon." *BioLaw* 2 (May 1991): S549-S563.

Campion, Edward W., Axel Bang, and Maurice I. May. "Why Acute Care Hospitals Must Undertake Long-Term Care." *New England Journal of Medicine* 308 (1983): 271–277.

Center for Research and Educational Services (CARES). *Aging in North Carolina*. Chapel Hill, NC: CARES, 1989.

Clarke, Gary J. "The Role of the States in the Delivery of Health Services." *American Journal of Public Health* 71 (January 1981): 59–69.

Conlan, Timothy. "Politics and Governance: Conflicting Trends in the 1990s?" *Annals of the American Academy of Political and Social Science* 509 (1990): 128–138.

———. *New Federalism: Intergovernmental Reform From Nixon to Reagan*. Washington, DC: The Brookings Institution, 1988.

Coye, Molly J. et al. "Funding AIDS Services and Prevention from Public and Private Sources, New Jersey's Experience." *AIDS & Public Policy Journal* 3 (1988): 20–28.

Daniels, Norman. *Just Health Care*. Cambridge: Cambridge University Press, 1985.

Dougherty, Charles J. "Setting Health Care Priorities: Oregon's Next Steps." *Hastings Center Report* 21 (May–June 1991): 1–9.

Eisenbert, John M. *Doctor's Decisions and the Cost of Medical Care.* Ann Arbor, MI: Health Administration Press, 1986.

Elazar, Daniel J. "Opening the Third Century of American Federalism: Issues and Prospects." *Annals of the American Academy of Political and Social Science* 509 (1990): 11–21.

————. *The American Constitutional Tradition.* Lincoln, NE: University of Nebraska Press, 1988.

————. *American Federalism.* 3d ed. New York: Harper & Row, 1984.

————. *American Federalism: A View From the States,* 2d ed. New York: Thomas Y. Crowell, 1972.

Elazar, Daniel J., and J. Zikmund. *The Ecology of American Political Culture: Readings.* New York: Thomas Y. Crowell, 1975.

Erikson, Robert S., Gerald C. Wright, and John P. McIver. "Political Parties, Public Policy, and State Policy in the United States." *American Political Science Review* 83 (1989): 729–750.

Fabricant, Solomon. *The Trend of Government Activity in the U.S. Since 1900.* New York: National Bureau of Economic Research, 1982.

Falcone, David., and Boi Jon Jaeger. "Case Management of Health Services for the Elderly: Apologies and Promises." *Advances in Research* 12 (1988): 1–8.

Falcone, David, Elise Bolda, and Sandra Crawford Leak. "Waiting for Placement: An Exploratory Analysis of Determinants of Delayed Discharges of Elderly Hospital Patients." *Health Services Research* 26 (August 1991): 339–374.

Feder, Judith. *Medicare: Politics and Policy.* Lexington, MA: DC Heath,1977.

Fleming, Gretchen V., and Beth K. Yudkowsky. *Preventive Health Care for Medicaid Children: Related Factors and Costs.* Baltimore: Health Care Financing Administration, 1990.

Fox, Daniel M., and Elizabeth Fee eds. *AIDS: The Making of a Chronic Disease.* Berkeley, CA: University of California Press, 1991.

————. "Contemporary Historiography and AIDS," in Daniel M. Fox and Elizabeth Fee. *AIDS: The Making of a Chronic Disease.* Berkeley, CA: University of California Press, 1991.

————. "Policy and Epidemiology: Financing Health Services for the Chronically Ill and Disabled, 1930–1990." *Milbank Quarterly* 67 (August 1989): 257–287.

Fox, Daniel M., Patricia Day and Rudolf Klein. "The Power of Professionalism: Policies for AIDS in Britain, Sweden and the United States." *Daedalus* 118 (1988): 93–112.

Fox, Daniel M., and Daniel C. Schaffer. "Interest Groups and ERISA: The Politics of Semi-Preemption." *Journal of Health Politics, Policy, and Law* 14 (1989): 239–260.

Fox, Daniel M., and Emily H. Thomas. "AIDS Cost Analysis and Social Policy." *Law, Medicine, & Health Care* 15 (1987): 186–203.

Fried, Charles. "Equality and Rights in Medical Care." *Hastings Center Report* 6 (February 1976): 29–34.

Friedman, Emily. "The Uninsured: From Dilemma to Crisis." *JAMA* 265 (15 May 1991): 2491–2495.

Fries, James. "The Sunny Side of Aging." *JAMA* 263 (1990): 2354–2355.

Garrison, Louis P. "Medicaid, the Uninsured, and National Health Spending: Federal Policy Implications." *Health Care Financing Review* (Annual Supplement): 167–70; National Center for Health Statistics, 1989.

Goggin, Malcolm L., Ann O'M. Bowman, James P. Lester, and Laurence J. O'Toole, Jr. *Implementation Theory and Practice: Toward a Third Generation.* Glenview, IL: Scott, Foresman/Little, Brown, 1990.

———. *Policy Design and the Politics of Implementation: The Case of Child Health Care in the United States.* Knoxville: University of Tennessee Press, 1987.

———. "The 'Too Few Cases/Too Many Variables' Problem in Implementation Research." *Western Political Quarterly* 38 (1986): 328–347.

Gold, R.B., A.M. Kenney, and S. Singh. *Blessed Events and the Bottom Line: Financing Maternity Care in the United States.* New York: Alan Guttmacher Institute, 1987.

Gornick, Marian, Jay N. Greenberg, Paul W. Eggers, and Allen Dobson. "Twenty Years of Medicare and Medicaid: Covered Populations, Use of Benefits, and Program Expenditures." *Health Care Financing Review* (Annual Supplement, 1985): 13–59.

Governor's Commission On Health Care. "Report to Governor Neil Goldschmidt on Improving Access to Health Care for All Oregonians." Salem, OR: Office of Health Policy, 1 September 1988.

Gray, Virginia. "Innovation in the States: A Diffusion Study." *American Political Science Review* 67 (1973): 1174–1185.

———. "Rejoinder to 'Comment' by Jack Walker." *American Political Science Review* 67 (1973): 1192–1193.

Gray, Virginia, L.T. Jacob, and K. Vines. *Politics in the American States: A Comparative Analysis.* Boston: Little Brown, 1983.

Grumbach, K., T. Bodenheimer, D.U. Himmelstein, and S. Woolhandler. "Liberal Benefits, Conservative Spending: The Physicians for a National Health Program Proposal." *JAMA* 265 (15 May 1991): 2549–2554.

Hadorn, David. "The Oregon Priority-Setting Exercise: Quality of Life and Public Policy." *Hastings Center Report* 21 (May–June 1991): 11–16.

———. "Setting Health Care Priorities in Oregon: Cost Effectiveness Meets the Rule of Rescue." *JAMA* 265 (1 May 1991): 2218–2225.

Hagstrom, Jerry. "Liberal and Minority Coalitions Pleading Their Cases in State Capitals." *National Journal* (23 February 1985): 426–428.

Hall, P. *Governing the Economy: The Politics of State Intervention in Britain and France.* New York: Oxford University Press, 1986.

Hansen, Karen. "A Painful Prescription." *State Legislatures* (November–December 1988): 20–24.

Hasnain, Romana, and Michael Garland. *Health Care in Common: Report of the Oregon Health Decisions Community Meeting Process.* Portland, OR: Oregon Health Decisions, 1990.

Health Care Financing Administration. "National Health Expenditures, 1986–2000." *Health Care Financing Review* 8 (Summer 1987): 1–36.

Health Service Commission. "Preliminary Report." Salem, OR: 1 March 1990.

Hedrick, William H., and L. Harmon Zeigler. "Oregon: The Politics of Power." In

Interest Group Politics in the American West, edited by R.J. Hrebenar and C.S. Thomas. Salt Lake City: University of Utah Press, 1987.

Heifetz, Ronald, and Riley Sinder. "Political Leadership: Managing the Public's Problem Solving." In *The Power of Public Ideas,* edited by Robert Reich. Cambridge, MA: Harvard, 1988.

Herbers, John. "The New Federalism: Unplanned, Innovative and Here to Stay." *Governing* 1 (October 1987): 28–37.

Hill, Ian T. "Improving State Medicaid Programs for Pregnant Women and Children." *Health Care Financing Review* (Annual Supplement 1990): 75–87.

———. *Broadening Medicaid Coverage of Pregnant Women and Children: State Policy Responses.* Washington, DC: Health Policy Studies, Center for Policy Research, National Governors' Association, 1987.

———. *Implementing a Workable Presumptive Eligibility Program: The Experience in Arkansas.* Washington, DC: Health Policy Studies, Center for Policy Research, National Governors' Association, 1987.

———. "Medicaid Eligibility Thresholds for Families and Pregnant Women Information Update." Washington, DC: National Governors' Association, 8 September 1987.

———. *Medicaid Eligibility: A Descriptive Report of OBRA, TEFRA, and DEFRA Provisions and State Responses.* Baltimore: Office of Research and Demonstration, Health Care Financing Administration, U.S. Department of Health and Human Services, Medicaid Program Evaluation Working Paper 5.2, 1984.

Holahan, John, and G. Keney. "The Nursing Home Market and Hospital Discharge Delays." *Inquiry* 27 (1990): 73–85.

Hughes, Dana, Kay Johnson, Sara Rosenbaum, Janet Simons, and Elizabeth Butler. *The Health of America's Children: Maternal and Child Health Data Book.* Washington, DC: Children's Defense Fund, 1988 and 1989 editions.

Hutchison, Tony. "The Medicaid Budget Tangle." *State Legislatures* 16 (March 1990): 15–19.

Inglehart, Ronald. "The Renaissance of Political Culture." *American Political Science Review* 82 (1988): 1203–1230.

Institute of Medicine Staff. *Prenatal Care: Reaching Mothers, Reaching Infants.* Washington, DC: National Academy Press, 1988.

———. *Preventing Low Birthweight.* Washington, DC: National Academy Press, 1985.

Intergovernmental Health Policy Project, State AIDS Reports (February–March 1989).

Jennings, Bruce. "A Grassroots Movement in Bioethics: Community Health Decisions." *Hastings Center Report* 18 (Special Supplement June–July 1988): 1–16.

Jensen, M. "Organizational Theory and Methodology." *American Political Science Review* 58 (1983): 319–339.

Jewell, Malcolm E. "The Neglected World of State Politics." *The Journal of Politics* 44 (August 1982): 638–657.

Johns, Lucy, and Gerald Adler. "Evaluation of Recent Changes in Medicaid." *Health Affairs* 8 (1989): 171–181.

Justice, Diane, Lynn Etheredge, John Leuhrs, and Brian Burwell. *State Long Term Care Reform: Development of Community Care Systems in Six States.*

Washington, DC: National Governors' Association, 1988.

Kane, Robert A., L. Illston, Rosalie L. Kane, and John Nyman. *Meshing Service with Housing: Lessons from Adult Foster Care and Assisted Living in Oregon.* Final Report to the John A. Hartford Foundation, 1990.

Kane, Robert L., and Rosalie A. Kane. *A Will and a Way: What the United States Can Learn from Canada About Caring for the Elderly.* New York: Columbia University Press, 1985.

Kimball, Merit C. "Fluid Odds on Oregon Medicaid Waiver." *Health Week* (11 March 1991): 12.

———. "Children's Health: A System Full of Woe." *Health Week* 4 no. 17 (1990): 138–140.

Kincaid, John. "The State of American Federalism—1987." *Publius* 18 (Summer 1988): 1–15.

Kirkman-Liff, B.L. "Health Insurance Values and Implementation in the Netherlands and the Federal Republic of Germany: An Alternative Plan to Universal Coverage." *JAMA* 265 (15 May 1991): 2496–2502.

Kizer, Kenneth. "California's Approach to AIDS," *AIDS and Public Policy Journal 3* (1988): 1–10.

Klingman, David, and William W. Lammers. "The 'General Policy Liberalism' Factor in American State Politics." *American Journal of Political Science* 28 (1984): 598–610.

Lakin, K.C., J.N. Greenburg, M.P. Schmitz, and B.K. Hill. "A Comparison of Medicaid Waiver Applications for Populations That Are Mentally Retarded and Elderly/Disabled." *Mental Retardation* (22 August 1984): 182–192.

Lambert, C., and Bill Finger. "Targeting Older Persons for Services: An Overview of the Aging Network." *North Carolina Insight* 8 (1985): 9–31.

Larson, S. A., and K.C. Lakin. *Policy Research Brief.* Vol. 1, no. 2. Minneapolis, MN: Research and Training Center on Community Living in the University of Minnesota's Institute on Community Integration (1989).

Laubacher, Steven. "Administrative Initiative in Policy Implementation: Mental Retardation Deinstitutionalization Policy in Texas." Ph.D. diss., University of Houston, 1990.

Laumann, O., J.H. Gagnon, S. Michaels, R.T. Michael, and J.S. Coleman. "Monitoring the AIDS Epidemic in the United States: A Network Approach." *Science* (15 June 1989): 1186–1189.

Lester, James P., J.L. Franke, Ann O'M. Bowman, and Kenneth W. Kramer. "Hazardous Wastes, Politics, and Public Policy: A Comparative State Analysis." *Western Political Quarterly* 36 (1983): 257–285.

Lewin, John. "From Vision to Reality: Insurance Plan Establishes Hawaii as the Health State." *Hawaii Health Messenger* 52 no. 2, State Department of Health (1989).

Lisle, E. "Perspectives and Challenges for Cross-National Research." In *Comparative Policy Research: Learning from Experience.* New York: St. Martin's Press, 1987.

Luebke, Paul. *Tarheel Politics: Myths and Realities.* Chapel Hill: University of North Carolina Press, 1990.

MacStravic, Robin Scott. *Forecasting Use of Health Services: A Provider's Guide.* Rockville, MD: Aspens Systems Corporation, 1984.

Maggard, Heather Fairburn. "Medicaid Eligibility: New State Options." Washington, DC: National Conference of State Legislatures, 1987.

Mahood, Henry R. *Interest Group Politics in America: A New Intensity.* Englewood Cliffs, NJ: Prentice Hall, 1990.

Manton, Kenneth. "The Interaction of Population Aging and Health Transitions at Later Ages: New Evidence and Insights." In *Health Care and Its Costs,* edited by Carl Schramm. New York: W.W. Norton, 1987.

Marmor, Theodore. *The Politics of Medicare.* Chicago: Aldine, 1973.

Masters, Robert D. *The Nature of Politics.* New Haven: Yale University Press, 1989.

Mathematica Policy Research, Inc. *The Evaluation of the National Long-Term Care Demonstration: Final Report.* Princeton, NJ: 1986.

McManus, Margaret. "Medicaid Services and Delivery Settings for Maternal and Child Health." In *Affording Access to Quality Care: Strategies for Medicaid Cost Management.* Washington, DC: Health Policy Studies, Center for Policy Research, National Governors' Association, 1986.

Mechanic, David. "Some Dilemmas in Health Care Policy." *Health and Society* 59 (1981): 1–15.

Mendleson, Margaret A. *Tender Loving Greed.* New York: Knopf, 1974.

Merrill, Jeffery C. "State Initiatives for the Medically Uninsured." *Health Care Financing Review* (Annual Supplement 1990): 161–166.

Moe, T. "The New Economics of Organization." *American Journal of Political Science* 28 (1985): 739–777.

Morehouse, Sara M. *State Politics, Parties and Policy.* New York: Holt, Rinehart and Winston, 1983.

Morell, Virginia. "Oregon Puts Bold Health Plan on Ice." *Science* 249 (3 August 1990): 468–471.

Nathan, Richard P. "Federalism—The Great 'Composition.' " In *The New American Political System,* 2d Version, edited by Anthony King. Washington, DC: American Enterpreise Institute, 1990.

Nathan, Richard P., and Fred C. Doolittle. *Reagan and the States.* Princeton: Princeton University Press, 1987.

National Association of Insurance Commissioners. "Medical/Lifestyle Questions and Underwriting Guidelines." *Model Regulation Service* 60 (July 1989): 3–8.

National Center for Health Statistics. "Advance Report of Final Mortality Statistics, 1988." *Monthly Vital Statistics Report* 39, no. 7 (1990): 1–47.

———. *Births, Marriages, Divorces, and Deaths for August 1990.* Hyattsville, MD: Public Health Service, 1990.

———. *Health, United States, 1989.* Hyattsville, MD: Public Health Service, 1990.

New York State Department of Health. *Universal Health Care: Voices from the States.* Albany, NY: New York State Department of Health, 1990.

Office of Medical Assistance Programs. "Waiver Application for Oregon Medicaid Demonstration Project, Discussion Draft." (Salem, OR: Department of Human Resources, 26 April 1990).

Office of Technology Assessment, U.S. Congress. *AIDS And Health Insurance: An OTA Survey.* Washington, DC: U.S. Government Printing Office, 1988.

———. *Neonatal Intensive Care for Low Birthweight Infants: Costs and Effec-*

tiveness. Washington, DC: U.S. Government Printing Office, 1987.

Osborne, David. *Laboratories of Democracy*. Boston: Harvard Business School Press, 1990.

Padgett, J. "Managing Garbage Can Hierarchies." *Administrative Science Quarterly* 25 (1980): 583–604.

Peat, Marwick, and Mitchell. *Study of Routine Costs Of Treating Hospitalized AIDS Patients*. New York: Greater New York Hospital Association, 1986.

Peterson, P. *City Limits*. Chicago: University of Chicago Press, 1981.

President's Commission for the Study of Ethical Problems in Medicine and Biomedical and Behavioral Research. *Securing Access to Health Care*, Vol. I, (Washington, DC: Government Printing Office, 1983).

Przeworski, Adam, and Henry Teune. *The Logic of Comparative Social Inquiry*. New York: Wiley, 1970.

Redfoot, Donald. "Dignity, Independence and Cost Effectiveness: The Success of the Congregate Housing Services Program." *A Report to the Subcommittee on Housing and Consumer Interests of the Select Committee on Aging of the U.S. House of Representatives*. Washington, DC: Government Printing Office, 1987.

Reeves, Mavis Mann. "The States as Polities: Reformed, Reinvigorated, Resourceful." *The Annals of the American Academy of Political and Social Sciences* 509 (May 1990): 83–93.

Reich, Robert E., ed. *The Power of Public Ideas*. Cambridge: Harvard, 1990.

Riesenfeld, Stefan A. "Prepaid Health Care in Hawaii." University of Hawaii, Legislative Reference Bureau, Report No. 2, 1971.

Rockefeller, J.D. "A Call for Action: The Pepper Commission's Blueprint for Health Care Reform." *JAMA* 265 (15 May 1991): 2507–2510.

Rosenbaum, Sara. "Financing Maternity Care for Low-Income Women. Results of a Nationwide Medicaid Survey." Washington, D.C: Children's Defense Fund, 1985.

Rovner, Julie. "Medicaid: A Safety Net Riddled With Holes." *CQ Weekly Report* 46 (20 February 1988): 366.

Rowe, Monica, and Stephanie Keintz. "National Survey of State Spending For AIDS." *Intergovernmental AIDS Reports* (September–October 1989): 1–10.

Scheerenberger, R.C. *Deinstitutionalization and Institutional Reform*. Springfield, IL: Charles C. Thomas, 1976.

Schneider, Saundra K. "Governors and Health Care Policy in the American States." *Policy Studies Journal* 17 (Summer 1989): 901–926.

———. "Intergovernmental Influences on Medicaid Program Expenditures." *Public Administration Review* 47 no. 6 (1988): 479–484.

Schwarz, Mildred, and Michael Thompson. *Divided We Stand: Redefining Politics, Technology and Social Choice*. Philadelphia: University of Pennsylvania Press, 1990.

Scitovsky, Anne, Mary Cline, and Philip Lee. "Medical Care Costs of Patients with AIDS in San Francisco." *JAMA* 256 (1986): 3103–3106.

Seage, Jerome R., Stewart Landers, M. Anita Barry, Jerome Groopman, George A. Lamb, and Arnold M. Epstein. "Medical Care Costs of AIDS in Massachusetts." *JAMA* 256 (1986): 3107–3109.

Sharkansky, Ira. *The Maligned States*. New York: McGraw-Hill, 1978.

South Carolina Department of Health and Environmental Control. "Medicaid

High Risk Channeling Project Procedures Manual." Columbia: South Carolina Department of Health and Environmental Control, 1986.

———. "Response to Federal Request for Additional Information Concerning the Establisment of a High Risk Channeling Project Within the South Carolina Medicaid Program." Columbia: South Carolina Department of Health and Environmental Control, 1985.

———. "Request for Federal Waiver to Establish a High Risk Channeling Project within the South Carolina Medicaid Program." Columbia: South Carolina Department of Health and Environmental Control, 1984.

Southern Regional Task Force on Infant Mortality. *Final Report: For the Children of Tomorrow.* Washington, DC: Southern Governors' Association and the Southern Legislative Conference, 1985.

Southwick, Karen. "Women Confront Second-Class Care." *Health Week* 4 no. 16 (1990): 1, 40–42.

Starr, Paul. *The Social Transformation of American Medicine.* New York: Basic Books, 1982.

Stason, William B. "Oregon's Bold Medicaid Initiative." *JAMA* 265 (1 May 1991): 2237–2238.

Stevens, Robert B. and Rosemary Stevens. *Welfare Medicine in America: A Case Study of Medicaid.* New York: Free Press, 1974.

Stone, Deborah. *Policy, Paradox, and Political Reason.* Glenview, IL: Scott, Foresman and Company, 1988.

Sundquist, James. *Making Federalism Work.* Washington, DC: The Brookings Institution, 1969.

Sussman, David, and Marilyn Wann. "Controlling Medicaid Costs: A Lingering Concern in States." *Health Week* 4 no. 9 (1990): 1, 41.

Tellis-Nayak, V., and M. Tellis-Nayak. "An Alternative Level of Care: Retrospective Payment System and the Challenge of Extended Care." *Social Science and Medicare* 23 (1986): 655–671.

Thompson, Frank. "The Enduring Challenge of Health Policy Implementation." In *Health Politics and Policy,* 2d ed., edited by T. Littman and L. Robins. Albany, NY: Delmar Press, 1991.

———. "New Federalism and Health Care Policy." *Journal of Health Politics, Policy and Law* 11 (1986): 647–666.

Thompson, Michael, Richard E. Ellis, and Aaron Wildavsky. "Political Cultures." *Working Paper* 90–124. Institute of Governmental Studies. Berkeley: University of California, 1990.

Todd, James S., S.V. Seekins, J. A. Krichbaum, and L. K. Harvey. "Health Access America—Strengthening the U.S. Health Care System." *JAMA* 265 (15 May 1991): 2503–2506.

Turshen, Meredith. *The Politics of Public Health.* New Brunswick: Rutgers University Press, 1990.

U.S. Bipartisan Commission on Comprehensive Health Care. "Special Report: The Pepper Commission Report on Comprehensive Health Care." *New England Journal of Medicine* 323 no. 14 (4 October 1990): 1005–1007.

U.S. Department of Health and Human Services (USDHHS). *Hospital Studies Program Hospital Cost and Utilization Project.* Research Note. Washington, DC: USDHHS, 1988.

U.S. General Accounting Office. *Prenatal Care: Medicaid Recipients and Uninsured Women Obtain Insufficient Care.* Washington, DC: General Accounting Office, 1987.

Van Horn, Carl E. "The Quiet Revolution." In *The State of the States,* edited by Carl E. Van Horn. Washington, DC: CQ Press, 1989.

Vladeck, Bruce. *Unloving Care: The Nursing Home Tragedy.* New York: Basic Books, 1980.

Wachtler, Sol. "Constitutional Rights: Resuming the States' Role." *Intergovernmental Perspective* 15 (Summer 1989): 23–25.

Wagner, J.L., R.C. Herdman, and D.W. Alberts. "Well-Child Care: How Much Is Enough?" *Health Affairs* 8 no. 3 (1989): 147–157.

Walker, Jack. "Comment: Problems in Research on the Diffusion of Policy Innovations." *American Political Science Review* 67 (1973): 1186–1191.

———. "Diffusion of Innovation." *American Political Science Review* 63 (1969): 880–899.

Wegner, Eldon. "A Framework for Assessing Health Needs." *Social Process in Hawaii* 32 (1989).

Weissert, William, Cynthia Cready, and Jane Pawelak. "The Past and Future of Home and Community-based Long-term Care." *The Milbank Quarterly* 66 (1988): 309–388.

White, C.C., J.P. Koplan, and W.A. Orenstein. "Benefits, Risks and Costs of Immunization for Measles, Mumps and Rubella." *American Journal of Public Health* 75 no. 7 (1985): 739–744.

Wilson, Keren B. "Assisted Living: The Merger of Housing and Long Term Care Services." *Long Term Care Advance* 1 (1990): 1–11.

Wright, Gerald C., Jr., Robert Erikson, and John P. McIver. "Public Opinion and Policy Liberalism in the American States." *American Journal of Political Science* 31 (1987): 980–1001.

———. "Measuring State Partisanship and Ideology of Survey Data." *Journal of Politics* 47 (1985): 469–489.

Yudkowsky, Beth K., and Gretchen V. Fleming. "Preventive Health Care for Medicaid Children." *Health Care Financing Review* (Annual Supplement 1990): 89–96.

Ziegler, L. Harmon. "Interest Groups in the States." In *Politics in the American States: A Comparative Analysis,* edited by Virginia Gray, Herbert Jacob, and Kennedy Vine. Boston: Little, Brown (1983).

Index

AIDS
  AZT and, 32, 34, 39, 42, 142
  as chronic illness, 28, 45
  cost of care for, 16, 26, 28, 31
  and the federal government,
    30–31
  groups affected by, 25, 27,
  home care and, 34, 35, 40
  long-term care and, 41–42
  number of cases of, 18, 27–28, 32
  private insurance and, 35
  state problems created by, 27, 30,
    31–33
  See also Medicaid
AIDS, policy responses to,
  in New York, 34, 40–41
  in New Jersey, 35
  in Michigan, 35
  by state governments, 33–44
Aging policy
  and demographic trends, 74
  long-term care and, 74–75, 96
  in North Carolina, 73, 75, 80–83, 86,
    87, 88, 96–97
  nursing home care and, 31, 74, 76,
    78–79, 83, 86–87, 90
  in Oregon, 73, 75–78, 83–87,
    88–91, 96–97
  Oregon model on, exportability of,
    91–96
  Pepper Commission and, 168, 192
  role of hospitals in, 74, 76, 78–79,
    99n

Aid to Families with Dependent
  Children, 8, 58–59, 112, 122,
  138–139
American Association of Retired
  Persons, 74
American Medical Association, 191
Ariyoshi, George, 152–153

Biotechnology, regulation of in
  Hawaii, 148, 164, 166
Blue Cross/Blue Shield, 31, 174, 184–185
Bush Administration, health policy of,
  x, 5–6, 10, 12, 192

Caplan, Arthur, 137
Case management, 36–38, 40, 54–55,
  76–78, 83, 11–113
Centers for Disease Control, 27
Certificate-of-Need, 104, 162, 141
Children's Defense Fund, 56, 134, 143
Clarke, Gary, 6
Community Health Nursing Program,
  162
Consolidated Budget Reconciliation
  Acts (COBRA)
  COBRA '85, 57, 62, 70n
  COBRA '86, 29

Dukakis, Michael, 21, 176, 182, 188

Elazar, Daniel, 92–93
Environment and health, 4, 15, 149,
  165, 167

95x